## CHRISTIAN SMITH

(PhD, Harvard University) is the William R.
Kenan Jr. Professor of Sociology and director of
the Center for the Study of Religion and Society at the University of Notre Dame. He is the
award-winning author or coauthor of numerous
books, including *Souls in Transition: The Religious
and Spiritual Lives of Emerging Adults*.

# THE BIBLE MADE
# IMPOSSIBLE

# THE BIBLE MADE IMPOSSIBLE

*Why Biblicism Is Not a Truly Evangelical*
*Reading of Scripture*

## CHRISTIAN SMITH

**BrazosPress**
*a division of Baker Publishing Group*
Grand Rapids, Michigan

© 2011 by Christian Smith

Published by Brazos Press
a division of Baker Publishing Group
P.O. Box 6287, Grand Rapids, MI 49516-6287
www.brazospress.com

Printed in the United States of America

Library of Congress Cataloging-in-Publication Data
Smith, Christian, 1960–
    The Bible made impossible : why biblicism is not a truly evangelical reading of Scripture / Christian Smith.
        p.   cm.
    Includes bibliographical references (p.    ) and indexes.
    ISBN 978-1-58743-303-0 (cloth)
    1. Bible—Evidences, authority, etc. 2. Bible—Hermeneutics. 3. Evangelicalism.
I. Title.
BS480.S569 2011
220.1—dc22                                                                          2011004345

Scripture quotations are from the Holy Bible, New International Version®. NIV®. Copyright © 1973, 1978, 1984, 2011 by Biblica, Inc.™ Used by permission of Zondervan. All rights reserved worldwide. www.zondervan.com

11   12   13   14   15   16   17        7   6   5   4   3   2   1

# Contents

# Introduction

This book addresses Christians, especially evangelicals, who believe that the Bible is a divine word of truth that should function as an authority for Christian faith and practice, and who want to espouse a coherent position that justifies and defends that belief. My contention here is that the American evangelical commitment to "biblicism," which I will define and describe in detail below, is an untenable position that ought to be abandoned in favor of a better approach to Christian truth and authority.

What follows is not an attack on Christian authority or the Bible. It is rather a critical interrogation of certain aspects of *one specific account* of biblical authority that I think reason and evidence show is impossible to defend and employ with integrity. The kinds of reason and evidence I bring to bear here are not those of the irreligious, skeptical unbeliever; rather, they are the sort of considerations Christians need to engage. The goal of this book is not to detract from the plausibility, reliability, or authority of the Christian faith or from scripture. The goal is to persuade readers that one particular theory of Christian plausibility, reliability, and authority—what I call biblicism—is inadequate to the task.

I am aware that the term "biblicism" is often used pejoratively, as a disrespectful slight suggesting ignorance and lack of sophistication. I intend the use of the term here in a rather more neutral, descriptive sense, denoting a particular tradition of approach to scripture, as described in greater detail below. I contend that the biblicism that characterizes the thinking and practice of much of American evangelicalism is not so much "wrong" as it is *impossible*, even taken on its own terms. It simply does not work as proposed and cannot function in a coherent way.

In order for evangelical biblicism to *appear* to work, therefore, those who believe in it have to engage in various forms of textual selectivity, denial, and contortion—which actually end up violating biblicist intentions. Most of these are practiced covertly, not in any sneaky way, but simply as the learned, taken-for-granted, and therefore largely unintentional habits of a particular subcultural style of thinking and behaving. Contemporary Christians who want to be theologically orthodox, biblical, and evangelical (in the best sense of the word) can and must do better. But before anyone is motivated to do better, we must confront the real problems with the current, inadequate biblicist account.

To be clear, I am not suggesting that all American evangelicals are biblicists. Some are not. And some others mix biblicism with other forms of authority, such as personal "leadings of the Spirit." Many simply assume a kind of background biblicism without giving it much systematic thought. Many academic and more thoughtful evangelicals also tend to be more selective and careful in the way they articulate their biblicism. Furthermore, while I am focused here on evangelicals in particular, nearly all American Protestant fundamentalists are also biblicists, as are many if not most charismatic and pentecostal Christians.[1] I am suggesting, therefore, that biblicism of the kind I describe below represents the epistemological center of gravity of much of American evangelicalism (and conservative Protestantism more generally) and so warrants the kinds of questions raised in this book.

By "biblicism" I mean a theory about the Bible that emphasizes together its exclusive authority, infallibility, perspicuity, self-sufficiency, internal consistency, self-evident meaning, and universal applicability. Different communities within American evangelicalism emphasize various combinations of these points differently. But all together they form a constellation of assumptions and beliefs that define a particular theory and practice. My argument as follows does not question the doctrine of the divine inspiration of the Bible.[2] Nor am I here discounting the crucially important role that the Bible must play in the life of the church and the lives of individual Christians. I am not suggesting that the Bible is just a set of historical writings set in particular cultures, or the record of human subjective experiences of the divine that has little to say to contemporary people without being translated into terms that modern people can accept. Instead, what I say here is simply that the biblicism that in much of American evangelicalism is presupposed to be the cornerstone to Christian truth and faithfulness is misguided and impossible. It does not and cannot live up to its own claims.

I must also insist that my motives, goals, and arguments have nothing to do with promoting or representing theological liberalism. I am no theological liberal. While I believe that orthodox Christians need to engage intellectually and socially with theological liberals, I am and always have been a skeptic of theological liberalism as a project. I view the program of liberalism as an unworthy corrosion of historically orthodox, evangelical (again, in the best sense of that word) Christianity. I view theological liberalism—despite its good intentions—as naive intellectually, problematic in its typical ecclesial expression, and susceptible to unfortunate and sometimes reprehensible social and political expressions. It was no accident, for example, as Karl Barth explained at the time, that the prominent leaders of theological liberalism in the German church together publicly endorsed the causes of both Kaiser Wilhelm in World War I in 1914 and Hitler and the Nazis in 1933. When the church lacks a sovereign word of God that is not defined in terms of human subjectivity, experience, and culture, such ill-fated political moves become hard to resist. The theological liberal program lacks internal resources to help expose idolatry and so recurrently falls prey to the latest cultural movements and political fashions. I would go so far as to agree with J. Gresham Machen that theological liberalism is not one particular branch of Christianity; it is rather actually a very different religion from Christianity.[3]

However, *opposing theological liberalism does not necessitate biblicism as the only viable alternative*, as some seem to believe. This notion is an unfortunate legacy of the American modernist-fundamentalist battles of the early twentieth century. Slapping the "liberal!" label on others is still a knee-jerk reaction of many evangelicals against any argument that on first glance does not seem identical to or more conservative than their own position. This tendency has much more to do with the sociological process of maintaining safe identity boundaries and avoiding truly challenging intellectual engagements than it does with sustaining Christian faith with appropriate confidence, integrity, and trust in God.[4] In any case, to be clear, I deny any attempts to label the argument of this book "liberal."

My argument in what follows focuses not merely on theories about what the Bible is believed to be and how it ought to function as an authority. It also focuses on how in practice the Bible is often *actually* read and used as an authority and on the results that this produces. I will suggest that the problematic results are not mere accidents or worst practices within an otherwise sound approach, but they are rather the inevitable outcomes of bad biblicist theory. In this I do not assume that empirical facts about what actually happens are all that are ever worth knowing. A great deal of Christianity is of course about conforming problematic empirical experience to what is ultimately true in and about reality. However, actual empirical human practices and experiences of Bible reading, interpretation, and application—especially when they are widespread and endemic—tell us a great deal about the adequacy of our *theories* about the Bible.

In what follows I will not engage a number of issues that have long occupied certain kinds of critics and defenders of the Bible. One of those concerns "higher criticism" of the text, such as whether the purported author of a certain text really was that author or whether the events described in a text "really" happened in that way. Those may or may not be interesting and important issues, but they do not concern me here. Neither will I engage the exercise of finding long lists of scriptural texts that appear to contradict each other, to which some sophomoric skeptics devote themselves in order to try to undermine the Bible's coherence and authority.[5] That merely mirrors the worst kind of fundamentalist literalism, to which few thoughtful evangelicals subscribe, and betrays pitiable misunderstandings of how human language works.

My line of reasoning in this book will run as follows. First, I will argue that most biblicist claims are rendered moot by a more fundamental problem (which few biblicists ever acknowledge) that undermines all the supposed achievements of biblicism: the problem of *pervasive interpretive pluralism*. Even among presumably well-intentioned readers—including many evangelical biblicists—the Bible, after their very best efforts to understand it, says and teaches very different things about most significant topics. My suggestion is that it becomes beside the point to assert a text to be solely authoritative or inerrant, for instance, when, lo and behold, it gives rise to a host of many divergent teachings on important matters. Authority implies and requires definitive instruction, direction, or guidance. As the nineteenth-century Princeton Seminary theologian Charles Hodge stated, "If the Scriptures be a plain book, and the Spirit performs the functions of a teacher to all the children of God, it follows inevitably that they must agree in all essential matters in their interpretation of the Bible."[6] But definitive instruction, direction, or guidance is precisely what pervasive interpretive pluralism precludes.

So, theorists about the Bible can assert theoretical claims of scriptural authority and infallibility as much as they want. But those ring hollow because of the ubiquitous variety and combinations of "biblical" teachings that sincere readers of the Bible think it teaches on nearly every subject. To be clear, the problem is not that theoretical claims to biblical sufficiency or authority are proved to be wrong or erroneous per se; rather, they are defeated *in relevance* by the undeniable lack of interpretive agreement and consistency among those who share the same biblicist background. That defeat in relevance then gives rise to questions about the truth of those theoretical claims. Biblicists might offer a variety of responses to this problem, to be sure, but none of them, I will suggest, are adequate to address the difficulty. So, pervasive interpretive pluralism remains a debilitating problem for the relevance of biblicist theory.

Having made that primary case, I will then turn more briefly to a subsidiary examination of the larger question of the defensibility of biblicism generally. My argument focuses on the fact that the Bible contains a variety of texts that are problematic in different ways and that biblicist (among other) readers rarely know how to handle. Some are texts that frankly almost no reader is going to live by, however committed in theory they may be to biblicism. Others are texts that need explaining away by appeals to cultural relativity (although no principled guidelines exist about when that explanation should and should not be applied). Some are passages that are simply strange. And some are texts that seem to be incompatible with other texts.

In order not to let these problematic texts endanger their formal theory of the Bible, biblicists tend to respond in three ways. The first is simply to *ignore* the problematic texts, essentially pretending that they do not exist. The second is to "interpret" the problematic texts as if they say things that *they do not in fact say*. The third is to develop elaborate *contortions* of highly unlikely scenarios and explanations—of the sort to which nobody would ever resort in any other part of life—which seem to rescue the texts from the problems.[7] But, from the viewpoint of the biblicist perspective itself, these strategies should be illegitimate. Reliance on them to sustain a biblicist position is self-defeating. In addition, I will show, first, that biblicism itself is not a self-evident, much less necessary, teaching of the Bible about itself, and, second, that biblicism has some problematic, pernicious pastoral consequences for many thoughtful youth raised in biblicist traditions.

I conclude with three chapters advancing a number of proposals for overcoming American evangelical biblicism. My proposals assume that biblicism can be escaped not by turning away from an evangelical approach to the Bible but rather by becoming *even more truly evangelical* in the reading of scripture. Contrary to the fears of some biblicists, leaving biblicism behind need not mean losing the best of evangelicalism but, instead, can mean strengthening an evangelical hermeneutic of scripture.

How I came to write a book about biblical authority and scriptural interpretation is sometimes beyond me. (I have no doubt that some readers, by the time they get well into the book, will wish I had never written it.) I did not start off with that intention in mind, but it began simply with me (someone who tends to think better when writing) merely drafting out some thoughts and questions for myself and perhaps to bounce off a few friends for their reactions. Needless to say, it grew from there. I am not a biblical scholar or a theologian professionally—although I have studied at three Boston Theological Institute schools (Gordon Conwell, where I took a course on Christology from David Wells; Harvard Divinity School, where I studied historical theology with Margaret Miles and Ian Siggins, among others; and Andover Newton, where I took an excellent course on scripture with Gabriel Fackre) and have spent much of my life reading in theology.

Professionally, I am a sociologist. For purposes of writing this book, that is both an asset and a liability. It is an asset, I believe, because it gives me a perspective that is different from many who deal with these topics for a living and so enables me to perhaps see things that some others may not. Being a sociologist—particularly one not employed at an evangelical institution with doctrinal standards statements determining the viability of my employment—also frees me to say things in print that I think are true without the accompanying worry that I will lose my job as a result. I know that there are at least some employees at evangelical institutions who share the concerns I lay out in this book but who cannot give voice to them because of the internal political problem this would create.[8] I am fortunate not to have to worry about such matters.

But being a sociologist is also in some ways a liability in writing this book, since I do not have the expertise in certain complex areas of scholarship upon which this book touches. I do not claim to bring such expertise to my argument; rather, the force of my case, such as it is, grows merely from the asking of some very simple questions and the refusal to settle for what I think are inadequate standard answers. Sometimes what needs to be asked or said—especially in contexts of well-established and taken-for-granted routines that at least some powerful people have a stake in maintaining—is not all that sophisticated but is instead quite elementary. Pervasive interpretive pluralism is the proverbial massive elephant in the room of evangelical biblicism that nobody talks about. I want to talk about it.

I should also say up front, for purposes of full disclosure, that, since completing the writing of this book, I have joined the Catholic Church. My reasons for becoming Catholic—an evangelical Catholic, I might add—were many, and only partly related to the issues raised here.[9] This fact of my autobiography, however, takes nothing away from the importance and legitimacy of this book's argument for American evangelicalism—a movement about which I still care, in certain ways admire, and want to see realizing its best potential. Toward that end, for evangelical Protestants who intend to remain evangelical, the argument of this book stands strong and deserves to be engaged and answered. The constructive suggestions with which I conclude this book hold true for evangelical Protestants, and, to be clear, no reader needs to become Catholic in order to embrace any or all of them.

Finally, it should go without saying that just because I cite a certain author or publication, that does not mean that I accept and endorse everything he, she, or it says. Oftentimes one wants to connect with certain specific ideas or perspectives of another without implying a full-scale endorsement of the other's entire intellectual program. Most scholars know this. But, since among American evangelicals issues surrounding the nature of the Bible are so sensitive and politically charged, it is probably necessary for me to avoid guilt-by-association by saying it explicitly: merely because I cite a certain author or publication, that itself does not mean that I accept and endorse everything he, she, or it says.

I owe a debt of thanks to Mark Regnerus, Brian Brock, Mark Noll, Stanley Hauerwas, Richard Flory, Stan Gaede, Rich Mouw, Katie Spencer, Trish Snell, Peter Mundey, Scot McKnight, Charles Cosgrove, Bill Webb, Roger Olson, Jeff McSwain, Douglas Campbell, Meredith Whitnah, Kevin Vanhoozer, Peter Enns, Craig Allert, Roger Lundin, Robert K. Johnson, Bob Brenneman, Kent Sparks, and David Sikkink for critical feedback on early versions of this manuscript. As is customary to say, and is true here also, this book was strengthened considerably by these people's helpful feedback; yet, none of them is to be held responsible—even by association—for any of its mistakes, inaccuracies, confusions, oversights, or oversimplifications, of which I am aware there may be more than a few.

Finally, I owe a large debt of gratitude to my fellow B4B partners: Jeff McSwain, Douglas Campbell, Allan Keoneke, and (for one very enjoyable year) Brian Brock (as well as sometimes Jeremy Begbie, Allan Poole, and Peter Hausman)—to whom I dedicate this book, whether they like that or not. Nobody could hope to enjoy a more fun, stimulating, and edifying group of theological companions while meeting at Whole Foods to hash out life-changing theology. May they and their work prosper, especially Jeff's at the Reality Ministries Center in downtown Durham, North Carolina.

# PART 1

# THE IMPOSSIBILITY
# OF BIBLICISM

# 1

# Biblicism and the Problem
# of Pervasive Interpretive Pluralism

The "biblicism" that pervades much of American evangelicalism is untenable and needs to be abandoned in favor of a better approach to Christian truth and authority. By untenable I do not simply mean that it is wrong, but rather that it is literally impossible, at least when attempted consistently on its own terms. It cannot actually be sustained, practiced, and defended. Biblicism is one kind of an attempt to explain and act on the authority of the Bible, but it is a misguided one. In the end it cannot and in fact does not work.

A better alternative to biblicism is needed that takes seriously scriptural authority but in a way that does so beyond the framework of biblicism. Before any biblicist or semibiblicist is going to be motivated to seek a postbiblicist alternative to biblicism, however, they must first become convinced of biblicism's untenability. Seeing that biblicism really is a dead end may motivate a constructive search for something better. This chapter and the next three seek to persuade readers that biblicism is a dead end, best to be abandoned.

## What Is Biblicism?

Many functional biblicists in America have not heard of the term "biblicism" or do not know that it describes them. That does not

3

matter. What does matter are the real belief system and the practices it animates. Whether called by that name or not, biblicism is prevalent and powerful in American Protestantism, particularly among conservative Protestants. As John Frame, professor of theology at Reformed Theological Seminary (Orlando, Florida) concludes in a thoughtful paper titled, "In Defense of Something Close to Biblicism," "although Protestant theology under the *sola Scriptura* principle is not biblicist, it is not always easy to distinguish it from biblicism."[1] The word "biblicism" turns out to mean different things to different people. It is therefore important to be clear about the meaning I intend here.

All that I write below is intended to reference the following definition. By "biblicism" I mean a particular theory about and style of using the Bible that is defined by a constellation of related assumptions and beliefs about the Bible's nature, purpose, and function. That constellation is represented by ten assumptions or beliefs:

1. Divine Writing: The Bible, down to the details of its words, consists of and is identical with God's very own words written inerrantly in human language.
2. Total Representation: The Bible represents the totality of God's communication to and will for humanity, both in containing all that God has to say to humans and in being the exclusive mode of God's true communication.[2]
3. Complete Coverage: The divine will about all of the issues relevant to Christian belief and life are contained in the Bible.[3]
4. Democratic Perspicuity: Any reasonably intelligent person can read the Bible in his or her own language and correctly understand the plain meaning of the text.[4]
5. Commonsense Hermeneutics: The best way to understand biblical texts is by reading them in their explicit, plain, most obvious, literal sense, as the author intended them at face value, which may or may not involve taking into account their literary, cultural, and historical contexts.
6. Solo Scriptura:[5] The significance of any given biblical text can be understood without reliance on creeds, confessions, historical church traditions, or other forms of larger theological hermeneutical frameworks, such that theological formulations can be built up directly out of the Bible from scratch.

7. Internal Harmony: All related passages of the Bible on any given subject fit together almost like puzzle pieces into single, unified, internally consistent bodies of instruction about right and wrong beliefs and behaviors.
8. Universal Applicability: What the biblical authors taught God's people at any point in history remains universally valid for all Christians at every other time, unless explicitly revoked by subsequent scriptural teaching.
9. Inductive Method: All matters of Christian belief and practice can be learned by sitting down with the Bible and piecing together through careful study the clear "biblical" truths that it teaches.

The prior nine assumptions and beliefs generate a tenth viewpoint that—although often not stated in explications of biblicist principles and beliefs by its advocates—also commonly characterizes the general biblicist outlook, particularly as it is received and practiced in popular circles:

10. Handbook Model: The Bible teaches doctrine and morals with every affirmation that it makes, so that together those affirmations comprise something like a handbook or textbook for Christian belief and living, a compendium of divine and therefore inerrant teachings on a full array of subjects—including science, economics, health, politics, and romance.[6]

Biblicism is not a comprehensively formalized position always explicated in exactly these ten points and subscribed to identically by all adherents. Different people and groups emphasize and express a variety of these points somewhat differently. Some may even downplay or deny particular points here and there—there are, for example, highly biblicist denominations and seminaries that are unapologetically confessional. The point is not that biblicism is a unified doctrine that all of its adherents overtly and uniformly profess. The point, rather, is that this constellation of interrelated assumptions and beliefs informs and animates the outlooks and practices of major sectors of institutional and popular conservative American Protestantism, especially evangelicalism.

Evangelical biblicism has a long history in America—one revealing how much popular biblicism was driven not by fellowship with the historic church but by the particular sensibilities of life in a postrevolutionary, nineteenth-century, individualistic, republican democracy.[7] However intensely and with whatever variations it may be expressed by different groups, biblicism is the foundational belief and practice of many tens of millions of American Christians—perhaps as many as a hundred million (according to General Social Survey data, about one-third of all adult Americans say that they believe that "the Bible is the actual word of God and should be taken literally, word for word").[8] Biblicism can readily be found in the belief statements of scores of denominations, seminaries, and parachurch ministries; seen in the words of myriad Christian authors and speakers; heard in the messages of innumerable pulpits and Bible studies; and observed in the practices of countless personal devotions.

### Popular, Institutional, and Scholarly Examples of Biblicism

To put a finer point of particularity on the "ism" about which I have generalized above, I next cite some examples of specific expressions of biblicism. I draw here from an almost limitless supply of possible examples, both academic and popular, using numbers in brackets (e.g., [5]) throughout—at the risk of oversimplifying and overlabeling—to indicate when any of the ten biblicist themes noted above are expressed or implied. I begin with popular or "folk" expressions of biblicism[9] and then move on to more scholarly and institutional examples.

Biblicism is everywhere in evangelical popular culture, including, for instance, on the Internet. One Bible website dedicated to helping readers in "selecting the best Bible translations," for example, is entitled "God's Handbook to Life" [10].[10] Another Christian music and lyrics website devotes a page to "The Bible, God's Word—Our Manual for Life" [10], which says that the Bible "contains the solution for every problem you are facing today [3]. The Bible is an encyclopedia on all subjects you can think of under the sun" [10].[11] Likewise, *Faith and Fitness Magazine* on its website calls the Bible "His Instruction Manual—Our Guidebook for a Healthy Life" [10], explaining that the Bible is designed by God to provide us a blueprint for living life. It's like an owner's manual for a piece of exercise equipment [9 implied]. We can make the best use of the equipment if we read the owner's manual so we are aware of how to use all the special capabilities and how all the "buttons and whistles" work. When it breaks down, we can look in the manual to know how to repair it [10].[12]

Similarly, the author of the "Bible Authors" webpage says that

the Bible was written through more than 40 men, but it fits together perfectly as if written by one man [7] because the author of all 66 books is the Holy Spirit [1]. The Bible was written over a time span of about 2,000 years, and it is totally accurate in matters of History, Prophecy, and every issue of life. There are no contradictions in the Bible [7]. . . . The Bible contains the mind of God [1]. . . . It is the traveler's map, the pilgrim's staff, the pilot's compass, the soldier's sword [4, 5 implied], and the Christian's charter . . . [that] condemns all who trifle with its holy contents. The Word of God is your absolute, infallible guide for life. Just like every major purchase is accompanied by an owner's manual which tells you how to operate it, if you do not go by the book, it won't work. The Bible is God's owner's manual for your life [10]. God would not save you and call you to service without clear, exact directions. You must go by the book.[13]

As another example, popular evangelical pastor and author John F. MacArthur Jr. writes that the Bible is "the only reliable and sufficient worship manual."[14] Folk biblicism is also expressed in products such as automobile bumper stickers and T-shirts, as with the following actual instances, all currently for sale:

- God said it, I believe it, that settles it!
- BIBLE—Basic Instruction Before Leaving Earth
- Vote Responsibly—Vote the Bible!
- Confused? Read the Directions! [picture of Bible]
- Have You Read My #1 Best Seller [picture of Bible]? There Is Going to Be a Test. —God
- Have Truth Decay? Brush Up on Your Bible
- Hey Bible Hater! You'd Fit Right in with Communist-Atheist Regimes, Dictatorships, and Islamic States!

- Got Scripture?
- Certified Bible Thumper!

[themes 1, 4–8, and 10 implied]

Biblicism also pervades the evangelical book-publishing market, which entails both popular evangelical markets and formal evangelical institutions (Thomas Nelson, Harvest House, NavPress, InterVarsity Press, etc.). The following are examples, drawn from among a longer list of similar books, almost all of which are currently still in print, all of whose titles listed here are, for present purposes, well worth reading word for word:

- *Bible Answers for Almost All Your Questions*
- *Biblical Principles for Starting and Operating a Business*
- *100 Biblical Tips to Help You Live a More Peaceful and Prosperous Life*
- *Cooking with the Bible: Recipes for Biblical Meals*
- *The Bible Cure for Cancer*
- *The World According to God: A Biblical View of Culture, Work, Science, Sex, and Everything Else*
- *The Biblical Guide to Alternative Medicine*
- *Bible Answers for Every Need*
- *Bible Prophecy 101: A Guide to End Times in Plain Language*
- *What Does the Bible Say about . . . The Ultimate A to Z Resource to Contemporary Topics One Would Not Expect to Find in the Bible, Fully Illustrated—Discover What the Bible Says about 500 Real-Life Topics* [pictures on the cover include golfing, pets, flower arrangements, and a whistle]
- *How to Make Choices You Won't Regret—40 Minute Bible Studies*
- *Queen Esther's Secrets of Womanhood: A Biblical Rite of Passage for Your Daughter*
- *Handbook for Christian Living: Biblical Answers to Life's Tough Questions*
- *Scientific Facts in the Bible: 100 Reasons to Believe the Bible Is Supernatural in Origin*

- *Friendship Counseling: Biblical Foundations for Helping Others*
- *Principles for Life: Using Biblical Principles to Bring Dynamic Psychological Healing*
- *Business by the Book: Complete Guide of Biblical Principles for the Workplace*
- *Bible Solutions to Problems of Daily Living*
- *The Biblical Connection to the Stars and Stripes: A Nation's Godly Principles Embodied in Its Flag*
- *God's Blueprint for Building Marital Intimacy*
- *Crime and Community in Biblical Perspective*
- *A Crown of Glory: A Biblical View of Aging*
- *Gardening with Biblical Plants*
- *Biblical Psychology*
- *One Blood: The Biblical Answer to Racism*
- *Leadership Communication: A Scriptural Perspective*
- *Diagrams for Living: The Bible Unveiled*
- *What the Bible Says about Parenting: Biblical Principles for Raising Godly Children*
- *God Honoring Finances: What the Bible Tells You about Managing Money*
- *Success in School: Building on Biblical Principles*
- *Christian Dress and Adornment—Biblical Perspectives*
- *Feeling Good about Your Feelings: How to Express Your Emotions in Harmony with Biblical Principles*
- *Getting the Skinny on Prosperity: Biblical Principles That Work for Everyone*
- *Off to Work We Go: Teaching Careers with Biblical Principles*
- *Incoming: Listening for God's Messages—A Handbook for Life*
- *Biblical Strategies to Financial Freedom*
- *Revelations That Will Set You Free: The Biblical Roadmap for Spiritual and Psychological Growth*
- *Scripture Based Solutions for Handling Stress*
- *Bad Girls of the Bible and What We Can Learn from Them*

- *Success by Design: Ten Biblical Secrets to Help You Achieve Your God-Given Potential*
- *The Awesome Book of Bible Facts*
- *Learn the Bible in 24 Hours*
- *Body by God: The Owner's Manual for Maximized Living*
- *Biblical Foundations for Manhood and Womanhood*
- *Beyond Positive Thinking: Success and Motivation in the Scriptures*
- *Biblical Economics: A Commonsense Guide to Our Daily Bread*
- *Holding Hands, Holding Hearts: Recovering a Biblical View of Christian Dating*
- *Politics and the Christian: A Scriptural Treatise*
- *Seven Secrets to Bible-Made Millionaires*
- *Prophecy 20/20: Profiling the Future through the Lens of Scripture*
- *Weather and the Bible: 100 Questions and Answers*[15]

  [Implied in these titles are biblicist themes 1–10.]

Clearly, masses of American Christians are biblicists who expect the Bible to be able to speak with authority on a nearly limitless range of topics, and they are willing to spend lots of money to purchase and read about those "biblical" teachings. Numerous Christian authors and publishing houses, both marginal and mainstream, are also clearly unabashedly biblicist, as evidenced in the kind of publications they write and put on the market.[16]

This fact helps to explain some of the more misguided public uses of biblicism. Take, for example, the recent case of disgraced governor of South Carolina (a highly conservative Protestant state) Mark Sanford's public appeal to the example of King David's remaining in monarchical power after his sin with Bathsheba and against Uriah. Sanford used the David and Bathsheba story as justification for his (Sanford's) remaining governor after he disappeared for some days in June 2009 in order to continue his illicit affair with a woman from Argentina. The exposure of the affair and Sanford's explanation proved highly embarrassing on many fronts. Sanford said in a televised cabinet meeting about his remaining in gubernatorial power: "I have been doing a lot of soul searching on that front. What I find interesting is the story of David, and the way in which he fell mightily, he fell in very significant ways, but then picked up the pieces and built from there." He followed up with this written statement: "I remain committed to rebuilding the trust that has been committed to me over the next 18 months, and it is my hope that I am able to follow the example set by David in the Bible—who after his fall from grace humbly refocused on the work at hand." Sanford's friend and Bible study teacher, Warren "Cubby" Culbertson, reportedly gave him these ideas.[17]

Evangelical biblicism is also used by some believers to justify the creation of conservative Christian subcultural alternatives to mainstream healthcare finance industries. Consider, for instance, the following ad published on the inside front cover by the "Christian Care Medical Sharing" company, Medi-Share, in the premiere issue of the evangelical parachurch ministry Focus on the Family's magazine, *Thriving Family* (November/December 2009). This was published at the height of national healthcare reform debate in 2009. "With apologies to Washington," the ad states, "the best plan for healthcare reform was written 2000 years ago." Pictured is a white-haired man in a business suit with briefcase—most likely a member of Congress—sitting on the steps of the Capitol building and reading a Bible. The ad copy continues, "When it comes to your healthcare, the best answers won't be found in the halls of Congress. They're in the pages of God's Word. And you can apply them to your life simply by joining Medi-Share." That organization, the ad also says, promotes and supports "healthy biblical lifestyles, making member costs affordable." Thus, the Bible not only proclaims the good news about salvation in Jesus Christ but it also provides the "best answers" blueprint for national healthcare reform and instructions for healthy lifestyles.

More generally, a defining feature of much of evangelicalism's approach to scripture for ordinary believers is reflected in the "inductive Bible study," a method presupposing that laypeople can sit down with the Bible and inductively draw from it the clear, relevant, and universal truths it teaches [4, 5, 8, 9]. If we could listen in to the private devotions and personal "quiet times" of millions of ordinary evangelical believers around the country, we would also hear biblicist assumptions and practices at work. And biblicism pervades a large amount of "expository preaching" from evangelical pulpits, which

generally proceeds on the assumption that a minister can select virtu-
ally any passage of scripture and adduce from the text an authoritative, relevant, "applicable" teaching to be believed and applied by the
members of his or her congregation [4, 5, 6, 8, 9, 10].

All this popular biblicism has deep historical roots in America,
reflected, for instance, in such popular tracts as Thomas Bingham's
1817 *The Sufficiency of the Holy Scriptures, in the Memoir of William Churchman a Poor Cripple, Who Never Read Any Book but the
Bible*, and Dwight L. Moody's declaration, "I will read no book that
will not help me understand The Book."[18]

Popular, local, folk, and personal biblicism, however, are not free-
floating and self-generating. They are contextualized and cultivated,
if not sometimes outright justified and authorized, by more formal,
institutional, and scholarly expressions of biblicism on which they
ultimately depend. Take, for instance, the "2000 Baptist Faith and
Message" of the massive Southern Baptist Convention, which professes the following:

> The Holy Bible was written by men divinely inspired and is God's
> revelation of Himself to man. It is a perfect treasure of divine instruc-
> tion [10]. It has God for its author, salvation for its end, and truth,
> without any mixture of error, for its matter [1]. Therefore, all Scripture
> is totally true and trustworthy. It reveals the principles by which God
> judges us, and therefore is, and will remain to the end of the world, the
> true center of Christian union, and the supreme standard by which all
> human conduct, creeds, and religious opinions should be tried [8].[19]

The Evangelical Free Church in America's statement of faith says,
"As the verbally inspired Word of God, the Bible is without error in the
original writings [1], the complete revelation of His will for salvation,
and the ultimate authority by which every realm of human knowledge
and endeavor should be judged" [2, 3, 10 implied].[20] Likewise, Trinity
Evangelical Divinity School's (Deerfield, Illinois) statement of faith
avows, "We believe the Scriptures, both Old and New Testaments, to
be the inspired Word of God, without error in the original writings
[1], the complete revelation of His will [2] for the salvation of men
and the Divine and final authority for all Christian faith and life."[21]

Wheaton College's statement of faith similarly says that, "the
Scriptures of the Old and New Testaments are verbally inspired

by God and inerrant in the original writing [1], so that they are fully trustworthy and of supreme and final authority in all they say" [9 implied].[22] Moody Bible Institute declares under "Our Beliefs" that "Everything at Moody falls under the authority of the Bible, which declares timeless truth that is relevant today" [8].[23] The faith statements of other evangelical seminaries and theology schools—including Gordon Conwell, Dallas Seminary, Covenant Seminary, Biola's Talbot School of Theology, Concordia Seminary at St. Louis, and Asbury Seminary—are similar.[24] To take a more obscure and upstart example, consider the "Biblical Foundation Statement" of Gutenberg College—a small Christian "great books" school in Eugene, Oregon, which actually uses the label "biblicist" to describe itself:

> We believe that no creed, no orthodoxy, no consensus, no tradition, nor any other extra-biblical source of teaching that attempts to claim what the Bible teaches should ever dictate how we understand and interpret the Bible [6]. We believe that our doctrines, beliefs, faith, practice, understanding, and knowledge should be brought into conformity to what the actual text of the Scriptures actually teach; but we do not believe that our doctrines, beliefs, faith, practice, understanding, and knowledge need be brought into conformity to any spiritual authority other than the Bible. . . . We grant absolute authority to the Bible and make it our working assumption that everything the Bible asserts—no matter how seemingly trivial or unimportant—should be assumed to be true [3]. We believe that the Bible is without error in anything whatsoever that it does, indeed, assert.[25]

By comparison, back to a more mainstream illustration, Westminster Theological Seminary (Philadelphia) frames its view of scripture confessionally. In a recent statement adopted and published by its board of trustees,[26] for example, Westminster Seminary asserted that the Westminster Standards[27] are "a summary and just exhibition of that system of doctrine and religious belief which is contained in Holy Scripture" [9]. The truths that are affirmed in those standards, the statement declares, "are true for all times, all places, all languages, and all cultures" [8], precisely because they are believed to be scriptural. (The statement does affirm that "the Westminster Standards are fallible, that is, that it is possible in principle that they may err, and, further, that they are open to revision." Yet, the larger content and tone of the statement, Westminster's historical legacy, and the fact that, according to the statement, "the meaning of any particular teaching in the Standards is determined by the Board" [a Reformed quasi-papal Magisterium?], suggest that the likelihood that such a possibility of detecting or admitting error or revisions is effectively nil.)

The statement further declares that "the Holy Scripture is to be believed and obeyed, because it *is* the word of God" [1]; "what Scripture says, God says"; that "what Scripture affirms to its ancient addressees is always true" [8]; and the Bible is "without error in all it affirms." According to the statement, God is the "primary author" who "in causing his word to be written down in the Bible . . . used human writers . . . [as] secondary authors" and "kept them from error." Moreover, the statement declares, "the Holy Scripture contains a system of doctrine. We deny that the Holy Scripture lacks doctrinal unity on any point of doctrine, or that it does not always agree with itself. We affirm that the Holy Scripture is harmonious in all its teachings" [7]. Thus, "each individual passage of Scripture is consistent in its affirmation with every other passage. . . . We deny that passages may contradict one another" [7].

Finally, while the statement acknowledges that "some things in Scripture are difficult to understand, and . . . we may not always be able to easily explain apparent contradictions," the implications of that have no evident effect in unsettling the confidence of the rest of the document.[28] Indeed, the statement claims that "Scripture makes known clearly those things necessary to be believed and observed for salvation, so that even the unlearned may come to sufficient understanding through due use of ordinary means" [4, 5]. More generally, the Westminster Confession of Faith, to which numerous Reformed evangelical denominations and seminaries explicitly subscribe,[29] says this of scripture: "The whole counsel of God concerning all things necessary for His own glory, man's salvation, faith and life, is either expressly set down in Scripture, or by good and necessary consequence may be deduced from Scripture" [2, 3].

Another example of biblicism is the landmark 1978 "Chicago Statement on Biblical Inerrancy"—signed by more than three hundred notable evangelical scholars and leaders—which states:

Holy Scripture, being God's own Word, written by men prepared and superintended by His Spirit, is of infallible divine authority in all matters upon which it touches [1]: it is to be believed, as God's instruction, in all that it affirms [and] obeyed, as God's command, in all that it requires. . . . Being wholly and verbally God-given, Scripture is without error or fault in all its teaching, no less in what it states about God's acts in creation, about the events of world history, and about its own literary origins under God, than in its witness to God's saving grace in individual lives [10 implied].

Therefore, the "statement" warns, "The authority of Scripture is inescapably impaired if this total divine inerrancy is in any way limited or disregarded, or made relative to a view of truth contrary to the Bible's own [6]; and such lapses bring serious loss to both the individual and the Church."[30] The signers of the Chicago Statement furthermore profess in Article XIV that "We affirm the unity and internal consistency of Scripture" [7].[31]

Evangelical parachurch organizations, which provide a major institutional component of American evangelicalism, also reflect some of the biblicism I have described here—despite the fact that in most ways they generally seek to build broad-based support with fairly generic statements of belief. The statement of faith of Campus Crusade for Christ, for instance, says, "The sole basis of our beliefs is the Bible, God's infallible written Word, the 66 books of the Old and New Testaments [6]. We believe that it was uniquely, verbally and fully inspired by the Holy Spirit and that it was written without error (inerrant) in the original manuscripts [1]. It is the supreme and final authority in all matters on which it speaks" [3].[32] The evangelical men's movement Promise Keepers similarly says that "God uniquely revealed and inspired the Bible, so that it alone is God's Word written [1], hence the Holy Scriptures are the only inerrant authority for what we believe [2, 6] about God's moral law, salvation from sin and how we should live" [8].[33]

Likewise, Back to the Bible ministries states, "We believe that the Bible . . . is the revelation of God to mankind, is verbally and fully inspired by Him, is sufficient for the knowledge of God and His will that is necessary for the eternal welfare of mankind [2], is infallible and inerrant in its original manuscripts, and is the supreme and final authority for all Christian faith and conduct" [6].[34] And the parachurch organization Great Commission Churches says in its statement of faith: "The sole basis of our beliefs is the Bible [6] . . . uniquely, verbally, and fully inspired by the Holy Spirit and was written without error in the original manuscript [1]. It is the supreme and final authority in faith and life in every age" [8].[35] I could provide much more evidence of biblicism to be found in the formal statements of countless denominations, seminaries, and other organizations, as well as declarations of scholars, though hopefully these examples will suffice.

Formal statements of faith and theological declarations represent the more respectable face of evangelical biblicism. Popular Internet sites, books, T-shirts, and bumper stickers reflect the kitschier side. But they are both different parts of the same larger biblicist culture. Biblicist leaders and scholars[36] at reputable Christian denominations, seminaries, colleges, and parachurch ministries may dismiss or disdain the popular biblicism embodied in folk Christianity, but popular biblicist kitsch is the fruit of the larger biblicist culture that at least some of those leaders and scholars sustain. There are of course more and less sophisticated versions of biblicism. Yet in the end they are typically different versions and expressions of a broad, similar, shared historical and cultural epistemological tradition. What they generally fail to see is that "to say that the Bible is authoritative is [only] to begin a discussion, not to end it."[37]

## The Problem of Pervasive Interpretive Pluralism

Consider the following four hypothetical scenarios. Imagine first an official state road map that four people all wanting to drive to the same destination consult for directions; each person decides on a different route as the best one to take to that destination. Picture next a pair of army-certified binoculars that five commanding officers who are meeting in war council use to assess their distant enemy's position, strength, and movements; each officer reports quite different accounts of what they see of their enemy's situation, and each one therefore recommends different battle strategies. Then imagine a manufacturer-authorized owner's manual for a fancy new camera that all the shutterbug members of a family study carefully; each individual comes away insisting on very different methods for proper use of the camera. Finally, consider a well-known cookbook containing a recipe that all the contestants in a particular cooking-skills competition must prepare; the contestants, though they vow that they cooked up the same recipe from the same cookbook, each produce a dish that is in some way distinct from all the others.

These four hypothetical scenarios depict something like the quandary in which biblicist believers find themselves. The very same Bible—which biblicists insist is perspicuous and harmonious—gives rise to divergent understandings among intelligent, sincere, committed readers about what it says about most topics of interest. Knowledge of "biblical" teachings, in short, is characterized by *pervasive interpretive pluralism.*

What that means in consequence is this: in a crucial sense it simply does not matter whether the Bible is everything that biblicists claim theoretically concerning its authority, infallibility, inner consistency, perspicuity, and so on, since in actual functioning the Bible produces a pluralism of interpretations. Analogously, the road map may indeed be officially published by the state department of transportation, the binoculars may actually be officially certified by the military, the camera's owner's manual may be manufacturer-authorized, and the cookbook may be well known and the recipe clearly specified—all of that may be so. But it simply does not matter. That is because those apparent facts did not actually accomplish the important things that make them relevant, which being official, certified, authorized, and specified are meant to achieve—namely, clear, consistent, and focused instruction, direction, information, and guidance for users.

Furthermore and very importantly, none of the differences among users that arose in these scenarios will ever get resolved simply by their focusing and insisting on the believed official, certified, or authorized qualities of the road map, binoculars, owner's manual, and cookbook per se. Merely asserting those believed facts itself contributes nothing to solving the *functional* problems of multiple, diverse, and incompatible "readings" of or through them. Likewise, neither do increasingly insistent declarations of biblicist beliefs about the inerrancy, reliability, harmony, and perspicuity of the Bible actually address the fact and problem of pervasive interpretive pluralism concerning scripture, which is a major problem.

This is not a new critique. It is in fact a mere restatement of the same argument made by the evangelical biblical scholar Robert K. Johnson in 1979, at the height of what was then evangelicalism's contentious "battle for the Bible." In his book *Evangelicals at an Impasse: Biblical Authority in Practice*, Johnson offered this astute observation:

> That evangelicals, all claiming a common biblical norm, are reading contradictory theological formulations on many of the major issues they are addressing suggests the problematic nature of their . . . understanding of theological interpretation. To argue that the Bible is authoritative, but to be unable to come to anything like agreement on what it says (even with those who share an evangelical commitment) is self-defeating.[38]

Quoting Professor Geoffrey Bromiley, then of Fuller Theological Seminary—one of the "moderate" evangelical voices of the time—Johnson asked a simple question: "The Bible is infallible and authoritative. But if there are different possibilities of interpretation, where is one to find that which is infallible and absolute?" Johnson then opens his case-study analysis of the problem with this observation and query:

> Evangelicals, all claiming a common biblical norm, are reading contradictory theological formulations on many of the major issues they address. . . . If evangelicals cannot discover a way to move more effectively toward theological consensus, can they still maintain in good conscience their claim to biblical authority as a hallmark?[39]

The evangelical historian Mark Noll in 1986 agreed with Johnson's point, calling "contemporary disagreements on what an infallible Bible means for daily living" a "formidable" difficulty facing evangelical views of the Bible.[40] Similarly, N. T. Wright observes, "It seems to be the case that the more you insist that you are based on the Bible, the more fissiparous you become; the church splits up into more and more little groups, each thinking that they have got biblical truth right."[41] Likewise, Kevin Vanhoozer admits that "inerrancy—the belief that the Bible speaks truly in all that it affirms—does not necessarily generate interpretive agreement among those who hold to it. . . . It is one thing to posit the Bible's truthfulness in all that it affirms, quite another to say what the truth of the Bible *is*."[42] Similarly, D. A. Carson notes that "I speak to those with a high view of Scripture: it is very distressing to contemplate how many differences there are among us as to what

Scripture actually says. . . . The fact remains that among those who believe the canonical sixty-six books are nothing less than the Word of God written there is a disturbing array of mutually incompatible theological opinions."[43]

As far back as 1958, Geoffrey Bromiley had observed—anticipating the present book's view—that "We have to recognize that the Bible is . . . a fruitful source of dissension and disunity in and among churches, so that *acceptance of its authority does not solve at once the problem of unity*. . . . The interpretation of the Bible gives rise to a whole series of more or less important and divisive differences. . . . These are obviously very real difficulties which cannot be ignored even if they cannot be fully embraced and answered. . . . Even in this sphere [of the Bible] there is the constant bias to disunity."[44]

As a matter of fact, this precise line of questioning actually goes back to at least 1849, when Mercersburg Seminary professor John Nevin wrote in an article titled "The Sect System":

> It sounds well, to lay so much stress on the authority of the Bible, as the only text-book and guide of Christianity. But what are we to think of it, when we find such a motley mass of protesting systems, all laying claim so vigorously here to one and the same watchword? If the Bible be at once so clear and full as a formulary of Christian doctrine and practice, how does it come to pass that where men are left most free to use it in this way . . . they are flung asunder so perpetually in their religious faith, instead of being brought together?

Nevin continues:

> However they may differ among themselves as regard to what it teaches, sects all agree in proclaiming the Bible the only guide of their faith; and the more sectarian they are . . . the more loud and strong do they show themselves in reiteration of this profession. . . . It will not do to reply . . . that the differences which divide the parties are small, while the things in which they are agreed are great, and such as to show a general unity after all in the main substance of the Christian life. Differences that lead to the breaking of church communion, and that bind man's consciences to go into sects, can never be small for the actual life of Christianity, however insignificant they may be in their own nature. . . . However plausible it may be in theory, to magnify in such style the unbound use solely of the Bible for the adjustment of

Christian faith and practice, the simple truth is that the operation of it in fact is, not to unite the church into one, but to divide it always more and more into sects.[45]

Even before Nevin, various other observers of American Christianity's sectarian fragmentation expressed dismay about the many denominational divisions that biblicism produced. One, Joseph Smith, who later became the founder of the Church of Jesus Christ of Latter-Day Saints, wrote in retrospect:

> In the midst of this war of words and tumult of opinion, I often said to myself, What is to be done? Who of all these parties are right? Or, are they all wrong together? If one of them is right, which is it, and how shall I know? The teachers of religion of the different sects destroy all confidence in settling the question by an appeal to the Bible. At length I came to the conclusion that I must . . . ask of God.[46]

The rest of Smith's story is, as we know, history. Likewise, sectarian division helped to drive one Pennsylvanian minister, Richard McNemar, to abandon his Presbyterian orthodoxy in favor of the "certainty" afforded by direct revelations among the Shakers. McNemar ridiculed the divisions among the many Christian denominations around him thus:

> Ten thousand Reformers like so many moles
> Have plowed all the Bible and cut it [in] holes
> And each has his church at the end of his trace
> Built up as he thinks of the subject of grace.[47]

The British romantic poet William Blake put the problem even more succinctly:

> Both read the Bible day and night,
> But thou read'st black where I read white.[48]

In some sense, recognition of this problem of pervasive interpretive pluralism even goes back to the Reformation and Martin Luther. When he was writing polemics against the Catholic Church, Luther was forceful about the perspicuity of scripture, since he assumed that the Bible clearly demonstrated the theological beliefs he championed.

However, in due time, as the Reformation began to spin out of control (from his point of view) with the spread of Anabaptist and other sectarian groups, Luther had to back away from the perspicuity of only one "correct" view and recognize the potential to prove a wide variety of doctrinal positions from scripture, admitting, "I learn now that it is enough to throw many passages together helter-skelter, whether they fit or not. If this be the way, then I can easily prove from Scripture that beer is better than wine."[49]

In another, more general sense, this problem of pervasive interpretive pluralism goes all the way back to the recognition of the early church fathers Tertullian (AD 155–230) and Vincent of Lérins (early fifth century) about the impossibility of using scripture to persuade heretics of the error of their ways. Vincent wrote, "Owing to the depth of Holy Scripture, all do not accept it in one and the same sense, but one understands its words in one way, another in another, so that it seems capable of as many interpretations as there are interpreters."[50] According to Tertullian, scriptural "ambiguity" and the possibility of reading the Bible in different ways means that "a controversy over the Scriptures can clearly produce no other effect than help to upset either the stomach or the brain." Tertullian observed: "Though most skilled in the Scriptures, you will make no progress, when everything which you maintain is denied on the other side, and whatever you deny is (by them) maintained. As for yourself, indeed, you will lose nothing but your breath, and gain nothing but vexation from their blasphemy. . . . Our appeal, therefore, must not be made to the Scriptures."[51]

Christians engaging other Christians with whom they disagree is of course different from arguing with heretics, so this is not to suggest that such engagements with other believers should not appeal to scripture. The relevant underlying parallel logic, however, is that scripture taken at face value itself often cannot resolve differences in interpretation, because of its multivocal, polysemous, and multivalent nature, which I discuss in detail below.

To my knowledge and that of Robert K. Johnson (personal correspondence), these observations and questions have been essentially ignored by biblicists in the debate. I know of no satisfactory reply to Johnson's critique or Nevin's question, and neither does Johnson. That is, I suspect, because there *is* no satisfactory answer that does not inevitably endanger the biblicist position. Thirty years ago,

Johnson identified a flaw in biblicism that seemed to be fatal but that was not taken seriously. So the issue must continue to be pressed, for the sake of intellectual honesty and theological integrity in Christian scholarship and practice.

Christians—including different biblicists—come away from their long, hard, well-intentioned studies of scripture convinced that the Bible teaches things that are very different and often incompatible from those that other readers of scripture believe. These differences concern matters both theological and moral, on issues that are considered both secondary and essential.

Biblicists are quick to minimize these differences. Most ("real") Christians, they say, believe essentially the same things on most of the matters of real importance. Vern Poythress, for instance, writes in a book addressing the multiple perspectives evident in the Bible, "We must realize that our own understanding of the Bible's teaching is not perfect or infallible. Because of error or deficiency in understanding, Christians may disagree *slightly* among themselves over *certain* aspects of their common world view."[52] But that gross understatement, we must admit, is flat wrong, as I show below. On most matters of significance concerning Christian doctrine, salvation, church life, practice, and morality, different Christians—including different biblicist Christians—insist that the Bible teaches positions that are divergent and often incompatible with one another.[53]

One strategy for dealing constructively with this problem is to try to turn this unavoidable "necessity" of disagreement into a virtue. The inability of Bible-reading evangelicals to come to anything like a common mind about a host of topics is turned into published scholarly debates conducted under the guise of helpful theological orientation and education. Typical of the results of this strategy are the popular "Three Views," "Four Views," and "Five Views" book series. Thus, the Christian market today offers books with these titles:

- *The Nature of Atonement: Four Views*
- *Understanding Four Views on Baptism*
- *Perspectives on the Doctrine of God: Four Views*
- *Who Runs the Church? Four Views on Church Government*
- *Four Views on Hell*
- *Divorce and Remarriage: Four Views*

- *Four Views on Salvation in a Pluralistic World*
- *Four Views of Christ*
- *Women in Ministry: Four Views*
- *Four Views on Eternal Security*
- *Revelation: Four Views*
- *Divine Foreknowledge: Four Views*
- *Understanding Four Views of the Lord's Supper*
- *Predestination and Free Will: Four Views*
- *The Meaning of the Millennium: Four Views*
- *War: Four Christian Views*
- *Four Views of the End Times*
- *Are Miraculous Gifts for Today? Four Views*
- *God and Time: Four Views*
- *Show Them No Mercy: Four Views of God and Canaanite Genocide*
- *Four Views of Moving Beyond the Bible to Theology*
- *Psychology and Christianity: Four Views*
- *Science and Christianity: Four Views*
- *What about Those Who Have Never Heard? Three Views on the Destiny of the Unevangelized*
- *Three Views on the Rapture*
- *Three Views on the Millennium and Beyond*
- *How Then Should We Choose: Three Views on God's Will and Decision-Making*
- *Three Views on the New Testament Use of the Old Testament*
- *The Genesis Debate: Three Views on the Days of Creation*
- *The Lord's Supper: Five Views*
- *The Historical Jesus: Five Views*
- *Perspectives on Christian Worship: Five Views*
- *Five Views on Apologetics*
- *Church, State, and Public Justice: Five Views*

Another popular evangelical book compares two, three, or four alternative, Bible-based, evangelical views on each of seventeen

theological concerns about which contemporary evangelicals disagree—in theory creating more than *five million* unique, potential
theological belief positions that any given person might espouse,
composed of possible combinations of the alternative views.[54] The
disagreements, to be specific, are over inerrancy (inerrantism versus
infallibalist), providence (Calvinist versus Arminian), divine fore-
knowledge (Arminian versus Calvinist versus Open views), Genesis
(the young earth, day-age, restoration, and literal views), divine image
in humanity (the substantival, functional, and relational views),
Christology (classical versus kenotic), atonement (penal substitution, Christus Victor, and moral government views), salvation (TULIP
versus Arminian), sanctification (Lutheran, Reformed, Keswick, and
Wesleyan), eternal security (eternal versus conditional), the destiny of
the unevangelized (the restrictive, universal opportunity, postmortem
evangelism, and inclusive views), baptism (believer's versus infant
baptism), the Lord's Supper (spiritual presence versus memorial),
charismatic gifts (continuationism versus cessationism), women in
ministry (complementarian versus egalitarian), the millennium (premillennialism, postmillennialism, amillennialism), and hell (the classical view versus annihilationism).

The differences that these books above chronicle concern some
relatively minor topics, admittedly, in the eyes of many—although
obviously not minor enough to have made the differences go away as
beliefs of interest. But some also address major issues, including the
doctrines of God, Christ, revelation, atonement, salvation, baptism,
the Lord's Supper, creation, hell, war, divorce, and remarriage. On
all of these biblical and theological issues, we can identify three or
four different views, not because those who hold them are trying to be
contentious but because they read the Bible and come away convinced
that their different views are correct.

It will not suffice to respond simply by reciting the mantra, "In
essentials, unity; in nonessentials, liberty; in all things, charity," because many of these matters that sustain multiple "biblical" views
that cause division *are* essentials—particularly as viewed by many
biblicists. There simply is not unity on many essentials. Furthermore,
this response assumes more fundamentally that evangelicals at least
agree on what the essentials *are*, which they do *not*. For certain kinds
of Reformed believers, the sovereignty of God understood in a certain

way and double predestination are clearly essentials of the faith—while for others they are not. For Bible-centered Anabaptist Christians, biblical pacifism and nonviolence are central to the gospel—while other believers serve in the US military with clean consciences. For some biblicists, the penal satisfaction theory of the atonement expresses the pure essence of salvation—but for others it is an unbiblical and misguided doctrine. So, not only are Christians divided about essential matters of doctrine and faithful practice; they are also sometimes divided on what even *counts* as essential.

Such four-views and three-views books may provide theological inquirers helpful surveys of historical Christian disagreements about matters of significance—which does serve a good purpose and can be interesting. But in the end the books themselves may distract us from the larger, more serious problem they represent: *that on important matters the Bible apparently is not clear, consistent, and univocal enough to enable the best-intentioned, most highly skilled, believing readers to come to agreement as to what it teaches. That is an empirical, historical, undeniable, and ever-present reality. It is, in fact, the single reality that has most shaped the organizational and cultural life of the Christian church, which now, particularly in the United States, exists in a state of massive fragmentation.*

The fact that Christians have worked for centuries and sometimes millennia to try to sort through these differences has not mattered. The fact that the Bible *itself* implores Christian believers to come to unity with one another and be of the same mind as one another, in view of their one Lord, one faith, and one baptism (John 17:23; Rom. 15:5; Eph. 4:2–5, 13; Phil. 2:2; Col. 3:12–15), has not mattered. The differences have not been overcome. And we have little reason to believe that they will be overcome anytime soon—whether or not we have an inerrant, harmonious, and perspicuous Bible. Appealing to the same scriptural texts, Christians remain deeply divided on most issues, often with intense fervor and sometimes hostility toward one another.

Thus, Craig Branch, a Birmingham Theological Seminary faculty member and ruling elder in the Presbyterian Church of America, observes: "As evangelical Christians we claim that the inspired, infallible, and inerrant Bible reveals God's truth. . . . Yet Bible scholars, Bible teachers, and students from many different denominations and traditions (sometimes even within the same denomination) differ on

. . . doctrines. The doctrines range from significant to peripheral. Yet they all claim to be based on the Bible."[55]

Kenton Sparks observes:

> Recall that among committed inerrantists we will find those who believe in "predestination" and "free will," in "premillennial" and "postmillennial" eschatology, in "infant baptism" and "believer's baptism," in the "elder rule" and "congregational rule." On almost every important interpretive question in every biblical book, we find a wide variety of "inerrantist" readings. So it is clear that inerrancy does not guarantee a correct reading of Scripture, nor does it prevent all sorts of exegetical tomfoolery. . . . Even though evangelicals deny the diversity of Scripture, the theological diversity within evangelicalism is a good and ready indicator of Scripture's truer nature. . . . It is hardly conceivable that evangelicals could assent to so many differing and contradictory viewpoints if the Bible spoke as clearly and univocally as we are wont to suppose.[56]

So the question is this: if the Bible is given by a truthful and omnipotent God as an internally consistent and perspicuous text precisely for the purpose of revealing to humans correct beliefs, practices, and morals, then *why is it that the presumably sincere Christians to whom it has been given cannot read it and come to common agreement about what it teaches*? I know of no good, honest answer to that question. If the Bible is all that biblicism claims it to be, then Christians—especially those who share biblicist beliefs—ought to be able to come to a solid consensus about what it teaches, at least on most matters of importance. But they do not and apparently cannot.

Quite the contrary. Christians, perhaps especially biblicist Christians, are "all over the map" on what the Bible teaches about most issues, topics, and questions. In this way, the *actual functional outcome* of the biblicist view of scripture belies biblicism's *theoretical claims* about the Bible.[57] Something is wrong in the biblicist picture that cannot be ignored.

# 2

## The Extent and Source
## of Pervasive Interpretive Pluralism

Before we are ready to move on to more constructive responses, we must press the matter of pervasive interpretive pluralism harder. Is it really as extensive as I claim? And, if so, of what is it the result? And are there any good ways within the biblicist framework to reply to it?

### Facing the Extent of Pluralism

The many four-views and three-views books noted in the previous chapter address only some of the myriad issues, topics, doctrines, and questions about which Christians—including biblicists—disagree on biblical grounds.[1] Divergent views based on different readings of the Bible also involve many other significant topics—including the role of "good works" in salvation, proper worship protocols, the value of reason and rationality in faith, supersessionism (whether God's "old covenant" promises to the Jews have been replaced by the "new covenant"), marital submission and equality, the legitimacy of creeds and confessions, the nature of life after death, the possible legitimacy and nature of ordained ministry, the morality of slavery, the theological significance of Mary, the ethics of wealth, views of private property, creation and evolution, the nature of depravity and

original sin, salvation of the Jews, use of statues and images in devo-
tion and worship, the status of Old Testament laws, the importance
of a "conversion experience," the perseverance of the saints, church
discipline, birth control, tithing, dealing with the "weaker brother," the
meaning of material prosperity, abortion, corporal punishment, capital
punishment, asceticism, economic ethics, the wearing of jewelry and
makeup, celibacy, drinking alcohol, homosexuality, the "anti-Christ,"
divinely chosen nationhood, swearing oaths, the ontology of church,
believers' relations to culture, church-state relations, and—last but
not least—the nature and purpose of the Bible itself.

What I have written so far should suffice for informed readers to
grasp my meaning. However, because biblicists seem so ready to try
to defend their theory of the Bible by sidestepping or minimizing the
nature and extent of interpretive and theological differences among
sincere and informed Bible readers, I will press the point home by
developing a handful of specific and significant cases of interpretive
pluralism. This may risk beating the proverbial dead horse. But I
prefer to err on the side of presenting too much rather than too little
evidence, because many biblicists seem accustomed to easily ignoring
or dismissing the "biblical" convictions of others who read the Bible
differently than they happen to, or to minimizing those disparities by
suggesting that they are only slight variations on what are commonly
shared Bible-based interpretations and convictions. Yet the differences cannot be ignored, dismissed, or minimized. They are real and
concern important matters. The following examples indicate only
some of those differences.

*Church Polity*: Does the Bible teach a free-church congregational
system, a Presbyterian church government, an Episcopal church polity,
or something else? The answer, it seems, is yes, yes, yes, and yes. Where
two or three are gathered there is Christ with them (Matt. 18:20).
Appoint elders in every town (Titus 1:5). If anyone sets his heart on
being a bishop, that is a noble thing (1 Tim. 3:1). Not to mention:
Jesus made Peter (or was it Peter's confession?) the rock upon which
he built his church (Matt. 16:18). The Christian church today exists in
the fragmented form of literally untold thousands of denominations,
dioceses, conventions, and individual congregations. Baptists alone
are comprised of hundreds of denominations and groupings. There
are extrabiblical, sociological reasons explaining the continuation of

the variety of church polities, each with their own canon laws, constitutions, and manuals of order. But usually beneath these reasons stand genuine differences concerning scriptural teaching about what a "biblical" church looks like. If that was not so, then Christianity would have far fewer divisions, "reformations," and schisms, and the church would enjoy much greater unity.

*Free Will and Predestination*: Christians, especially Protestants, with any awareness of church history and theology know about the apparently irresolvable debate between believers over human free will versus the bondage of the will. The Bible-based argument has been running for centuries. Can people make a choice to embrace God? Or must God alone irresistibly call them out of their spiritual slavery and darkness? Are believers sovereignly predestined to salvation? Or is salvation an offer and decision made to and by every person? Christians disagree, sometimes vehemently. They disagree among other reasons because the Bible contains plenty of evidence to support both sides and more. Arminius lined up a lot of scripture to back up his case; that cannot be denied. But so did the Calvinists who opposed him. Thus, the debate has been interminable. Each side is certain that its view is biblical, yet holds its position at the expense of having to exert mighty efforts to reinterpret away the rather plain meaning of the Bible passages that seem to support the other side.[2] Other Christians, tired of the argument, simply decide either to ignore the matter or to split the difference by asserting that somehow all the contradictions are true in a divine mystery beyond human understanding. That may be, but as a final position it hardly ends up offering us clear biblical instruction on a matter of no small theological importance. Again, the promise of biblicism is unfulfilled.

*The Fourth*[3] *Commandment*: "Remember the Sabbath and keep it holy." All Christians agree that this is one of the Ten Commandments. What does the command mean? What practically does it require? And, for that matter, which day of the week actually *is* this day to be kept holy? Does it remain Sabbath in Jewish terms? Or has it become "The Lord's Day" in the new covenant? Biblicists have quite different answers. Sabbatarians, for instance, make a case for a first-day observance of the Sabbath, but many other Christians disagree. Groups like Seventh-day Adventists, Seventh-Day Baptists, the United Church of God, the Living Church of God, and the True Jesus Church, advocate a seventh, not first, day observance of the Sabbath. Yet others say the old covenant command has been abolished altogether—the Sabbath was "a shadow of the things that were to come; the reality, however, is found in Christ" (Col. 2:17; also see Gal. 4:10–11). Okay, well, whatever day should be observed, what does it mean to "keep it holy"? Does it literally mean using the day exclusively to worship, pray, read scripture, and physically rest? How about eating out at a restaurant? Watching sports on television? Holding a job that sometimes entails work on this day? Enjoying a pleasurable trip to the shopping mall? Bible-reading Christians, including biblicist Christians, are all over the map on this. Again, scripture can apparently be interpreted in many ways.

*The Morality of Slavery*: The bloodiest and one of the most tragic episodes in all of American history was a civil war fought by myriad Bible-believing Christians on both sides, many of whom were equally convinced that the scriptures taught the rightness of slavery, on the one hand, and the imperative of abolition, on the other.[4] Previous decades of heated debate by biblical scholars and ministers who trusted the Bible as God's authoritative word simply could not resolve the conflict by an appeal to the divine texts. If anything, the more strictly biblicist approach supported the proslavery position.[5] On a basic, important moral question addressed in the Bible, the scriptures proved impotent in providing a definitive teaching that sincere believers might have agreed on and thus perhaps avoided war.

The civil war was in its deepest meaning a "theological crisis."[6] It required raw, gory, military might—and took the lives of 620,000 soldiers, not counting incalculable other casualties—to "settle" the matter. As to the adversaries, "both," observed President Abraham Lincoln in his Second Inaugural Address in 1865, "read the same Bible and pray to the same God."[7] Furthermore, it was precisely in the decades after the civil war that "biblical" Christianity was discarded by a majority of American intellectuals as doubtful, and it was displaced by pragmatism, positivism, and materialism.[8] If ever there had been a time when the Bible needed to teach a clear word on an urgent moral issue, the 1850s and early 1860s was it. But no clear word was forthcoming. Mortal enemies instead found clear biblical support for their opposing and irreconcilable convictions.

*Gender Difference and Equality*: The marketplace contains no lack of books explaining "the" biblical view of manhood and womanhood, conceived within the biblicist framework.[9] The only problem is that different contemporary books reading the same biblical texts come to very different, often contradictory conclusions. One set of scholars finds that the Bible teaches a traditional view of gender difference in which men should have authority over women in marriage and church. Another finds that the Bible teaches feminist gender equality and the full participation of women in ministry. One book purports in its title to present *the biblical foundation of manhood and womanhood*. Another's title invites the reader to *discover the truth of biblical equality*. The next offers itself by title as *a response to evangelical feminism*. Then yet another promises to tell us *what Paul really said about women*.

All these books appeal to the Bible as the authority backing their views. And many make what are reasonable cases for their divergent positions. Given this pluralism of arguments, we might ask: in what sense does or can the Bible actually function as an instructive, issue-clarifying authority for the open-minded Bible believer who simply wants to know what the scriptures teach about gender roles, marriage relations, and the place of women in church ministry? In actual practice, it does not and apparently cannot serve as such an authority.

The Bible seems to say many things that can be reasonably read and theologized in various ways. In studying the various sides of this heated debate, one gets the distinct feeling that it is actually the divergent *prebiblical* interests of the many interpreters—both traditionalist and feminist—that drive their scriptural readings, as much as the texts themselves. That too presents problems for biblicism. But the more pertinent point here is this: apparently smart, well-intentioned scripture scholars in fact do read the same set of texts and come away making arguably compelling cases for opposing if not incompatible beliefs on a matter of significance for Christian personal and church practice.

*Wealth, Prosperity, Poverty, and Blessing*: When I was a freshman at Wheaton College in 1979, I took a wonderful course with Professor Bob Webber on "Christ and Culture." One of the assigned readings was Ronald Sider's *Rich Christians in an Age of Hunger*,[10] a bombshell of a book that demonstrated, if nothing else, that the Bible is jam-packed full of scripture verses making it very clear that God cares very much about poverty and hunger. To save money I bought a used copy of the book from another student who had been assigned to read it the semester before. Taking possession of the book, I discovered that page after page had angry notes scrawled in the margins "yelling" at Sider about how dumb and wrong he was—including scrawled in the "biblical passages" chapters. Many pages had actually been torn out (and then shoved back in) in apparent fury over the book's argument. I was surprised and amused. Why would an evangelical student become so incensed about a book that made such a clear biblical case about poverty and hunger? Despite the book's scriptural-evidence overkill, we know that more than a few "Bible believers" at the time of its 1977 publication scorned and attacked the book. One author even wrote a Bible-based counterargument titled, *Productive Christians in an Age of Guilt Manipulation: A Biblical Response to Ronald Sider.*[11]

Yet these are only two among a host of other books about biblical teachings on money, poverty, wealth, prosperity, blessing, and generosity. Some agree in their teachings, but many do not. Some say the Bible teaches material prosperity and financial riches as blessings from God for faithfulness, which believers ought to aspire to win. Others report that the Bible teaches the need for voluntary simplicity or poverty, a kind of new lay monasticism. Yet others claim that the Bible effectively teaches a prudent responsibility and balance concerning money, which fits a middle-class American lifestyle and sensibilities quite well. All appeal to multiple passages of scripture to make their cases, however in tension or at variance with one another their cases turn out to be.

*War, Peace, and Nonviolence*: Across church history, Christians have found in the Bible support for the mutually exclusive positions of nonresistant pacifism, crusades, and just wars, to name the major alternatives. And many American Christians today find clear biblical justification for serving in the US military—which, by virtue of not evaluating possible wars on a case-by-case basis, doesn't neatly fit any of those three historic models. Violence, war, and peace are massively important human moral concerns, and different ethical Christian positions taken on them inevitably make an imprint on the theological character of the gospel preached. Thus, the good news of the evangelical Mennonite is very, very different from the good news of the conservative Republican evangelical.

What *is* clear in all this, however, again, is that, upon a careful study of the biblical bases of the various alternative positions, it is entirely possible for well-meaning and informed students of scripture to justify very different "biblical" views on the matter—it actually happens, and has so for centuries of church history. And, given biblicist assumptions, fully embracing any one "biblical" position on war also necessitates ignoring, discounting, or dramatically reinterpreting those scriptural passages that inconveniently contradict the position embraced. Biblicism is thus again skewered on at least one of the many horns of the beast of pervasive interpretive pluralism.

*Charismatic Gifts*: Should Christians be exercising charismatic gifts of the Spirit today? That is, ought Christians to expect that at least some believers today should and will "speak in tongues," prophesy, be "slain in the spirit," be overcome with "holy laughter," and perform miraculous healings and other "signs and wonders"? Or were charismatic gifts of the Spirit provided only to the first Christians during the time of the apostles in order to help establish a solid foundation of the early church, but then ceased with the closing of the apostolic era? Believers in the latter view argue that supernatural signs and wonders were not meant by God for all times. In contrast, entire evangelical denominations—pentecostal and charismatic—are founded on the conviction that charismatic gifts of the Spirit do and must continue to be exercised by Christians today who want to live the full gospel. Other evangelical denominations explicitly teach as a matter of polity that supernatural signs and wonders have ceased and that to exercise them is to be misled into unbiblical error. Each side marshals lots of Bible verses to argue its case, and each ends up, in my view, making a fairly convincing case.[12] It is hard to see how both can be correct, though. And what one believes makes a big difference in what church and Christian life should look like. So then which one is right? Scripture itself does not seem capable of adjudicating the matter.

*Atonement and Justification*: At the heart of Christian faith stands the cross on which Christ died for the salvation of the world—or at least some humans in the world. But what exactly did the cross—presumably along with the incarnation and resurrection—accomplish? Christians have appealed to scripture and disagreed about this for nearly two thousand years.[13] Biblicists and others who claim to take the Bible seriously still disagree today. Many biblicists have championed the so-called penal satisfaction theory of the atonement as the truly biblical view, arguing that the blood and death of Christ satisfied the holy wrath of God, paying to the Father as judge the legal penalty (death) for human sin. Some, however, especially of a more Anabaptist leaning, claim that the cross is centrally about the nonviolent movement of God and his kingdom in history. Still others emphasize the healing and cleansing nature and effect of the cross. Yet others simply find in scripture a vast mélange of images and metaphors for the meaning of the cross, none of which, they claim, holds theological primacy. For them, the Bible simply presents a "kaleidoscopic" or "mosaic" set of views about the atonement. Then again, recently a theological storm has broken over the so-called new perspective on Paul concerning the doctrine of justification—both (or more) sides of which appeal to many scriptural texts for support.[14] And none of this is to mention other views less appealing to most biblicists, including the so-called classical or Christus Victor view, seeing the cross as a quasi-military victory over Satan and the kingdom of darkness; or the so-called subjective view of atonement, understanding the cross as setting a moral example of God's boundless love for the lost, which transforms those who believe. These views also draw on a variety of apparently supportive biblical texts.

The cross, atonement, and justification are clearly not "secondary" theological issues. Yet, it is a historical, empirical, undeniable fact that biblicist and other Christians have been unable to come to anything like a common mind about what the Bible actually teaches on those central matters. Instead, scripture has given rise to a multiplicity of divergent beliefs and commitments.

*God-Honoring Worship*: How does God want or how might he allow his people to worship him? Bible-reading Christians disagree. May clergy wear vestment robes and burn incense? Must all pictures and images be removed from sanctuaries? May worship include musical instruments? What does the Bible teach? Different things, it seems. The various answers cluster around three general principles, all claiming to honor scripture.

One is the so-called regulative principle, which argues that only those things that are instituted by command, teaching, or example in the Bible or are derived by "good and necessary consequence" from the Bible are permitted in worship. In short, God institutes in the Bible everything required for church worship and prohibits all other possibilities. This is the view of many Presbyterian, Reformed,

Anabaptist, Restorationist, and some Baptist churches. Lutherans, Anglicans, Methodists, and many other sorts of evangelical churches disagree, holding instead to the so-called normative principle of worship, which says that worshipers may use elements of worship that are not prohibited by the Bible, whether or not they are positively commanded by scripture.[15]

Then again, some Christians argue for the so-called informed principle of worship, which says that what the Bible commands of worship is required, what it forbids is prohibited, and what is not forbidden is allowable if deduced by an application of the good-and-necessary-consequence principle. But regulative-principle advocates argue that this is merely a more complicated restatement of their view. Many Christians today may not be aware that these are even issues of debate. But they do cause controversies and have consequences.

The regulative principle helps to explain why churches that subscribe to it can feel stripped down and bare to those not used to it. And the normative principle explains why churches that follow it embrace more ornate and liturgical elements of worship, such as clergy vestments, stained glass, sacred images, processional crosses, incense, and so on. These principles sometimes lurk behind controversies over "contemporary praise-song" versus traditional styles of worship services. Differing biblical beliefs about proper worship have also generated controversies about the propriety in worship services of hymnbooks, corporate confessions of sin, liturgical dance, doxologies, benedictions, the recitation of creeds, and other issues. Some Calvinists have even argued that the Bible prohibits the use of any musical instrument in church.[16] Others claim that in biblical worship services only the psalms may be sung.

Many American evangelicals may not care about these disputes, but that essentially says that they unwittingly subscribe to the normative principle. Particularly interesting to note about these disagreements is that they revolve both around the right interpretation of specific Bible verses (e.g., Exod. 20:4–6; Lev. 10:1–3; Deut. 4:2; 12:29–32; 17:3; Josh. 1:7; 23:6–8; 1 Kings 18; 2 Kings 16:10–18; Matt. 4:9–10; 15:3, 8–13; John 4:23–24; Acts 17:23–25; Col. 2:18–23) and also around larger hermeneutical principles concerning the use of scripture as a whole, which no verses per se seem able to determine (although regulative-principle adherents disagree with that view). The debates, in other words, are both biblical and (I think) metabiblical—which helps to explain why they are also interminable.

*General Christian Relation to Culture*: What about a less specific theological issue? Perhaps the Bible gives rise to greater consensus at a broader level, on, say, a biblical view of the general relation of Christianity to its surrounding culture and society. In such broad terms, does biblicism fare better? Well, no. As with most other issues, Christians have been and are all over the map—and all with well-read Bibles in hand. I will not elaborate in depth, as readers no doubt understand the facts here. H. Richard Niebuhr's classic *Christ and Culture* made the point clear enough, along with other Bible-based books that have also attempted to address the matter.[17] Does the Bible teach that Christians should be against, of, above, or transforming culture, or is it all a paradox? Again, yes, yes, yes, yes, and yes. Or at least plenty of biblical texts exist that can, within a biblicist framework, build quite strong cases for each perspective. Once again, the Bible itself does not settle the matter in an authoritative way. If anything, it gives rise to a multiplicity of plausible "biblical" positions that have biblicists lining up on all sides of the debate.

Evangelical biblicists are highly divergent from one another on many scriptural and theological issues and in their consequential cultural and institutional manifestations. For this reason, many scholars of American evangelicalism find it difficult to identify anything much that evangelicals share in common. Mark Noll, for instance, observes that "the groups and individuals making up the postwar evangelical movement unite on little except profession of a high view of scripture and the need for divine assistance in salvation."[18] Nathan Hatch has likewise emphasized American evangelicalism's "populist and decentralized structure," "its penchant for splitting, forming, and reforming," its "pluralism and decentralization," its "few church structures to which many of its adherents or leaders are subject," and its "instability that I [Hatch] think is problematic for theological integrity." He observes, "In truth, there is no such thing as evangelicalism. [It is made up of] extremely diverse coalitions dominated by scores of self-appointed and independent-minded religious leaders."[19] Other scholars similarly struggle to find in the "essentially contested concept" of "evangelicalism" anything more than a "family resemblance" or "mosaic" of pieces that together form a group by that name.[20]

A great deal of the work of the neo-evangelical movement in the United States since the 1940s has been trying to forge enough common ground on which to unite "for the sake of its gospel." But the Bible *itself*—and not simply a shared *theory about* the Bible—has proven to be a problematic basis for defining that common ground. Even in a book dedicated entirely to solidifying a consensus of shared evangelical theological beliefs—J. I. Packer and Thomas Oden's *One Faith: The Evangelical Consensus*—already by the second page of the introduction the authors admit to having to ignore the many areas of evangelical dissensus: "We have . . . attempted not to select passages [of key evangelical declarations and documents] on which evangelical consent is still under intense debate. . . . We decline to discuss secondary matters on which disagreements surface, such as variations on polity, modes and subjects of baptism, glossolalia, millennialism, theological epistemology, and specifics of exegesis."[21] Doing so is certainly necessary to sustain a case about evangelical consensus, but it does not make the disagreements go away.

American evangelicalism, I maintain, lacks a positive, shared, biblically grounded belief system and identity. The view of evangelicals in Britain, apparently, does not look much better.[22] Therefore evangelicalism has often, unfortunately, held itself together as a movement by reliance on the negative forces and mechanisms involved in fighting against alien groups and movements that seem threatening, such as liberal Protestantism and "secular humanism" (and, although to a lesser extent lately, Roman Catholicism).[23] Yet that dynamic does not reflect well the original vision of neo-evangelicalism's founders, such as C. F. H. Henry, Harold Ockenga, and Edwin Carnell. Something is wrong with this picture.

## Considering Possible Biblicist Replies

Biblicists or any other interested parties might respond to these problems with six possible replies. The first three are the kinds of responses that biblicists most likely would assume or say in response to the above. The last three are more speculative possibilities that might be proposed in order to salvage biblicism from the problem of pervasive interpretive pluralism—I know of no specific biblicists who do, but as theoretical possibilities they are still worth considering.

Some, to begin, might say in response to pervasive interpretive pluralism that truly sincere and informed students of scripture *can* come to understand the single, harmonious truth that the Bible teaches—and some do—but that most Christians who study the Bible actually do so with problematic motives, interests, or skills that prevent them from seeing the coherent truth. Less charitably stated: "We are right and the rest, unfortunately, are wrong." Let us call this the *blame-the-deficient-readers answer*. This view is often assumed, more or less consciously, by those who believe that their theological and moral views are *truly* biblical and others are misguided and in error.[24]

Second, biblicists might reply by claiming that none of these interpretive problems would apply to the "original autographs" of the original biblical manuscripts written by the hands of their first authors, but that something about the copying and translating of the original documents makes it more difficult for subsequent readers to grasp their true, single, coherent teaching. We might call this the *lost-original-autographs explanation*.

Third, some biblicists might reply that the Bible really does contain and teach one coherent truth, but that humans have suffered such profoundly damaging "noetic"[25] effects of sin—that is, the corruption of their capacities for inner thought and knowledge—that they simply cannot see the single truth in scripture clearly enough to understand and agree upon it. Let us call this the *noetically-damaged-reader reply*.

A fourth, more speculative, possible response to salvage biblicism from the problem of pervasive interpretive pluralism might be that God desires only some of those who call themselves by the name of Christ to understand biblical truth and so withholds the illumination of the Holy Spirit from many, but not all Christians, so that some cannot understand scripture rightly. Evangelicals who believe in double predestination might be prone in theory to believing this. A possible variant on that explanation, which might perhaps be favored by certain groups of Pentecostals, could be that Satan has gained such a powerful hold in the lives of so many Christians that he enjoys diabolical powers to cause them to misread the Bible and so believe in errors. We could call either of these the *supernatural-confusion explanation*.

Fifth, some might reply that the single, coherent divine word of truth in the Bible is so complex and multidimensional that it actually encompasses and is reflected in all the divergent and seemingly incompatible views of the truth that different Christians read in the Bible. The divergent scriptural interpretations that different biblicist readers hold thus represent something like the different parts of the proverbial elephant touched and reported on by the ten Indian blind men—each is right in his or her own way, but to get the full truth they need to put all their knowledge together. This we might call the *inclusive-higher-synthesis response.*[26]

Finally, someone might conceivably suggest that God has intentionally provided an ambiguous scripture that would purposively cause disagreement and division in order to achieve some greater good, such as perhaps forcing believers to continually struggle and work through doctrinal conflicts in order to learn humility, openness, and continual reliance on divine grace. This we might label the *purposefully-ambiguous-revelation thesis.*

Some of these reasons may be correct. I may actually be open, if not sympathetic, to the gist of more than one of them. But none rescues biblicism from pervasive interpretive pluralism, and that is the question at issue here. Each of these six replies is or should be unacceptable, *given biblicist assumptions*, and so, if adopted, forces significant revisions to biblicist beliefs. Take blaming-the-deficient-reader, for instance: it is no doubt true that in some cases some Christians do approach the Bible with certain faulty motives, interests, or skills, which distort their reading of scripture and lead them to draw erroneous and truly unbiblical conclusions.[27] Sometimes, for example, people look for "biblical" approval or permission for something problematic that they have already decided they want before opening up scripture. But that itself can hardly explain the divergent interpretations to which the Bible has recurrently given rise among well-meaning believers throughout church history and today.

Why and how, we might ask, would the Bible be so easily misread by so many believers if, as biblicism believes, it is divine, inerrant, internally harmonious, perspicuous, and intent on revealing infallible truth to humankind? The doctrine of scriptural perspicuity is particularly problematic here. If the truth of the Bible is really sufficiently understandable to the ordinary reader, then why do so many of them—and countless biblically and theologically trained scholars besides—find it impossible to agree on what that truth is?[28] This response places a huge burden of explanation on the bad intentions, biased interests, or poor scholarly skills of Christian Bible readers across two millennia—a burden the evidence cannot sustain.

What about the lost-original-autographs explanation? Unlike some of the following responses, which are somewhat far-fetched, this approach is not much off from the explanatory strategies of some biblicists. Usually an appeal to the "original autographs" is employed to rescue inerrancy in the face of certain quite apparent discrepancies in the text.[29] Take, for example, the 1978 "Chicago Statement on Biblical Inerrancy," Article X, which says:

> We affirm that inspiration, strictly speaking, applies only to the autographic text of Scripture, which in the providence of God can be ascertained from available manuscripts with great accuracy. We further affirm that copies and translations of Scripture are the Word of God to the extent that they faithfully represent the original. We deny that any essential element of the Christian faith is affected by the absence of the autographs. We further deny that this absence renders the assertion of Biblical inerrancy invalid or irrelevant.

This strategy could perhaps also be used to address the challenge of interpretive pluralism.

However, this move simply does not work. Suppose that any and every well-equipped theoretical reader of the original autographs of the original documents of sacred scripture would indeed find there a clear, unified, consistent system of doctrine and morality about which all readers could agree. What good does that do the *actual* Christian believers who do not possess the original documents—that is, nearly all Christians in church history—who want and need to understand Christian truth? Nothing. All that actually does is formally build a logically protective, unfalsifiable wall around a theory. But that proves completely unhelpful for the more pressing task of actually *knowing* what is true, real, wise, and good. People standing on a sinking ship in the middle of the ocean are not helped one bit by the in-fact-totally-correct observation that if they were on another ship they would not be sinking. Neither are Christians reading the actual Bible that they possess helped in any way by the idea that they would have greater clarity of understanding if they could only read the original autographs of the original manuscripts of the first scriptural writings. The lost-original-autographs explanation is not necessarily false. It is simply useless and irrelevant. It does not address and explain the present problem in any satisfying or constructive way.

Does the noetically-damaged-reader response prove any better at rescuing biblicism from pervasive interpretive pluralism? No. This explanation shipwrecks on the rocks of implying that God's chosen method of revealing truth and the power of God's Spirit to illuminate that truth are inadequate to the task. Perhaps God tried his best with biblical revelation, but unfortunately underestimated the damage of sin to humans' epistemic capacities? A biblicist cannot accept that. Certainly, some people lack the perceptual and mental capacities to make proper sense of the Bible. But those, we must believe, are abnormal exceptions. If biblicism is correct, then most ordinary people, and not simply an elite of scholarly specialists or the most brilliant readers, should be readily able to understand scriptural truth. Humans may be noetically damaged by sin. But the point of divine revelation and God's word is precisely to break through the limits of that damage from outside of the confines of those limits in order to convey truth to fallen humanity. The noetically-damaged-reader reply forces us to say that God's plan of revelation has worked rather poorly, which hardly provides a robust vindication of biblicism or the Bible.

The fourth possible response, the supernatural-confusion explanation, is theoretically possible on its own terms but proves unacceptable to biblicism in the end. Nothing in the biblicist outlook, which emphasizes the effectiveness of biblical infallibility, clarity, consistency, and truth disclosure, gives us reason to entertain it. Biblicists simply cannot believe on their own terms that God has an interest in purposely hiding doctrinal and moral truth from his people. Neither does scripture itself nor Christian tradition broadly give us reason to believe that diabolical forces have the capacity, against the illuminating power of the Holy Spirit, to prevent masses of Christians from properly reading and understanding divine truth. This reply just doesn't work, at least within biblicist terms.

Similarly, the inclusive-higher-synthesis response is theoretically possible when considered on its own terms, and some evangelicals may be inclined to believe it. God's ways and thoughts are indeed higher and different than those of humans. But this account may also run up against seemingly fatal problems. It seems to suggest, again, that God's method of revealing truth was less than adequate for the task involved, since in the end, despite having scriptural revelation, Christians do not know very definitely what the truth is. They see only small bits and pieces of it. This explanation tends to cut the legs out from under any reliable notion of doctrinal and moral coherence grasped and embraced at the human level, since the synthetic harmony that pertains at the level of divine understanding—assumed by this view—does not very well reach down to make sense within the best categories, logics, and understandings of human beings. The truth may be clear and coherent at a higher level, but by the time it reaches real people through the Bible it becomes ambiguous and fragmented. If this explanation is the answer to the problems noted above, then biblicism needs to back away from some of its defining claims.

Finally, what about the purposefully-ambiguous-revelation thesis? Again, in theory it could be true. It has some precedents in at least Luther and Augustine.[30] But most American biblicists would say that God is not a God of confusion, but of truth, order, and faithful care. Sin has already created plenty of darkness and confusion in the world. Why would God need or want to build more ambiguity and misunderstanding into the divine revelation given to those whom he is trying to speak to, enlighten, and save? If this explanation is needed to salvage biblicism from the problem of pervasive interpretive pluralism, then biblicism starts to defeat itself in the very act of trying to rescue itself.

In the end, these six possible biblicist responses fail to answer the question of why it is that, if everything biblicists say about the Bible is true, well-intentioned Christians to whom scripture has been given cannot read it and come to agreement about what it teaches. The hard question remains. It apparently cannot be answered from within biblicist parameters. Biblicism as a theory contains flaws that it cannot explain away, and such flaws seem to make it impossible for its believers to put it into practice with integrity and coherence. The problem of pervasive interpretive pluralism calls into question at least some of the beliefs of biblicism because it reveals how biblicism sets up expectations that simply are not met in practice.

## The Reality of Multivocality

To come to terms with pervasive interpretive pluralism, we should pay closer attention to the actual nature of human readings of scripture that produce contrary interpretations. What appear to be the common causes of the routinely divergent readings of the Bible? What actually happens, especially among biblicists, when well-intentioned believers sit down with the scriptural texts and make sense of them in ways that differ from the sense other believers make of the same texts? What is essentially at work—not in contending abstract theories about the Bible, but in the actual practice of Bible reading and interpretation itself—that gives rise to the pluralism of understandings of biblical truth at which Christians arrive and on which they insist?

What seems to happen, stated oversimply, is something like this. Christians, including most biblicists, sit down with the biblical text to try to grasp what it teaches and find that, lo and behold, it contains and reflects a vast and confusing array of terms, concepts, images, genres, styles, contexts, narratives, purposes, statements, and arguments.[31] They often do their finest to identify some overarching theme, consistent thread, or interpretive framework that will bring order and coherence to the texts. Let us call these interpretive "paradigms."[32] Sometimes these are identified in the attempt to provide a comprehensive grasp of the Bible as a whole. For some the overarching paradigm turns out to be salvation history. For others it is the covenant and election. For yet others the organizing frame is the idea of historical dispensations. Some say the paradigm is the idea of the kingdom of God. Some claim it is divine liberation from all forms of oppression. For some readers, it is the contrast between law and grace. Still for others the thread is simple, unconditional divine love and acceptance of humanity. Then again, others think that the best organizing paradigm revolves around the ideas of divine command, obedience, disobedience, judgment, punishment, and reward.

Sometimes, by contrast, Bible readers identify paradigms operating at an "intermediate" level of interpretation that are designed to make sense of a particular doctrinal or ethical issue. Some, for instance, believe scripture teaches peace and nonviolence. Others adopt the paradigm of a "consistent ethic of life." Yet others hear the scriptures revolving around the issue of the need for people to experience a public conversion, to invite Christ into their heart, to make a public profession of faith, in order to "go to heaven." Some believe the Bible centrally teaches the inexorable degeneration of human society and the singular call of believers to work to "win the lost" and "save souls." Still others read the Bible as calling for determined social and political reform that will help usher Christ's kingdom into history through an ever-expanding movement of justice and righteousness.

Most of these paradigms can seem to work, more or less. None of them decisively disqualifies or eliminates the others, at least as far as the adherents of other paradigms are concerned. In any case, no matter which metainterpretive paradigm Christians adopt, a great deal of scriptural text can be organized to make sense within it—some texts quite easily so and others only with some force and twisting. But, in all instances—and crucial for present purposes—there is always a significant set of texts that do not make sense, do not seem relevant, and do not harmonize or fit with the given larger thematic paradigm. Let us call those anomalous passages of scripture the "leftover" texts. The paradigms simply cannot integrate or make good sense of them. The leftover texts are outliers; they are incongruous and glitchy. For that reason, they are uncomfortable for the believers of the paradigms for which they are anomalous.

Another crucial fact about such leftover texts is this: those that are anomalous for one paradigm often turn out to be core texts in a different paradigm. What is leftover to one framework is fundamental to another. This is not surprising, since the paradigms were originally formed in part by the recognition that certain biblical themes suggest frameworks that best account for them. But no paradigm accounts for all the texts. And since the paradigms are alternative to each other and at least partially text-referencing, as described above, it makes sense that different constellations of texts fit certain paradigms well, yet remain anomalous leftovers for others.

The goal of any given legitimacy- and coherence-seeking paradigm vis-à-vis its leftover texts is to prevent them from discrediting itself as an adopted paradigm. This is generally accomplished in one of two ways. The first and easiest is simply to ignore the leftover texts, to learn to act as if they do not exist. Probably every biblical paradigm does this, though often—especially when most successful—without realizing it. The second means to avoid the discrediting effect of leftover texts is to formulate explicit, ad hoc explanations about why those texts actually do not say what they appear to say, to explain how what they "really" mean does not actually contradict the paradigm in question. Examples of both of these paradigm-protecting practices are myriad.

In the end, as a result, different groups of Christians end up invested in different interpretive paradigms, learn to ignore certain potentially threatening leftover texts, and are persuaded that the remainder of leftover texts can be explained away on an ad hoc basis when they are "rightly understood," read in proper context, or otherwise "correctly" interpreted. When all is said and done, the adherents of all of the paradigms are persuaded that their approach to biblical interpretation produces a comprehensive and consistent reading and understanding of the entire body of scripture. And since few of the paradigms appear susceptible to synthetic integration and many of the paradigm-protecting maneuvers required to take care of leftover texts entail denials of claims made by other paradigms, divergence, division, and fragmentation remain.

Consider an alternative image illustrating how biblical reading and interpretation seem to happen in real practice. This image switches away from organizing texts into intelligible meaning systems, as with above, to instead fitting pieces of an apparent whole into a recognizable visual picture. In this analogy, the Bible functions something like—to be clear, only *something like*, not exactly as—a particular, enormous jigsaw puzzle with a huge number of pieces that is sold in many stores. The job of the Bible interpreter in this analogy is to figure out how the scads of pieces dumped from the box and spread out all over a table fit together to make the finished puzzle picture.[33] The only difficulty is that this is a very unusual puzzle. For, as far as anyone working on it can figure out, different puzzle pieces can be fit together in different ways to make distinctly different pictures. Nearly all of them are portraits of people. One is of a scowling old man, another of a sweet young girl, yet another a pregnant woman, and still a fourth is a tired-looking police officer. Rumor has it that yet other portraits can be made. (Occasionally some put the pieces together into other kinds of pictures—of seascapes, pets playing, or flower arrangements—but most puzzle enthusiasts discount those pictures as silly, because they just don't look right and end up using only half the pieces in the box.)

So, in this way, the puzzlers discover that many of the pieces that make one portrait can be rearranged differently, with some pieces removed and others added, to make other portraits. Not only that, but in any given picture, enough of the pieces fit together to fill in most of the image, but not all of it. Every picture, no matter how well it is put together, still has some missing puzzle pieces. The sweet girl is missing part of an ear and a tooth. The pregnant woman is missing part of her foot and elbow. Furthermore, no matter how the pieces are fit together to make a nearly finished picture, there are always some pieces remaining that do not fit. In no picture do *all* the pieces correctly fit together. Some people try, but they end up bending and mangling those pieces. It just doesn't work.

Nevertheless, despite, or perhaps precisely because of, the unusual nature of this complicated puzzle, it is very popular. Untold numbers of people are keen to buy it, spread the pieces out, and work to put them together. Most hope to use up all of the pieces to make one grand, recognizable portrait. But nobody ever succeeds. What happens instead is that different puzzlers in time see that they can make different pictures and end up choosing to make the one that personally most appeals to them for whatever reasons. Often—either because they come to really like their preferred picture, or simply because they become tired of sorting out and working on the alternative portraits that they can and might fit together—different puzzlers become partisans of one or another of the possible portraits. Some are proud of being "scowling-man puzzlers," claiming that his is the *real* portrait that the puzzle makes when rightly put together. Others feel and say the same thing about the particular portraits they prefer.

Partiality to different puzzle portraits tends to run in families, as parents pass on the making of their own favorite pictures to their children. In most cases, however, puzzlers like to sweep the unused pieces that do not fit their portraits into Ziploc bags and put them into their closets.[34] Sometimes groups of puzzlers who all prefer to make the same portrait suggest that the leftover, unused pieces from those who make different pictures are actually not genuine, original pieces, but rather belong to other puzzles and were probably accidentally mixed into this puzzle box as a kind of contamination by careless hands. If other people who like to make different portraits knew the *real* portrait that this puzzle made, it is said, then they would realize the other glitchy puzzle pieces really don't belong and perhaps should be discarded to reduce confusion.[35] The only problem is, some people who like other portraits say the very same thing about the disagreeing people who make all the other puzzle pictures. In the end, nobody is convinced by the others. So the puzzlers continue to squabble.

If these descriptive accounts and analogies about how the Bible is actually read and made sense of by real Christians are essentially correct and revealing, then that tells us something very important. It tells us that the Bible is *multivocal* in its plausible interpretive possibilities: it can and does speak to different listeners in different voices that appear to say different things. Whatever biblicist theories say *ought* to be true about the Bible, in their actual, extensive experience using the Bible in practice, Christians recurrently discover that the Bible consists of irreducibly multivocal, polysemic, and multivalent texts (polysemy means "multiple meanings" and multivalence means "many appeals or values").[36] This means that the Bible often confronts the reader with "semantic indeterminacy."[37]

Specific *words* in the Bible are sometimes polysemic, as biblical scholars well know. For instance, the word "head" (*kephalē*) in Ephesians 5:23 ("the husband is the head of the wife as Christ is the head of the church") can plausibly be interpreted to mean either "authority" (as traditionalists interpret it) or "source," as in the "head" of a river (as egalitarians interpret it). The latter interpretation has the sense of husbands being a kind of source of life for wives by laying down their lives for them as Christ did for the church (cf. vv. 25–28).

Furthermore, very many *passages* in the Bible are polysemic. For example, to take a much-debated case relevant well beyond the circles of biblicists, the meaning of Matthew 16:18 ("And I tell you that you are Peter (*petros*), and on this rock (*petra*) I will build my church, and the gates of Hades will not overcome it"), has long been contested by those (Roman Catholics) who believe that the church is to be built upon Peter as a particular apostle, versus those (generally Protestants) who believe the church is to be built upon the *confession* of Peter (in v. 16, "You are the Christ, the Son of the living God")—among other argued positions. This is a debate the verse itself cannot, even in its larger context, resolve. This general fact of the polysemy of scriptural passages explains why ten different preachers can deliver ten quite different, more or less credible sermons on the exact same biblical passage.

Moreover, numerous passages *addressing the same issue* when considered together are often multivocal. Consider, for example, that the Gospels say quite different things about the role of signs and miracles in Jesus's ministry. The first three Gospels teach that no miraculous sign "will be given to [this generation] except the sign of the prophet Jonah" (Matt. 12:39; see also Luke 11:29; Mark 8:12). The Gospel of John, however, shows Jesus publicly providing many wondrous miracles, so that the people "followed him because they saw the miraculous signs he had performed" (John 6:2). More broadly, the evangelical biblical scholar Peter Enns does an excellent job of showing just how much multivocality—what he calls "theological diversity"—there is in the Old Testament as a whole.[38]

Therefore, when all of the multivocality of words, passages, and thematic groups of passages are added together, the *Bible as a whole* is exponentially more multivocal, polysemic, and multivalent. As a result, church history is replete with multiple credible understandings, interpretations, and conclusions about the Bible's teachings.[39] This makes scripture somewhat "semantically indeterminate," in that the exact *meanings* of its texts are *underdetermined by the words* of the texts themselves. Those who fail to see this multivocality and polysemy of scripture—who instead insist on the combination of perspicuity and internal consistency—can do so only by forgetting that they interpret the Bible from within a well-developed community of interpretation relying on particular (though, to them, invisible) hermeneutical tools and paradigms that many other biblicists do not share.

For a more extended example of the multivocal, polysemic, and multivalent nature of scriptural texts, we might consider the familiar story of Jesus talking to the Samaritan woman at the well, recorded in the Gospel of John 4:1–42. The story itself is not terribly complex as far as narratives go, and its author certainly had specific intentions in mind by putting it in writing. But the text's multivocality and polysemy are evident in the fact that it can and does give rise to a variety of different and sometimes discordant readings. Among those various readings—many of which I personally have over the years heard from diverse pulpits and read in various articles and books—are the following:

- Christians need to "get out of their comfort zones" in order to preach the gospel to those who are culturally different or who live in foreign lands but who are "ripe for the harvest."

- Jesus was a feminist, as evidenced by his willful violation of the repressive sexist cultural norms of his time.

- Once a person drinks of the "living water" by accepting Jesus Christ into their heart, they will never again "thirst" for the empty "waters" offered by "the world."

- Jesus continually disrupts our settled personal lives by encountering us with penetrating and troubling questions that lead us to repent.

- We know that Jesus was God because of the miracles he performed, including knowing details about this stranger's marital history and cohabiting relationship.

- Christianity ends not only the temple worship of the Jews but all empty institutionalized and ritualistic worship—God wants to be worshiped purely "in spirit and in truth."

- Jesus knows "everything we have ever done" and yet still loves and forgives us.

- The way to evangelize unbelievers is to build relationships, ask probing questions, and point them to Christ—pretty soon they will be telling the good news to their own people.

- Until the Holy Spirit gives illumination, sinful people, like the woman and the disciples, are hopelessly clueless about God's truth, even when it stares them in the face.

- The fact that Jesus was physically tired from his journey from Judea to Galilee proves that a docetic Christology (that Jesus was not fully human) is false.

- That the woman "left her water jar" to go and tell her townsfolk about Jesus models for Christians the kind of free and open-handed readiness to leave possessions behind in order to preach the good news around the world.

- God's kingdom is "upside down"—Jesus is always saying and doing the most unexpected things possible in order to challenge our assumptions about "normal" life.

- The worship of so-called Christians, such as Roman Catholics and Mormons, who think they know the truth but who actually believe false doctrine is not acceptable to God.

- By speaking the truth to a Samaritan woman at Jacob's well, Jesus was foreshadowing the gospel mission to the gentiles, which God would later unveil to Peter and commission to Paul.

- God cares about the integrity of people's marital and sexual relationships and so confronts them with their infidelities and calls them to repentance.

- Jesus's reply to his disciples about hunger and food shows us that more important than consuming physical food is eating the "food" of the word of God, especially by being consistent in having personal daily "devotions" or "quiet times."

- Jesus wants to break down all the fear-based walls that divide people—Jews and Samaritans, men and women, blacks and whites, heterosexuals and homosexuals—from one another, so they can live in love, acceptance, and fellowship.

Anyone familiar with preaching and writing in the American Christian church will know that none of these readings is particularly far-fetched. Different expositors—biblicist or otherwise—can and do read exactly these kinds of lessons from this single biblical text. Many of them are plausible, although some seem mutually exclusive. Different people will of course find some of them palatable and others ridiculous. My larger point, however, is that, with enough homiletic or writing skill, each reading is feasible, if not entirely credible. There are, indeed, major swaths of different kinds of Christians out there who would and do find any one of these readings compelling and edifying. Such different readings of scripture indeed *are* possible because the texts themselves are multivocal, polysemic, and multivalent in character.

What I have said thus far is, of course, not an original observation. Scholars of textual hermeneutics like Paul Ricoeur and Hans G. Gadamer have been telling us about the polysemy of texts for decades.[40] These scholars help us to see that most texts, unlike many scientific formulas and computer codes, involve "surpluses of meaning" that give rise to multiple understandings. Most texts are also at least somewhat "semantically independent" of their sources and so cannot be entirely controlled in their interpretation by their original authors.[41] Short of a divine miracle, the Bible therefore cannot function as an authority today, whether or not the Holy Spirit is involved, until it is interpreted and made sense of by readers. Every scriptural teaching is mediated through human reading and active interpretation, which involve choosing one among a larger number of possible readings. Thus every scriptural teaching is subject to the complexities and different outcomes of the interpretive process.

Donald Bloesch rightly notes, "Faith itself gives rise to criticism, for faith is discriminating. It distinguishes between the kernel and the husk, what is central and what is peripheral in the Bible. The truth of the Word of God is not self-evident even in the Bible, . . . it must be dug out through diligent searching that is at the same time faithful and critical."[42] John Goldingay notes, "An element of polyvalence or irreducible ambiguity characterizes parts of scripture—and all texts, to some degree."[43] As a result, while any given text clearly cannot be well interpreted as saying just any old thing at all, like a "wax nose," most texts can still be reasonably read to be saying more than one thing, conveying more than one meaning.[44] And in fact they usually are. This helps to explain the pervasive interpretive pluralism evident among Christians, perhaps especially biblicists, today.

Another way to express the point about multivocality somewhat differently is to say that theological and ethical interpretations and conclusions drawn from the Bible are sometimes, if not often, "underdetermined" by the text. For something to be underdetermined means there is not enough evidence to "nail it" convincingly and so settle debate. Such a lack of clear, validating evidence in any situation means that reasonable, qualified observers are unable to converge upon and together adopt one definite theoretical conclusion or interpretation about it; rather, the evidence seems able to reasonably but not definitively support more than one conclusion or interpretation.

Thus, in the natural and social sciences we sometimes say that a theory or interpretation is underdetermined (or sometimes "overdetermined") by the evidence. For example, the very best data that we might gather on the subject of, say, the causes of poverty in the United States may lead different smart scholars to draw divergent theoretical explanations of poverty. In which case, we say that "the evidence underdetermines the theory." The usual result in such cases is that we end up with multiple theories, and the available evidence seems unable to adjudicate in a way that leads different interpreters to converge in agreement on one theory. (When, by contrast, a theory, interpretation, or conclusion is "overdetermined" by the evidence, that means that reasonable, qualified observers have *more* than enough good evidence to draw the same conclusion or adopt the same theory—one could lose some of the available evidence and still be entirely justified in adopting the same conclusion or theory. An example of that might be the conclusion that a Marxist communist political economy is not a viable long-term project in the world today.)

When it comes to the Bible, the idea that a personal and loving God has created and redeemed the world, for example, is a theological conclusion that is overdetermined by the evidence of scripture. But a lot of other possible theological and ethical conclusions are not. They are, rather, often underdetermined by the biblical evidence. What exactly "the end times" will look like and how and when that will happen, for instance, is underdetermined by the available biblical evidence. That is why there are so many different views of the matter, each of which lacks the evidential support to "get the better" of its rivals. Numerous other Christian theological and moral beliefs—including most of those named above, about which Bible readers are unable to agree—also appear to be similarly underdetermined.

It is not that no biblical evidence can be garnered to support any one belief or conclusion. Each approach has at least some supporting evidence, which is what keeps it alive. But the textual evidence taken as a whole does not seem to be enough to clearly validate one "best" interpretation and so settle the debate, leading most or all reasonable Bible readers to converge on that view. As a result, different interpreters hunker down with their preferred interpretations, drawing attention to whatever evidence does seem to support it, yet often not admitting that their own interpretation, as well as everyone else's, is obviously underdetermined by the evidence overall. The result, again, is a multiplicity of interpretations on a host of issues, each enjoying enough evidential support to be plausible to at least some people but not enough to settle the matters and engender a reasonable consensus. In short, the result is pervasive interpretive pluralism.

The ideas of biblical multivocality, polysemy, and evidential underdetermination may not fit the biblicist theory about scripture. Biblicists instead tend to assume the single, univocal meaning of biblical texts. Notice, for example, how David Wells emphasizes the singularity of biblical meaning (not meanings), when he writes that his position on the Bible "assumes that words and meaning in scripture coincide and what secures this is [divine] inspiration. Meaning is not to be found above the text, behind it, beyond it, or in the interpreter. Meaning is to be found *in the text*. It is the language of the text which determines what meaning God intended for us to have."[45] My point here is not that Wells is wrong about words and meanings per se. My point is that he wrongly seems to assume that biblical texts give rise to only one single meaning that "God intended for us to have." That is an unsatisfactory view—in fact false—and assuming or asserting it simply does not make biblical multivocality and polysemy go away.

What we have instead is something like what evangelical biblical scholar Kenton Sparks describes: "At face value, Scripture does not seem to furnish us with one divine theology; it gives us numerous theologies. . . . The Bible does not offer a single, well-integrated univocal theology; it offers instead numerous overlapping but nonetheless distinctive theologies!" Sparks says that "the literary, historical, ethical, and theological diversity in Scripture . . . scholars have documented a thousand times over."[46] The evangelical Old Testament biblical scholar Christopher Wright states the matter even more strongly: "We are listening, not to a single voice, not even to a single choir in harmony, but to several choirs singing different songs with some protest groups jamming in the wings."[47]

The multivocality and polysemy of the Bible, and the diversity and division to which they give rise, are undeniable, historical, empirical, phenomenological facts. It is not that multiple possible meanings are necessarily read *into* scripture by readers' subjectivities (although sometimes they are) but rather that, even when read as good believers should read the texts, the words of scripture themselves can and usually do give rise to more than one possible, arguably legitimate interpretation. This very biblical multivocality and polysemy is exactly what explains a great deal of why Protestantism in particular—the tradition that, as the historical champion of *sola scriptura* and biblical perspicuity, has primarily fostered biblicism—is itself extremely fragmented doctrinally, ecclesiologically, and culturally. (The biblical multivocality and polysemy are also partly what explain in longer

terms why global Christendom is divided between the Oriental Orthodox Church, Eastern Orthodox Church, the Roman Catholic Church,
Protestantism, and Anabaptism—not to mention the many heterodox
and heretical movements that have claimed scriptural authority for
their teachings.) To deny the multivocality of scripture is to live in
a self-constructed world of unreality. Yet scriptural multivocality is
a fact that profoundly challenges evangelical biblicism. It must be
overcome or transcended, or biblicism is at least partly mistaken and
needs revising.

# 3

# Some Relevant History, Sociology, and Psychology

Before proceeding to an examination of subsidiary problems with American evangelical biblicism, it makes sense to step aside and briefly look at some historical, sociological, and psychological aspects of the matter.

## Philosophical Assumptions Underwriting American Biblicism

The historical roots of American evangelical biblicism's failure to grapple with the multivocality and polysemy of scriptural texts are many and would require an entire book to explicate. Most crucial among them, however, are certain teachings of Charles Hodge (1797–1878) and Benjamin Warfield (1851–1921), at their times both highly influential professors at Princeton Theological Seminary. Hodge's and Warfield's teachings were set within and governed by the then-reigning philosophy of Scottish commonsense realism and the Baconian inductive-empirical philosophy of science.[1]

To keep things brief, suffice it to say that the former philosophy emphasized the God-given capacity of human perceptions and mind to directly grasp the essential nature of objects perceived; the latter construed science as the task of gathering natural specimens as facts

55

and inductively arranging them in proper order for the purpose of better understanding the rational intelligibility of the world in the form of general laws. Both were intent to resist any kind of Kantian idealism—and the theological liberalism to which it often gave rise—that would split the knower from the known and invest the knower with autonomous epistemic authority to define the known through his or her own perception and "speculative" theorizing. Implicit in Scottish commonsense realism is a "picture theory" of language, which says that "words are directly knowable by the mind and, in addition, are direct representations of the objects to which they refer. Logically, therefore, words and sense impressions are identical in that each refers directly to objects. Those objects, in turn, are directly and with utmost certainty known by the mind."[2] The most important Scottish commonsense realist, Thomas Reid (1710–96), put it this way: "Language is the express image and picture of human thoughts; and from the picture we may draw some certain conclusions concerning the original [object to which language refers]."[3]

Relying upon this taken-for-granted philosophical backdrop, Hodge defined theology as a science whose method is to "begin with collecting well-established facts, and from them [to] infer the general laws which determine their occurrence." The source of all such theological facts is, of course, the Bible, which contains "all the facts which God has revealed concerning Himself and our relation to him. . . . The Bible contains all the facts or truths which form the content of theology, just as the facts of nature are the contents of the natural sciences."[4]

Furthermore, Hodge wrote, "The Bible is a plain book . . . intelligible by the people," who are "everywhere assumed to be competent to understand what is written."[5] Given this outlook, the task of theology consists of collecting the relevant facts from the Bible and inductively piecing them together according to the inherent logic of their own "internal relations" into the more general whole representing systematic Christian doctrine. Happily, this assumed philosophical background guaranteed that the biblical facts—represented in passages of scripture—would be self-evident and clear, even univocal, in their meaning, their relation to other biblical facts, and their relation to the world. The key to achieving this was to get human subjectivity, interpretation, and "speculation" out of the way and so to let the facts simply speak for themselves.

Oddly, it did not seem to trouble Hodge that Scottish commonsense realism entailed a highly optimistic view of human knowledge that was inconsistent with his own Augustinian-Calvinist heritage, which emphasizes the epistemologically and noetically devastating effects of original sin.[6] It served his purpose at the time, namely, to resist the corrosive effects of German idealism and theological liberalism. This conflict did not seem to bother Warfield either, who continued the same theological project at Princeton into the next generation. Warfield, for instance, emphasized the democratic perspicuity and commonsense hermeneutics of scripture, writing, "We have the Bible in our hands, and we are accustomed to reading it. . . . The proof of this is pervasive and level to the apprehension of every reader. It would be an insult to our intelligence were we to presume that we had not observed it, or could not apprehend its meaning."[7] Warfield also wrote: "We follow the inductive method. When we approach the Scriptures to ascertain their doctrine . . . we proceed by collecting the whole body of relevant facts." Because Warfield assumed the complete internal coherence and communicative transparency of scripture, he was able to assert, "The issue is not, what does the Bible teach? but, Is what the Bible teaches true?"[8] Given his doctrine of biblical inspiration, the answer for Warfield was, obviously, yes.

These quotes of Hodge and Warfield are among their weakest; elsewhere they do write with greater sophistication on these matters.[9] But as their teachings later passed through the scorching flames of the modernist-fundamentalist battles of the early twentieth century, it was often their weaker, more simplistic ideas that shaped the thinking of subsequent generations of evangelicals. The problematic influence of Hodge and Warfield on evangelical biblicism is evident today.

For instance, Wayne Grudem's *Systematic Theology*, which has become a standard text in many theology classes in evangelical seminaries, colleges, and universities, says, "Systematic theology involves collecting and understanding all the relevant passages in the Bible on various topics and then summarizing their teachings clearly so that we know what to believe about each topic. . . . It attempts to summarize the teachings of Scripture in a brief, understandable, and very carefully formulated statement."[10] G. K. Beale's attempted refutation of Peter Enns's Old Testament scholarship in his *The Erosion of Inerrancy in Evangelicalism: Responding to New Challenges to Biblical Authority*

actually suggests that the Bible does not need to be interpreted, that—
in contrast to a "subjective" view, in which the scriptural interpreter
makes "precarious" judgments about truths scripture teaches—the
truths of the Bible are objectively evident.[11]

Such views are intelligible only within the larger presupposed
framework of Scottish commonsense realism, the Baconian theory
of science, and the picture theory of language. Yet these eighteenth-
and nineteenth-century philosophies and outlooks have subsequently
proved to be untenable—and for good reasons. They simply do not
work, not for evangelicals or for anyone else. They are erroneous.
Perception, knowledge, science, and language do not function in the
real world the way these theories say they do. To build scriptural
theological orthodoxy on them is therefore to build on a foundation
of sand.

Language, for instance, does indeed correspond in some way to
objects and does represent thoughts—but not in any simple, direct,
unambiguous, picturelike way. Language operates as a different dimension of reality than most material and mental objects, and in its
usage often entails significant ambiguity, complexity, and polysemy.
Furthermore, "the facts"—natural, biblical, or otherwise—usually do
not simply present themselves to human perceivers and knowers as
obvious, unmediated entities. All human knowledge is *conceptually*
mediated in ways that require the active interpretation and significa-
tion of the knower. Interpretation, among other things, means judging
among the various possibilities the best or most compelling meanings
that are attributable to the signs or texts. And that is not an infallible
process—it requires uncertain human judgment.

All interpretations are also shaped by the particular historical and
cultural locations and interests of the interpreters. Often what may be
the best interpretation is underdetermined by the relevant empirical
sign, text, or evidence—so more than one possible interpretation is
reasonably plausible, and thus different interpreters find themselves
convinced to adopt different interpretations. Moreover, science is not
simply about inductively and objectively piecing together specimens
gathered from the world in order to identify big-picture laws. Rather,
for starters, science always operates within informing theoretical paradigms and epistemic communities of inquiry, which govern definitions
of problems to solve and the kind of evidence that might solve them.

Furthermore, science (as correctly defined by critical realism) is ultimately about explaining causal processes that are normally not empirically observable, which requires heavy loads of theoretical work, including not only the logical operations of induction and deduction but also retrodiction and abduction. The latter turn out to be the least definitive ways of knowing and so open up multiple possibilities for interpretation and disagreement. In most scientific work, it is usually what is going on *behind* the evident facts that is most interesting and important—yet that is not always entirely clear to the observer.

Digging two centuries deeper than Hodge and Warfield, Carlos Bovell's *By Good and Necessary Consequence* provides a fascinating genealogical study of "biblicist foundationalism."[12] In it Bovell shows through historical analysis that the "by good and necessary consequence" clause of the Westminster Confession of Faith—which contributes an important intellectual plank supporting contemporary evangelical biblicism—was not an inheritance from early church fathers or even the original Protestant Reformers. Rather, it was quite a novel theological move by the Westminster divines in response to a widespread seventeenth-century philosophical skepticism, with origins in the late Renaissance, that defined all reliable knowledge as deductively derived from absolutely certain premises. The ideal model for such indubitable knowledge was mathematics. Thus, it was a particularly skeptical philosophical context in the seventeenth century that drove Protestant theologians of the day to derive all Christian theological knowledge from scriptural propositions and their logical deductions in a way that mimicked Cartesian foundationalist epistemology—a move that is both philosophically naive and out of place in the contemporary context. This larger intellectual lineage, Bovell shows, can be traced from Westminster through Hodge and Warfield and up to contemporary evangelical biblicist assumptions and practices today.

All of this means that the philosophical assumptions on which Hodge and Warfield built their theologies of the Bible are seriously problematic. This need not lead us to general epistemic skepticism or force us into Kantian idealism, arbitrary subjectivism, or theological liberalism—there are better alternatives to those options. One in particular, I think, is critical realism. But neither do these problems let stand as acceptable Scottish commonsense realism, Baconian inductive-empirical science, or the picture theory of language.

To insist in the name of Christian theological orthodoxy on preserving these outdated and flawed philosophical positions in order to underwrite a particular approach to the Bible is counterproductive and intellectually obscurantist. If anything, the fact that biblicism was built upon these naive philosophical positions shows from yet another angle how problematic it is. Again, biblicism simply does not work, even taken on its own terms. This brief historical inquiry helps to explain why: biblicism presupposed a set of philosophical assumptions about language, perception, knowledge, and science that were rightly abandoned by informed thinkers a long time ago. Biblicists apparently have not yet entirely realized that or come to terms with its implications.

### Why Pervasive Interpretive Pluralism Is Not More Troubling to Biblicists: Sociological and Psychological Conjectures

If what I have said in this book so far is true, one would think that biblicists would be deeply troubled by interpretive pluralism and the implications it has for the biblicist theory of scripture, revelation, and truth. But for the most part they are not. Most biblicists carry on with unperturbed confidence in biblicist assumptions and beliefs, paying little attention to the ramifications of multiple counterclaims about rival biblical teachings. Why and how can this be? The answers are multiple, and I can offer only conjectures about some of the possibilities here.

One possibility concerns the structure of social networks among biblicists. We know sociologically that the principle of "homophily" (love for and attraction to what is similar to oneself) is one of the strongest forces operating in social life. As a result, biblicists (and most other Christians) who interpret the Bible in the same way have a very strong tendency to cluster together into homogeneous social networks of similarly believing people. One name for that when it is institutionalized is "Protestant denominations." Most people—including most biblicists—tend to live in relatively "small" worlds, in the subcultures and social circles with which they are most at home and comfortable. Homophily is powerful this way—even the most seemingly "cosmopolitan" people tend actually to live in parochial worlds. In fact, empirical research shows that evangelicals tend to live in more religiously homogeneous worlds than most (though not all) other religious Americans.[13] For biblicists these relatively small worlds can function as effective "plausibility structures" to sustain the "reality" and believability of their particular assumptions and convictions[14]—as the same small worlds that most everyone else, including atheists and adherents of every other belief system, do for them.

We also know sociologically that people's personal perceptions, concerns, and evaluations are strongly shaped by the social networks in which their lives are embedded. The more homogenous a person's social network is, the more likely he or she is to take the characteristics and assumed viewpoints of the people in that social network for granted, and they increasingly lose touch with the distinctive, visceral realities of the lifestyles and beliefs of people in other, different social networks. As experienced with the matter under consideration here, most biblicists know *in theory* that other Christians out there read the Bible differently and think that it teaches different things. But, lacking ongoing, significant social contact and interaction with many of those other Christians, the differences between them can easily recede into abstract notions operating far in the background of everyday life concerns.

When a believer lives largely within the world of the Presbyterian Church of America, for example, others, such as independent Freewill Baptists, evangelical Mennonites, and orthodox Anglicans, can seem millions of miles away. Moreover, people—biblicist and otherwise— can and often do limit the diversity of their network ties to minimize people quite unlike them, precisely in order to reduce the existential discomfort of having to deal with contradictory beliefs, values, and commitments that such ties normally entail.

Another reason why pervasive interpretive pluralism may not trouble more biblicists is the common tendency among them to minimize the real differences of interpretation and the significance of those differences. Ask a biblicist about the matter and a common response is, "Well, yeah, but most of those disagreements are about minor issues. On important matters most of us pretty much read the Bible as teaching similar things." Such a response is natural for American evangelicals, who comprise a transdenominational religious movement that has sought to transcend its differences in order to work together toward certain common activities and goals, particularly evangelism, world missions, and "ministries of mercy." It is also a highly useful response for protecting biblicism from the problems of interpretive pluralism.

But this response is in the end a form of denial. It is simply not true. It is like a member of a dysfunctional, conflict-ridden family telling her friends that, "Yeah, we all get along pretty well in our family." Disagreements among biblicists (and other Bible-referring Christians) about what the Bible teaches on most issues, both essentials and secondary matters, are many and profound. If biblicists hope to maintain intellectual honesty and internal consistency, they must acknowledge them and explain them.

A third possible reason why pervasive interpretive pluralism may not trouble biblicists as much as we might expect it to—a reason moving in the opposite direction and at a different level from the previous one—concerns the social functions gained by interacting with groups one disagrees with in particular ways. Establishing difference from others is a primary way that people and groups come to understand their own identities and continue to mobilize resources. Having an "other" from whom one is different helps one to know who one is and why one is committed to that particular self. The Duke and North Carolina basketball programs, for instance, need each other, even as they hate each other, simply to help promote the being and identity of Duke and North Carolina. The same with Notre Dame and Michigan or USC football. I have argued at length elsewhere that this general identity-formation-through-difference-and-tension mechanism helps to explain the vitality of many religious groups in the United States, especially American evangelicals.[15]

If this is correct, then it has two consequences for the religious groups involved. First, different communities of faith come to "need" others with whom they disagree in order to help sustain their internal identity commitments. Every group within a larger religious ecology becomes dependent on those they oppose in part to sustain their own existence and sense of distinct self. Once that kind of sociological dynamic is generated, rivals become perversely invested in the ongoing existence of each other, however much they oppose each other, because the other serves the identity and commitment purposes of the self, whether personal or collective. Biblicists may thus oddly come somewhat subconsciously to resist the idea of the biblical differences among them actually being settled. For without the many stimulating skirmishes and conflicts that those differences generate—such as "biblical patriarchs" resisting "biblical feminists," vice versa, and the like—life in the faith would come to seem so much less vital and interesting. So, biblicists may not be very troubled by interpretive pluralism because many draw much of the strength of their ecclesial and perhaps personal lives from policing the symbolic boundaries that those differences create.

Second, building in-group identity and commitment through difference from out-groups has the almost inevitable effect of each group ceasing to take the substantive claims and positions of those out-groups seriously. The point becomes not to understand the other's reasons, perspectives, and beliefs, or to honor them as fellow believers and come to a deeper understanding and perhaps resolution of differences. The point, rather, is to remain on guard from being contaminated by the out-group or allowing them to grow in influence. And in that process the other is very easily turned into an impersonal, two-dimensional caricature. Out-groups are reduced to an abstract "them" whose beliefs are abridged into a few bullet points of greatest disagreement, which need not actually be taken seriously on their own terms but rather simply need to be refuted and discredited as a means to validate the views of one's own group. In this way, differences between Christian groups cease to be existentially troubling facts that divide Christians. Instead they become dismissible ideas of people far away, ideas already known to be wrong.

The above two points are reinforced by the complicating third point that many American evangelicals—especially those shaped by the church-growth movement—assume that numerical growth in a congregation indicates spiritual strength and vitality, which, in turn, indicates possession of the truth. Numerical growth, the assumption suggests, can be taken as an empirical indicator that the Holy Spirit is present and working and leading a congregation into the right beliefs. God must be "blessing" such a spiritually vibrant and faithful church with increased numbers of visitors and members. The logic is faulty, of course. If it were true, then it would commend evangelicals to convert to Mormonism, which has very impressive growth statistics.[16] Swelling membership roles may have nothing at all to do with spiritual vitality or faithfulness or truth—particularly not in a mass-consumerist, therapeutically driven culture such as ours in the United States. For present purposes, however, the larger point is simply this: various Christian groups "benefit" from conflict, disunity, and fragmentation and use such disagreement and distinction from others to build and sustain their in-group strength. This practice, even if common, is highly problematic when considered in light of what the Bible says about Christian unity.

A fourth possible reason explaining why biblicists are not more troubled by pervasive interpretive pluralism is rather more simple. It concerns "cognitive transitivity" between cultural objects. Stated simply, this reason is reflected in the following syllogism: Overcoming biblical and theological differences toward Christian unity sounds like "ecumenism." Ecumenism sounds like liberal Protestantism. And liberal Protestantism is bad. Therefore overcoming biblical and theological differences toward Christian unity is itself suspect by association with liberalism. Better, suggests this emotional-cognitive logic, to be divided in absolute commitment to truth than to be unified in flaccid, liberal compromise. In this way, the experience of pervasive interpretive pluralism and division becomes (again, perversely) a badge of honor on behalf of orthodoxy and integrity. *We may be utterly fragmented*, biblicists tell themselves, *but at least we have not compromised.*

There is another possible explanation that is more psychological than sociological. I have no interest in psychoanalyzing individual biblicists, but I think it is fair to say that the general psychological structure underlying biblicism is one of a particular need to create order and security in an environment that would be otherwise chaotic and in error. That orientation seems itself to be driven by fear of disorder and discomfort with things not being "the way they ought to be." Aversion to disorder and falsehood is a common human trait. But some people evidence it more strongly than others. I suspect that there is a correlation between this trait and attraction to biblicism.

To be clear, this is not some kind of psychologically reductionistic way to deny that biblicists genuinely believe theologically and biblically what they profess to believe. They of course do. But beliefs are always set in historical, sociological, and psychological contexts—in this case, for instance, the heritage of the modernist-fundamentalist battles of the early twentieth century—which shape them and perhaps help motivate them in ways that are not always recognized. Understood in this way, then, biblicism may represent a particular effort to prevent what biblicists perceive to be ever-menacing external and internal threats to order, security, and certainty. This response would not be inexplicable or crazy, given the real challenge of sustaining what is believed to be an orthodox gospel in a modern and postmodern world of change, unbelief, liberalism, and relativism. Yet as a fundamental psychological orientation, most evangelicals would also concede that it seems to fail to reflect a robust belief in God's sovereign, benevolent control and faith that the Holy Spirit will ultimately lead the church into truth. In its worst expression, the psychological complex driving biblicism expresses an outright lack of trust in God and a grasping for human control. And that hardly seems biblical.

In any case, if this explanation has any merit, biblicism's need to create order and security to shield against chaos and error could be so powerful that it overrides concerns about pervasive interpretive pluralism. In fact, in such cases, biblicism may itself function psychologically as a primary mechanism for denying or containing the apparent chaos and error generated by pervasive interpretive pluralism.

Whether any or all five possible explanations for the lack of evident distress among biblicists about pervasive interpretive pluralism are valid does not much matter for my larger argument. Even so, pondering for a moment the puzzling fact that most biblicists seem quite content to live with extensive disagreement about what is "biblical" on most issues may help to shed light on the larger matter in question.

In any case, it is time to return more directly to biblicism's problems in the next chapter.

# 4

# Subsidiary Problems with Biblicism

The main thrust of my argument so far concerns the fatal implications of pervasive interpretive pluralism for evangelical biblicism. I have not engaged biblicism on the fronts of divine inspiration and inerrancy, and nothing in my case questions scriptural inspiration per se. I have little interest in systematically questioning the matter of inerrancy directly, a debate that seems largely fruitless.[1] Let us then for the sake of argument concede that divine inspiration and textual inerrancy need not be directly challenged. The central problem is that biblicism is discredited by pervasive interpretive pluralism. The undeniable fact of entrenched, ubiquitous disagreements among biblicists about what scripture teaches on most issues, large and small, represents a fatal blow to biblicism.

Most evangelical biblicists today somehow manage to continue to pretend that pervasive interpretive pluralism does them no harm, but that denial exacts heavy costs in undercutting intellectual honesty and theological credibility. Even if they realize that they have been self-defeated, evangelical biblicists often continue to defend the theory that they are committed to protecting. Yet if pervasive interpretive pluralism undermines biblicism, then the problematic front of evangelical biblicism has been breached and additional criticisms may reveal some of its other flaws, which include the following.

## Blatantly Ignored Teachings

Biblicists believe that scripture as a whole provides a divine authority that Christians must obey, and all the more so when its teachings are didactic, direct, repeated, and unambiguous. But in actual practice this view is routinely flouted. There are myriad biblical passages that contain clear commands and teachings (which the logic of biblicism would compel readers to follow) but that most biblicists do not obey and have absolutely no intention of obeying. I will spare the reader a long list of examples and offer a mere four telling cases.

First, in five different instances in five New Testament Epistles, the Bible contains this directive instruction: "Greet one another with a holy kiss" (Rom. 16:16; 1 Cor. 16:20; 2 Cor. 13:12; 1 Thess. 5:26; 1 Pet. 5:14). There is no denying that these are clear, imperative teachings of scripture—much more overt, in fact, than scriptural teachings against, say, premarital sex and abortion. But scarce are the biblicists who have any intention of obeying by kissing one another in holy greeting—at least those who live north of the Rio Grande. It simply does not happen and is not going to happen. Yet it is hard to see *based on biblicist standards* how ignoring the instruction is not blatant disobedience to a clear biblical teaching. Holy-kiss greetings would not be hard to practice. But the biblical command simply goes in one ear and out the other, as if it had simply not been taught in scripture. On purely logical grounds, the fact that biblicists ignore clear biblical commands does nothing itself to impeach or condemn biblicist theory—it could simply be that biblicism as a theory is correct and yet that biblicists as people are selectively disobedient. But I do not think that is the case. The blatantly ignored teaching observed here reveals more than unevenness in Christian obedience. It reveals, rather, a flaw in biblicism itself.

To keep this section brief, I offer only three more examples without extensive commentary. First Corinthians 14:34 says, "Women should remain silent in the churches. They are not allowed to speak, but must be in submission, as the Law says" (also see 1 Tim. 2:12). Many biblicists appeal to this verse to make many claims about women, authority, marriage, and church life—most of which turn out to have little if anything to do with the actual content of the passage. But *no* biblicist actually obeys what this verse clearly says. I know of no church, biblicist or otherwise, in which women are actually not permitted to speak. If biblicism were correct, it is not clear why biblicists do not follow this teaching.

Next, in Matthew 5:39, Jesus teaches his disciples, "Do not resist an evil person." The command is quite plain, spoken by Christ himself. But few if any are the biblicists (or anyone else other than the Amish, perhaps) who do or intend to obey it. It is simply read over and ignored or dramatically reinterpreted. Again, from a biblicist perspective it is not evident why that should be, but that it is so raises real questions about biblicism.

Finally, Jesus commanded his disciples, "Now that I, your Lord, have washed your feet, you should also wash one another's feet. I have set you an example that you should do as I have done for you" (John 13:14–15). Once again, the members of some churches do wash one another's feet. But most do not and never will, no matter what the Bible seems to clearly teach about it. Something is amiss in biblicists' selective seriousness about scriptural teachings, evidenced by these and other similarly ignored passages.

## Arbitrary Determinations of Cultural Relativism

One important and in many cases I think legitimate way that biblicists deal with the challenge of certain "difficult" Bible passages—including perhaps some of those just mentioned—is to claim that their relevance for contemporary believers is relativized by historical and cultural differences. What may have been important within the culture to whom a scriptural text was originally written may not apply in our culture today. Fair enough. But what is not fair, consistent, or honest is the fact that biblicists typically offer *no coherent account* explaining *which* Bible passages (1) are culturally relative, (2) remain in effect in principle but may be applied or expressed in very different ways depending on the particular culture, and (3) remain universally binding in their specifics for all believers at all times.

The relativizing of biblical teaching on grounds of historical and cultural differences therefore normally proceeds in an ad hoc, unsystematic, and often arbitrary manner. Various biblical commands are relaxed or tightened without a clear underlying rationale or justification, depending significantly, it seems, on the particular cultural and political interests and discomfort of those doing the relaxing and tightening. In other words, biblicists very often engage in what we might call "uneven and capriciously selective literalism." Sometimes the Bible says what it says and must be obeyed. Other times the obvious meaning of the passage is relativized by historical and cultural considerations. And it is often not clear for any given interpreter or across different interpreters which is which, when, and why.[2]

The contemporary relevance or irrelevance of some biblical passages is clear. The author of 1 Timothy's specific teaching about eating meat sacrificed to pagan idols, for instance, clearly can be directly relevant only in cultures that make such sacrifices in pagan temples. Likewise, the pastoral command to Timothy to start drinking wine in addition to water (1 Tim. 5:23) pertains to a particular situation of his unclean-water-borne stomach illness, and is not, it would seem, a general command to all Christians to drink wine. However, it is next to impossible to argue successfully that biblical teachings to love and forgive neighbors and enemies without measure pertain only to certain times, situations, or cultures. So, those are the more obvious extremes.

But many other scriptural passages are less clear than this. Take, for instance, the passage quoted above about women being silent in church. Is that a direct command to Christians now? Or was that a case of a particular command directed toward a specific situation that is not relevant for women and churches today? Or does it reflect a biblical teaching that is true at a level of general principle (and, if so, which principle?) but that must be applied variously depending on the specific historical and cultural situation? Different Bible readers believe each of these views, whether or not they are consistent in working them out. But let us suppose that one of the latter two views is correct. How might we know that? By what standard or principle could that be determined? And then what are the other implications of that standard if it is applied consistently? Nobody seems to know, or at least to agree. Yet these questions often matter a great deal.

Consider the broad range of problems this difficulty creates. May God's people never eat rabbit or pork (Lev. 11:6–7)? May a man never have sex with his wife during her monthly period (Lev. 18:19) or wear clothes woven of two kinds of materials (Lev. 19:19)? Should Christians never wear tattoos (Lev. 19:28)? Should those who blaspheme God's name be stoned to death (Lev. 24:10–24)? Ought Christians to hate those who hate God (Ps. 139:21–22)? Ought believers to praise God with tambourines, cymbals, and dancing (Ps. 150:4–5)? Should Christians encourage the suffering and poor to drink beer and wine in order to forget their misery (Prov. 31:6–7)? Should parents punish their children with rods in order to save their souls from death (Prov. 23:13–14)? Does much wisdom really bring much sorrow and more knowledge more grief (Eccles. 1:18)? Will becoming highly righteous and wise destroy us (Eccles. 7:16)? Is everything really meaningless (Eccles. 12:8)? May Christians never swear oaths (Matt. 5:33–37)? Should we never call anyone on earth "father" (Matt. 23:9)? Should Christ's followers wear sandals when they evangelize but bring no food or money or extra clothes (Mark 6:8–9)? Should Christians be exorcising demons, handling snakes, and drinking deadly poison (Mark 16:15–18)? Are people who divorce their spouses and remarry always committing adultery (Luke 16:18)? Ought Christians to share their material goods in common (Acts 2:44–45)? Ought church leaders to always meet in council to issue definitive decisions on matters in dispute (Acts 15:1–29)? Is homosexuality always a sin unworthy of the kingdom of God (1 Cor. 6:9–10)? Should unmarried men not look for wives (1 Cor. 7:27) and married men live as if they had no wives (1 Cor. 7:29)? Is it wrong for men to cover their heads (1 Cor. 11:4) or a disgrace of nature for men to wear long hair (1 Cor. 11:14)? Should Christians save and collect money to send to believers in Jerusalem (1 Cor. 16:1–4)? Should Christians definitely sing psalms in church (Col. 3:16)? Must Christians always lead quiet lives in which they work with their hands (1 Thess. 4:11)? If a person will not work, should they not be allowed to eat (2 Thess. 3:10)? Ought all Christian slaves always simply submit to their masters (reminder: slavery still exists today) (1 Pet. 2:18–21)? Must Christian women not wear braided hair, gold jewelry, and fine clothes (1 Tim. 2:9; 1 Pet. 3:3)? Ought all Christian men to lift up their hands when they pray (1 Tim. 2:8)? Should churches not provide material help to widows who are younger than sixty years old (1 Tim. 5:9)? Will every believer who lives a godly life in Christ be persecuted (2 Tim. 3:12)? Should the church anoint the sick with oil for their healing (James 5:14–15)? The list of such questions could be extended.

Again, the question is: are these universal Christian moral teachings applicable literally in all times and places, or ideas relevant for only

particular times and places, or universal teachings as general principles (again, which principles?) but to be applied in diverse ways as
appropriate to particular contexts? Biblicists offer too few guidelines
for the scriptural interpreter to know how to answer those particular
questions with any degree of principled consistency.[3] And so the precise instructions and applications of authoritative biblical teachings
are often left unclear.[4]

### Strange Passages

The Bible contains a number of passages that are simply strange. It
is hard to know what good use to make of them, particularly when
working within a biblicist theory. One such passage, for instance, is
Titus 1:12–13. Its context is this: the author of this Pastoral Epistle,
thought by biblicists to be the apostle Paul (so I will proceed here on
that basis), is writing to Titus, who had been sent to work in Crete
to take care of church business there, including dealing with people
who were disrupting the church. Paul is here citing the Cretan poet
Epimenides, who penned something similarly derisive about his people
around 600 BC—specifically, Κρῆτες ἀεί ψεύσται (Kretes aei pseystai),
"Cretans, always liars," as well, he wrote, as "evil beasts, idle bellies."[5]
In his instructions, Paul wrote this about the people to whom Titus
was ministering: "Even one of their own prophets has said, 'Cretans
are always liars, evil brutes, lazy gluttons.' This testimony is true."
Paul then instructed Titus to deal harshly with the natives, rebuking
those who were spreading falsehoods and creating trouble. Okay, so
what is the biblicist to make of this passage? In what sense is this part
of God's revealed and instructive truth? And what have Christians
today to learn from it?

In forty-nine years of churchgoing, I have never heard a sermon
preached on this passage. And for good reason. It reads almost like
a tasteless, private email message that was mistakenly forwarded by
the recipient to readers who were not meant to see it. Paul is here
endorsing ("This testimony is true") something like a racist stereo-
type—perhaps more accurately, an ethnic prejudice—an apparently
common slur against the entire nation of Cretans generally. He is
quoting a self-deprecating Cretan, admittedly, but then again one who
wrote nearly two-thirds of a millennia before his day. Further, Paul

himself is Jewish, not Cretan, so not really well positioned to make such critical statements legitimately. Let us begin by setting aside the strange fact that the making of such a proclamation violates many of Paul's own moral teachings in other Epistles—for instance, about living so as to break down the walls dividing alienated peoples (Eph. 2:13–15; Gal. 3:28); about thinking about what is good, lovely, and noble (Phil. 4:8); about love bearing, believing, and hoping all things (1 Cor. 13:4–7). Paul was an apostle, but that does not mean he was perfect—perhaps he still needed sanctification from the sin of ethnic prejudice. Still, Paul here is writing what became scripture.

Yet, we might observe that it simply cannot be the case that literally all Cretans of the day were *always* liars, evil brutes, lazy gluttons, as the text says. There must have been at least some Cretans who spoke truth, who pursued the good, who worked hard, or who ate in moderation. If not, Cretan society would have by then disintegrated. Presumably at least one member of the Christian church in Crete did not fit Paul's description. Perhaps the sentiment was actually true as a gross generalization painted in broad brush strokes, so maybe Paul was in fact speaking legitimately with poetic license or self-conscious hyperbole. What then? Well, Paul is still perpetuating here what certainly seems to be an insult against an entire nation's populace, a derogatory slight against the very people among whom he was working through Titus to establish the Christian faith.

What then ought we to learn here, given biblicist principles? That Christian missionaries are entitled by virtue of apostolic precedent and biblical example to hold ethnic prejudices against the people among whom they are planting churches? That Christian leaders may resort to bigoted characterizations of natives to motivate their missionaries on the ground to deal with troublemakers? That it is morally legitimate for Christians to perpetuate derogatory stereotypes about entire nations of people different from their own? That Cretans are innately morally inferior to other gentiles? Members of "Christian Identity" and neo-Nazi groups might be comfortable with those "biblical" take-home messages, but I am certain that few evangelical biblicists would be. Yet, given the assumptions and beliefs of biblicist theory, it is hard to know how else to learn the divine truth that this passage has to teach. Biblicism, it would seem, proves inadequate for making Christian moral sense of this biblical text.

Other passages of scripture, strange in different ways—when considered from a strictly biblicist perspective—include the following. In Genesis 6:1–4 the "sons of God" married the "daughters of men" in the days when the "Nephilim" (hybrid offspring of fallen angels and human women? giants? or what?) walked the earth (cf. Num. 13:33). Judges 11:29–39 shows Jephthah voluntarily slaying his only daughter to fulfill a vow made to the Lord to kill in a burnt offering "whatever comes out of the door of my house to greet me when I return" (v. 31) in exchange for God's help in his slaughtering the Ammonites. In 1 Samuel 16:23, an *evil* spirit *from God* came upon King Saul. Second Chronicles 18:22 says that "the Lord has put a lying spirit in the mouths of these prophets of yours." Psalm 137:8–9 says of the women of Babylon, "Happy is he who repays you for what you have done to us—he who seizes your infants and dashes them against the rocks."

In a less obvious though still relevant sense, it is unclear how biblicism—especially that which emphasizes anything like a "dictation theory" of divine inspiration—can make sense of passages in New Testament Epistles such as, "I have made a fool of myself" (2 Cor. 12:11), "I don't remember if I baptized anyone else" (1 Cor. 1:16), and "When you come, bring the cloak that I left with Carpus in Troas, and my scrolls, especially the parchments" (2 Tim. 4:13).[6] In what sense, we might wonder, are these inerrant words of God intended to instruct the contemporary (or even medieval) reader?

In yet a different way, William Webb points out the difficulties of this "grabbing the hot-looking women" passage of Deuteronomy 21:10–14:

> When you go to war against your enemies and the Lord your God delivers them into your hands and you take captives, if you notice among the captives a beautiful woman and are attracted to her, you may take her as your wife. Bring her into your house and have her shave her head, trim her nails and put aside the clothes she was wearing when captured. After she has lived in your house . . . for a full month, then you may go to her and be her husband and she shall be your wife. If you are not pleased with her, let her go wherever she wishes.

What honest sense can strong biblicists make of these kinds of passages?[7]

## Populist and "Expert" Practices Deviate from Biblicist Theory

Yet another problem with evangelical biblicism is that it is often not *practiced* by many people who believe in it, in the way its theory says it should be practiced. A number of recent empirical sociological and anthropological studies of scripture reading have focused specifically on how biblicist evangelicals—both popular book authors and ordinary church members—read and interpret scripture in real practice. Those studies make clear that, far from scripture functioning as an independent authority guiding the lives of believers, the Bible is often *used* by its readers in various ways to help legitimate and maintain the commitments and assumptions that they already hold before coming to the biblical text. In other cases, biblical texts often do not function as authorities driving discussions and applications of scriptural truths but are instead selectively engaged and made sense of primarily according to what happens to be personally, subjectively relevant to the reader at the time. In both instances, the authority of scripture conceived in biblicist terms is displaced by the prior functional weight of its interpreter's interests and presuppositions.

For example, in a fascinating ethnographic study of actual Bible reading in an evangelical church, titled *How the Bible Works: An Anthropological Study of Evangelical Biblicism*, Brian Malley reveals that biblicist expectations are routinely overridden by a variety of practices that are problematic for biblicist theory.[8] In Malley's study, evangelical readers focused much less on interpreting the actual meaning of the biblical texts than on simply establishing a "transitivity" between the texts and the readers' already existent beliefs. In other words, the proper biblicist logic of scriptural authority that is often *not* employed is this: "The Bible teaches propositional content X; I should believe and obey what the Bible teaches; therefore, I believe and obey propositional content X." Instead, the logic that is often actually employed is more like this: "I already believe, think, or feel Y; the Bible contains an idea that seems to relate to Y; therefore, my belief, thought, or feeling of Y is 'biblically' confirmed." This routinely required no genuine theological connection to what texts actually *said*, but rather merely established that *some* connection or other *could* be made. General hermeneutical principles were never referenced to attempt to resolve disagreements about what scripture teaches. What often counted as the best interpretation of any biblical passage was not what the text itself teaches, but instead simply what felt "relevant" to the reader's life. Bible readers elaborated a variety of possible meanings of the text, and brought in many considerations from beyond the text, until they hit on one meaning that struck them as most relevant for their personal experiences, at which point they stopped reading and effectively declared their interpretation complete. Authorial intent was often displaced in devotional readings, for instance, by various meanings that happen to "speak to" different readers, depending on their particular situations.

In group Bible studies, few ever spoke about *the* meaning of any passage in question but instead usually talked about what in the passage *impressed them* and what that might mean for their lives. At times, the church's pastor even confessed to struggling with how to use inappropriate texts to make points that served his homiletic purposes of preaching relevant topical sermons without stretching the texts too far beyond what they actually say. That is, the pastor was often compelled to offer *a* reading of the text that he knew was different from what he believed was *the* right reading of the text. In *Words Upon the Word: An Ethnography of Evangelical Group Bible Study*, author James Bielo reveals similar scriptural interpretive practices among biblicists that diverge significantly from those prescribed by biblicism.[9]

In a different, intriguing study of books about "biblical" family relationships written by evangelical "experts," sociologist John Bartkowski examines the actual interpretive practices of the authors in making their larger arguments. Analyzing books on "biblical marriage relationships" by Larry Christenson and Ginger Gabriel, which arrive at very different conclusions, Bartkowski shows that "competing textual interpretations can be traced to the distinctive presuppositions readers bring to the texts. Specifically, contrasting interpretations . . . seem closely related to their particular 'prejudices' (in this case, assumptions about the essential nature of men and women) which evangelical readers import in the interpretive process."[10]

Bartkowski similarly examines the biblical interpretive work found in sets of books on "Christian parenting" written by James Dobson and Ross Campbell. He finds that "each of these specialists use the broader biblical themes of love/forgiveness or of sin/punishment to legitimate their specific disciplinary prescriptions," such that "while both of these prominent parenting specialists argue that their interpretations are 'literal' readings of biblical verses about the 'rod' of correction, they arrive at very different conclusions concerning the Bible's prescriptions for child discipline." Bartkowski sums up by stating, "the Bible as a text is capable of generating multiple readings—including multiple 'literal' readings—and can yield seemingly contradictory conclusions."[11] William Webb draws a similar conclusion about the "biblical" arguments for the parental spanking and corporal punishment of children advanced by teachers like James Dobson, Andreas Köstenberger, Albert Mohler, and Paul Wegner. Webb systematically shows just how little resemblance exists between what the Bible actually assumes and teaches about corporal punishment, and the methods and motives that these authors advocate. The Bible's idea of corporal punishment, for instance, assumes and entails the broad and frequent employment of physical strikes applied by parents to the backs of children who may be as old as (what we now call) teenagers, with a graduated increase (as needed) up to forty lashes, which express parental love but also anger, and the resulting bruises, welts, and wounds of which are seen as entirely legitimate. Modern "biblical" teachers like Dobson, Köstenberger, Mohler, and Wegner, by contrast, advocate spanking and corporal punishment primarily for preschool-age children, involving no more than one or two smacks to the buttocks, administered infrequently, that never produce bruises or welts, and that express only parental love, never anger. Webb concludes:

> In their defense of spanking today, [these authors] . . . make rhetorically explosive claims about their own unwavering faithfulness to Scripture. With a seriousness like that accorded to prophetic pronouncements, they contend that only their pro-spanking position upholds the authority of Scripture. They chide those who embrace noncorporeal methods for departing from what the Bible teaches. Of course, what they *fail to share with their readers is exactly how they themselves have moved away from what Scripture teaches on the subject* of corporeal punishment. They seemingly assume that what indeed honors biblical authority is only their own highly concretized and static approach to applying the biblical text. However, there appears to be a touch of irony in the fact that *they themselves freely choose what they wish to ignore within the corporeal punishment texts.*[12]

Finally, in a fascinating edited volume by James Bielo, a variety of social scientists reveal in their contributions the multiplicity of ways that different Christian biblicist groups in the United States and abroad go about actually using and interpreting the Bible, ways that often diverge from those prescribed by biblicist theory.[13] What is evident in all this is that Christian scripture has a "social life" of its own, which means that in actual practice it functions as an authority in many different ways, not all of which, even among avowed biblicists, actually toe the biblicist line in lived experience.

In short, because many readers are first driven in interpretation by their personal, cultural, and political *contexts*, the biblical texts actually often serve functionally even among biblicists as *pretexts* to legitimate predetermined beliefs and concerns, rather than as an independent authority as scriptural *text*. Its interpreting readers thus engage in as much or more *eisegesis* (reading the reader's meaning *into* texts) or "overexegesis"[14] as authentic exegesis (reading authorial meanings *out* of texts). Once again, none of these empirical observations necessarily discredit biblicism. It could be that biblicist theory is correct and that actual, empirical biblicist practices and experiences are often compromised. Life sometimes works this way.

In this case, however, I believe that the actual inconsistent and divergent interpretive practices observed among various kinds of real biblicist scripture interpreters do point to significant problems inherent to biblicism itself. Namely, biblicism is impossible to practice in actual experience—because of, among other reasons, the multivocality and polysemy of the texts. So even those who theoretically endorse biblicist assumptions and affirm biblicist beliefs inevitably read and interpret the Bible in nonbiblicist ways. If so, then the only question is whether such inconsistent biblicists are prepared to honestly admit the actual impossibility of carrying out their theory and to make the necessary revisions to their theories and practices, or whether they will stick to their unworkable theoretical guns and simply live with the intellectual and practical duplicities that are imposed by their de facto inconsistencies with regard to scripture.

## Lack of Biblicist Self-Attestation

Many evangelical biblicists ground the alleged truth of biblicism in the Bible's supposed own self-attestation about its divine authority and other attributes assumed by biblicism. This is a circular move, but not viciously circular, and, within a presuppositionalist epistemology, perfectly legitimate. There is not necessarily a problem appealing to an authoritative Bible to validate the authority of the Bible. But there is another problem with this approach. The problem is that what the Bible says about itself does not actually validate biblicism, as defined above. Or at least it does not do so explicitly and without the making of numerous dubious inferences and extensions of logic. Some biblicists are comfortable claiming that a teaching is biblical, even if it is not explicit in scripture, when it is obtained through a "good and necessary inference" from what *is* explicit in scripture.[15] The problem is, most of the received assumptions of biblicism as a theory are not necessarily good and necessary inferences of what the Bible explicitly says about itself. Let us briefly examine the relevant evidence.

First, when the apostles spoke and wrote of "scripture," they meant the Law and the Prophets and some of the Writings of the Hebrew Bible, what Christians call the Old Testament. The New Testament as we now have it in its present form of course did not exist, at the time of its original writing, as a collected, recognized canon of scripture. So what the New Testament says about "scripture" may not be assumed to apply to the entire New Testament itself. (Note, however, evidence of the process of early inscripturation indicated in 2 Pet. 3:15–16, where the author of that Epistle speaks of the apostle Paul's "letters" as comparable to "the other scriptures"—suggesting that by the time of that Epistle's writing [likely between the late first century and the mid-second century] at least some of Paul's letters were being viewed by at least some of the churches of that day as having a kind of scriptural status.)

Furthermore, nearly everything the New Testament says about the Old Testament scriptures refers to them foretelling the coming, life, death, and resurrection of Jesus. The scriptures were a preparation for and witness to the coming of Christ. In Christ, therefore, the scriptures were "fulfilled," as many New Testament texts say. Beyond this, sometimes Old Testament passages are used by New Testament authors to justify particular practices in Christian churches, such as providing material support to preachers and teachers (1 Tim. 5:18). But little of this speaks directly to the matter of biblicism per se.

Five texts about "scripture" matter most for biblicists. The first is John 10:35, in which Jesus says that "scripture cannot be broken."

The second is Romans 15:4, which states that "everything that was written in the past was written to teach us, so that through endurance and the encouragement of the Scriptures we might have hope." Third, 1 Timothy 4:13 says that, until Paul arrives to meet Timothy, Paul's instruction to Timothy was to "devote yourself to the public reading of Scripture." Fourth, 2 Timothy 3:15–17 observes of Timothy that "from infancy you have known the holy Scriptures, which are able to make you wise for salvation through faith in Christ Jesus. All Scripture is God-breathed and is useful for teaching, rebuking, correcting and training in righteousness, so that the man of God may be thoroughly equipped for every good work." Finally, 2 Peter 1:20–21 states, "No prophecy of Scripture came about by the prophet's own interpretation. For prophecy never had its origin in the will of man, but men spoke from God as they were carried along by the Holy Spirit."

What then is the Bible's own view of scripture, when read in biblicist terms? First, all scripture is "God-breathed," divinely inspired. Second, prophecies of scripture were never purely human products but rather spoken "from God" by men "carried along by the Holy Spirit." God is thus clearly the causal agent producing scripture both in its existence and (at least some if not all of its) content. Third, scripture cannot be "broken." Fourth, scripture is able to prepare believers for salvation through Christ. Scripture also has the purpose for believers of being useful for the teaching, discipline, and training in righteousness. And the goal of scripture's use is to encourage believers to have hope and to fully equip believers to produce good works. Finally, in at least one setting, a church pastor was to devote himself to scripture's public reading.

All of that says a lot, but what it says does not add up to the theory of biblicism as described above and practiced by many American evangelicals. What is clearly correct in biblicism, according to the Bible's self-attestation, is scripture's divine inspiration. Nothing in this book has questioned that belief. But none of these biblical passages themselves obviously or necessarily teaches divine writing, total representation, complete coverage, democratic perspicuity, commonsense hermeneutics, *solo scriptura*, internal harmony, universal applicability, inductive method, or the handbook model (as I described them above). To get from the apparently relevant scriptural texts to any of these ten biblicist beliefs requires supplementary argumentative work that relies on inferences and employs additional scriptural texts. Biblicists believe that this extra argumentative work succeeds, but I am persuaded that they are wrong.

For example, biblicists argue the following: "The Bible is inspired by God; God does not and cannot lie (Titus 1:2; Heb. 6:18); therefore everything in the Bible is true; therefore the Bible is inerrant." But this line of thought involves multiple instances of slippage and leaping.[16] The first unwarranted leap is from (rightly) believing that scripture is "God-breathed" to (erroneously) assuming that that necessarily endorses the belief of some biblicists in "divine writing," that the Bible, down to the details of its words, consists of and is identical with God's very own words written in human language. Those are not necessarily the same thing.[17] The second leap is to apply New Testament statements about God's inability to lie, which were meant in context to concern the questions of hope of eternal life and God's oath of promise to Abraham, to a more general and abstract issue about the ontological nature of the Bible. Nobody is interested in claiming that God does or can lie. But, lacking a well-established set of other connections concerning scripture, that itself does not necessitate an inerrancy doctrine of scripture.

In short, lacking a prior, independent belief in the biblicist "divine writing" assumption, it simply does not necessarily follow from the idea that God cannot lie to the idea that everything in the Bible is inerrant—unless one subscribes to a "dictation theory" of inspiration, which most thoughtful evangelicals do not.[18] There is a lot of room between lying and total inerrancy in revelatory communication.

Third, the logic here relies on simplistic notions of what "true" means, given the diverse literary nature of the Bible and many textual forms of conveying truths. Only the more unsophisticated of biblicists do not know that they must back away from these simplistic notions. For instance, the "Chicago Statement on Biblical Inerrancy" offers this qualification: "When total precision of a particular kind was not expected nor aimed at, it is no error not to have achieved it. Scripture is inerrant, not in the sense of being absolutely precise by modern standards, but in the sense of making good its claims and achieving that measure of focused truth at which its authors aimed."[19] It is thus also an unwarranted leap from "true" to biblicist versions of inerrancy.

In sum, the Bible itself does not lay out the full biblicist program or anything like it. The Bible contains passages showing, for example, a reader of scripture unable to understand what it teaches unless someone guides him (Acts 8:30–31). The theory of biblicism cannot itself be generated and justified by its own biblicist principles. What is specifically true in biblicism is belief in divine inspiration. Beyond that, there are many other nonbiblicist approaches to the Bible that recognize and fully honor what scripture attests about itself. Biblicism is only one of the possibilities—and one dependent on tenuous connections to the actual statements of scripture about itself. Again, this per se does not invalidate biblicism. It merely nullifies the assumption that evangelical biblicism rests on obvious biblical teachings. If biblicists see biblicism working on biblical grounds, it is because they very much *want* it to work and so *make* it work—I am tempted even to say *force* it to work—not because it naturally and clearly works of its own accord.

A significant gap exists between what the Bible has to say about scripture and what biblicism says. In order to bridge that gap, to get from actual biblical texts to biblicist theory, it is necessary to employ decidedly nonbiblicist methods, including eisegesis and the making of multiple inferences that the relevant texts hardly necessitate.[20] That the theory of biblicism cannot itself be generated and justified by its own biblicist principles suggests sociologically that biblicism is actually not driven by its purported, manifest interest, but by other latent concerns, motives, and interests that are at least somewhat auxiliary to the biblicist program.

## The Genuine Need for Extrabiblical Theological Concepts

Biblicism suggests that all of the pieces of the Christian doctrine and morality puzzle are right there in the Bible as propositions to be pulled out and put together in their logical ordering. Such a view is fed by evangelical Bible-only-ism and the handbook model of scripture. Yet a bit of reflection on orthodox Christian theology makes clear that numerous absolutely crucial doctrinal terms are not themselves found in the Bible but were invented or appropriated by the church during the patristic era. These doctrinal developments give conceptual expression to what was and is believed (by most) to be the best reading of scripture. I give three brief examples here.

The term "Trinity" is nowhere found in scripture, yet it is utterly central to orthodox Christian belief. The Bible does, of course, speak of God by many names, including the Father, Jesus Christ the Son, and the Holy Spirit. But to best render theologically what scripture seems to teach about divine ontology, the church was forced to move beyond the Bible to the extrascriptural concept of "Trinity." The adoption of the concept of Trinity itself does nothing to undermine the biblicist outlook—except perhaps that of a strictly anticreedal Baptist variety. But it does remind us that orthodox Christian theological reflection *requires* moving beyond the Bible to employ extrabiblical terms and concepts that are, strictly speaking, progressive doctrinal developments authorized by the church on scriptural grounds. That is a significant move.

The same is true of the Greek term *homoousion*, the use of which was required by the bishops and other leaders in the Council of Nicaea (AD 325) in order to most accurately represent the Catholic Church's orthodox Christology against the (also biblically supported) arguments of Arianism. About this, David Bentley Hart rightly notes:

> The ultimate defeat of Arius' position was . . . not because he stood on scriptural grounds weaker than those of his opponents. The Arians could adduce any number of passages from the Bible to support their case. . . . Each side could produce fairly cogent [biblical] arguments for why the other's interpretations of the verses in question were flawed. Here neither side enjoyed the advantage. Ultimately, though, the Arian position was untenable simply because it reduced to incoherence the Christian story of redemption as it had been understood, proclaimed, prayed, and lived for generations.[21]

It is worth noting that some opponents of that day and even today object to the term *homoousion* because it is strictly "unbiblical," in that the term itself is not found in the Bible. Theological orthodoxy says that this is true but irrelevant, since it is necessary to work theologically beyond the Bible in order to make best sense of the Bible. In the words of David Yeago, "The ancient theologians were right to hold that Nicene *homoousion* is neither imposed *on* the New Testament texts, nor distantly deduced *from* the text, but, rather, describes a pattern of judgments present *in* the texts, in the texture of scriptural discourse concerning Jesus and the God of Israel."[22] The crucial theological idea of *homoousion* is thus not strictly "biblical" in a biblicist sense but certainly is biblical in the theological sense. And that kind of realization, I suggest, opens doors to understandings that begin to erode the biblicist outlook.

Finally, an even more problematic theological concept for biblicism is the doctrine of divine creation ex nihilo, "out of nothing." Not only is the term "ex nihilo" not "biblical" in the strict sense noted above (unless one counts the "deuterocanonical" book of 2 Maccabees scriptural, in which the writer declares [7:28] that "God made [heaven and earth] out of what did not exist, and . . . mankind comes into being in the same way"—the first time the concept of ex nihilo is expressed explicitly in Jewish writings). The idea "out of nothing" also does not actually seem to fit the relevant biblical text of Genesis itself, which appears to suggest that God's creative activity began working on a preexistent "formless and empty" earth involving "darkness," "the deep," and "the waters" (Gen. 1:2). Clearly this passage does not force some kind of dualistic "doctrine of the eternity of raw matter." But the naive reader of Genesis 1:1–2 could well conclude that idea on purely "biblical" grounds.

What is required, once more, to come to an orthodox theology of creation is to work with a broader array of scriptural materials and extrabiblical theological reasoning—in order to avoid both Greek monism and dualism. This approach produced a key concept, ex nihilo, that is not only not found in the Bible itself but is also hermeneutically controlling of what the most relevant Bible passage says. That is what second-century Christian theologians did.[23] Again, my point is that, while most reasonable Christians find these theological moves to be obviously legitimate, it is not clear that they could flow naturally from a consistently practiced biblicist paradigm, which tends, if anything, to authorize evangelical tendencies toward naive primitivism.

## The Dubious Genealogy of the Bible-Only Tradition

One of the ironies of evangelicalism's practice of *solo scriptura* in America as a means to arrive at pure doctrine and practice is that the populist pursuit of Bible-only-ism started off as an ideological project not of conservatives but of heterodox liberal Protestants driven by Enlightenment ideals. Eighteenth-century American evangelicals did not particularly believe that the Bible could be read entirely alone, apart from theologically informed church teachings. Those early American evangelicals usually believed in the necessity of learning from the creeds and doctrines of the church, mediated by a well-educated minister, as a means to read the Bible properly.

By contrast, as historian Nathan Hatch observes, "the first Americans to underscore the right of private judgment in handling Scripture were, oddly enough, ministers who *opposed* the evangelical tenets of the First Great Awakening. As New Lights in New England worked to make people more theologically self-conscious . . . theological liberals became increasingly restive with strict creedal definitions of Christianity."[24] The liberals' motive was usually to overthrow what they viewed as the thick and oppressive dogmatic systems of orthodox Calvinism. To do so, these liberal Protestant leaders of the late eighteenth and early nineteenth centuries hammered away against doctrinally concerned evangelicals with the slogan of returning to "the Bible only" as a means to purify theology in order to arrive at the simplicity of biblical beliefs. Where they usually arrived, however, was unorthodox beliefs.

"In the late-colonial period . . . professions to follow *just the Scriptures* had been a staple of heterodox exegesis practiced by liberals."[25] The Boston liberal Protestant Charles Chauncey (1705–87), for example, insisted that his belief in universalism of salvation resulted from "studying the scriptures in [a] free, impartial, and diligent manner."[26] In 1813, the Congregationalist minister Thomas Worchester published a book titled *Divine Testimony Received without Any Addition or Diminution*, which claimed to be based solely on the Bible as the single and ultimate doctrinal authority. Williams observes that "many of his arguments in defense of biblical authority can easily be found among evangelical writers today. Worcester declared that the church had abandoned the simplicity of the gospel since the times of the apostles and had lain in darkness, error, and degeneracy."[27] Worcester's Bible-only theological method, however, led him to espouse the doctrine of Unitarianism.[28]

In 1850, Charles Beecher published *The Bible a Sufficient Creed*, which rejected received orthodoxy, denounced "creed-power," and advocated "the Bible, the whole Bible, and nothing but the Bible."[29] So liberal was Beecher that he was relieved of his preaching position as a New England Congregational minister. Hatch, Noll, and other historians provide numerous other corroborating examples. Yet it was precisely the Bible-only method of scripture reading of these heterodox liberal Protestants that conservative evangelicals in the nineteenth century adopted and turned to their own evangelical ends. Driving the rush into Bible-only-ism was not a well-considered theological rationale but rather the populist, individualistic, democratizing tendencies of the ideology of the Revolutionary and early Republic eras.

Reflecting more broadly on this odd linkage of liberal and conservative, Roger Lundin notes the connection between the "unlikely allies" of former liberal Protestant Bible readers and contemporary American evangelicals when it comes to reading scripture apart from historical tradition: "Schleiermacher and the evangelicals come together on key questions of interpretation through their common disregard of the constructive hermeneutical significance of history. . . . History can only be hindrance and not a help. . . . [With] no less than Schleiermacher, conservative biblical scholars have sought to read the Bible as though it had never been read before." This tendency Lundin situates within the long Cartesian inclination in Western (Protestant) modernity to continually, as "orphans" in a "parentless" (i.e., godless) world, try to "start history over again" in recurring moments of "self-fathering."[30]

Often lacking an appreciation of the importance of history, contemporary American evangelical biblicists typically fail to grasp the dubious heritage and problematic genealogy of their own Bible-only tradition. And that makes them all the more vulnerable to the potential misreadings and conflicts resulting from that tradition's antitraditionalism.

## Lack of a Biblicist Social Ethic

Many if not most evangelicals—in the spirit of Carl F. H. Henry's 1947 classic, *The Uneasy Conscience of Modern Fundamentalism*[31]— would say they believe that "Jesus is the answer" not only for people's personal needs but also for society's political, economic, and social problems. The difficulty is that biblicism is unable to deliver one coherent, much less comprehensive, social ethic to guide a compelling "biblical" response to contemporary social problems.

The reasons are many—including that the very idea of the possibility of Christian political influence or social action is alien to the New Testament—yet beyond the scope of this book to examine. The Bible offers some very general "principles," such as humans being created in God's image and the state being established by God to execute justice, along with some extremely specific (and perhaps culturally extraneous) instructions, such as the New Testament "household codes" (Col. 3:18–4:1; Eph. 5:21–6:9; Titus 2:1–10; 1 Pet. 2:18–3:7). This lack of biblical material with which to build a coherent social doctrine helps to explain why social ethics have been one of the weakest—and at times simply nonexistent—dimensions of American evangelicalism as a whole.

It also helps to explain why so many evangelicals are so highly vulnerable to being swayed by new and different winds of political change—for example, entertaining quite progressive social ideas during the 1970s, only then to be swept into a close identification with and support for the neoconservative Republican Party of the 1980s and 1990s. Evangelical scholars also clearly have difficulty identifying the Bible's social ethics. When theorists who take a basically biblicist approach try to derive a systematic Christian social ethic from scripture, they end up offering an incredibly wide range of proposals. These may include everything from Jim Wallis's left-of-center *Agenda for Biblical People* and Stephen Mott's progressive *Biblical Ethics and Social Change*, to James Skillen's more moderate Kuyperian "structural pluralism" in his *Political Order and the Plural Structure of Society*, all the way over to the neo-Calvinist, postmillennialist "theonomy" or "dominion theology" of the so-called Christian reconstructionists, such as R. J. Rushdoony, Gary North, Greg Bashan, David Chilton, and Gary DeMar.[32] (Not all these authors are biblicists themselves, necessarily, but their views are not infrequently appropriated by evangelical biblicists on biblicist grounds.) There are also a variety of other alternative scripture-based social ethics to be found in that mix, all claiming to be "biblical."

The problem here is one of pervasive interpretive pluralism again, but greatly complicated too by the sheer dearth of internally consistent scriptural substantive content with which one might construct a robust biblical social doctrine or ethic. In the end, biblicism seems to make the task of full-bodied constructive Christian social ethics undoable. And that is a very serious problem.

## Setting Up Youth for Unnecessary Crises of Faith

Finally, though hardly the least of concerns to me, biblicism also has the pastorally problematic tendency to set up some young, committed believers for unnecessary crises of personal faith, when some of them come to realize (rightly, yet without warning) that biblicism is untenable. Having been taught as youth to stake their faith fully on one (faulty) theory of the Bible, their faith can later founder and sometimes collapse when antagonistic nonbiblicists point out and press home real problems with biblicist theory.

Biblicism is in fact objectively vulnerable to certain critiques that range in their effects from being troubling to devastating—including, perhaps, some of those that I have elaborated above. Therefore, the faith "eggs" of those believers who place them all in the biblicist "basket" can be very easily smashed when they—for example, by going away to college—leave the "plausibility structures" of the sheltered, biblicist faith communities of their youth and are confronted with those real critiques.

My personal observation of this happening has been of many "Bible believing" evangelical and fundamentalist (mostly Baptist and Methodist) students from around the state of North Carolina who have their biblicist faith thrown into crisis and sometimes shattered, often as a result of taking certain religious studies courses at the University of North Carolina at Chapel Hill, particularly courses in New Testament with Dr. Bart Ehrman—a compelling professor who was himself once evangelical but is now agnostic, in part because of (he has told me personally) naive, biblicism-confronting, textual difficulties (as a graduate student at Princeton Seminary; grappling with the problem of evil and other issues also contributed to Ehrman's loss of faith). Carlos Bovell has also written forcefully about this and related problems.[33]

John Goldingay, focusing specifically on inerrancy, summarizes the concern this way: "A stress on [biblical] inerrancy cannot safeguard people from a slippery slope that carries them from abandoning inerrancy to an eventual reneging on all other Christian doctrines. Indeed, it more likely impels them toward such a slope. The claim that scripture is factually inerrant sets up misleading expectations regarding the precision of narratives and then requires such far-fetched defenses . . . that it presses people toward rejecting it."[34] I think the same dynamic applies not only to inerrancy specifically but to biblicism more generally.

In such cases, the difficulty is not necessarily the fact of the anti-biblicist critiques per se. The real problem is the particular biblicist theory about the Bible; it not only makes young believers vulnerable to being disabused of their naive acceptance of that theory but it also often has the additional consequence of putting their faith commitments at risk. Biblicism often paints smart, committed youth into a corner that is for real reasons impossible to occupy for many of those who actually confront its problems. When some of those youth give up on biblicism and simply walk away across the wet paint, it is flawed biblicism that is partly responsible for those losses of faith.

Insofar as these biblicism-caused outcomes are undesirable and unnecessary, we have another good reason to seek better alternatives to biblicism. In this Peter Enns is correct: "We do not honor the Lord nor do we uphold the gospel by playing make-believe."[35]

## Conclusion

The main focus of my critique of biblicism is the problem of pervasive interpretive pluralism, examined in the previous chapters. Once we face that difficulty, we can also then begin to acknowledge other serious problems with biblicism, such as those mentioned in this chapter. When we confront biblicism's many problems, we come to see that it is untenable. Biblicism simply cannot be practiced with intellectual and practical honesty on its own terms. It is in this sense literally impossible. Biblicism's fatal problems are not the sort of things with which faithful Christians ought to be comfortable. Biblicism is not the way forward for evangelicalism. There must be a better way to understand and read the Bible. What might that be?

# PART 2

# TOWARD A TRULY EVANGELICAL READING OF SCRIPTURE

# 5

# The Christocentric Hermeneutical Key

Evangelical biblicism is not an especially *evangelical* way to read the Bible. In practice, biblicism demeans scripture. On the surface, biblicism *appears* to champion a "high view" of the Bible, but its actual practices betray a rather low view of the Bible. Evangelicals who are truly evangelical can and ought to do better.

Most readers of this book know that the word "evangelical" originally comes from the Greek word *evangelion* (εὐαγγέλιον), which is formed by the union of the linguistic parts *eu-* "good" and *angelion* "message." To be evangelical, then, means having one's life centered on the terrifically good message that God is reconciling the world to himself in Jesus Christ (2 Cor. 5:17–19). That is indeed amazingly good news. But really and truly hearing, grasping, and making sense of that fantastic news for our lives is altogether different than, for example, simply following a life handbook of divine oracles or looking up information in a holy user's manual to help fix a problem. Go find any one of the user's manuals or handbooks in your garage or closet and think for a moment about whether even a divinely inspired manual for living life would really amount to gospel-like great news. It wouldn't.

A truly evangelical reading of scripture confronts us with a particular story and message that, if taken seriously, blow the doors off every assumption, outlook, and experience that we have ever had apart from Jesus Christ. The evangelical message of scripture shakes loose from us every misguided and idolatrous preconception about everything, literally everything, that we thought we knew, and then begins to rebuild us in light of the singularly radical fact of who God really is and therefore who we really are in relation to God and what he has done for us. The good news of the gospel of Jesus Christ is the most important thing we will ever need to hear and know, and it has the power to reframe and transform everything else.

Neither the Christian gospel itself nor the scriptures that announce the gospel to us are collections of biblical advice or "perspectives on" every ancillary "how-to" topic with which we might want help in our lives—including dressing well, running our finances, and raising our children. If we ever get to the point where the gospel has seriously formed our lives, we may then have some good gospel-informed ideas concerning how to think about money and parenting. But real evangelicals will always think about such issues, indeed all issues, through the single lens of the gospel of Christ—which means indirectly, not directly through some biblicist procedure of parsing allegedly "relevant" biblical propositions.

We are fortunate if scripture's good news, as disturbing as it is, reworks even part of our lives—and even more so if the gospel really gets a grip on us. Unfortunately, we tend to domesticate the amazing message with which scripture challenges us, and we work hard to protect ourselves from the good news doing its life-altering work on us. Indeed, I suspect that all too often evangelical biblicism in particular—under the well-meaning guise of defending a "high view" of scripture—does just that. Biblicism too often traps, domesticates, and controls the life-quaking *kerygma* (proclamation) of the gospel in order to provide the Bible reader with the security, certainty, and protection that humans naturally want.

The irony, if and when this happens, is tragic. Evangelicals—a people whose core identity is supposedly centered in God's earth-shaking good news to a literally lost world—turn the inspired and truthful witness to that good news into merely a holy handbook to help people live more manageable lives. The Bible—however highly it is lauded in theory—easily becomes in biblicism a tool in human hands used to facilitate the kind of secure, stable, and therapeutically satisfying lives we wish to live.

Sometimes, at the popular level, this looks like "helpful hints from scripture" that people use to manage their daily emotions and relationships. At more academic and official church levels, it might consist of establishing and defending watertight theological systems that provide all the answers (for those who believe them) and thus produce cognitive and emotional security in a very insecure world. As a result, in these ways, "the defense of Scripture can become more important than Scripture itself."[1] Either way, these approaches use scripture to achieve the biblicist's human-centered purposes rather than allowing the Holy Spirit to speak through scripture the God-to-people message that, even as it saves and comforts, also disrupts, challenges, and changes anyone who takes it seriously.

The primary purpose of the present book is to point out what appears to be a serious problem with biblicism, not to elaborate complete solutions to that problem. However, so as not to leave the misimpression that I am a hermeneutical nihilist or radical postmodern relativist, I hope to suggest that this critique can actually go somewhere constructive, and I will offer some viable alternatives to biblicism that I think retain some of the best of that for which biblicism stands. Biblicists may not like these alternatives or be willing to choose them, but they are worth consideration. If biblicists reject these possibilities, the burden is on them either to show how biblicism is actually possible (despite pervasive interpretive pluralism and its other problems), or to advance a better alternative.

If my larger critique above is even modestly sound, then what is needed to improve on biblicism is some kind of a stronger hermeneutical guide that can govern the proper interpretation of the multivocal, polysemous, multivalent texts of scripture toward the shared reading of a more coherent, authoritative biblical message. Such a stronger hermeneutical guide would also, of course, have to be consistent with, if not directly derived from, Christian scripture and tradition.

This chapter offers some ideas to readers who acknowledge biblicism's fatal problems as described in this book and who want to find an alternative approach to scripture that still remains essentially faithful to the sensibilities of the evangelical tradition. Readers who are not persuaded that pervasive interpretive pluralism and other problems make biblicism impossible will find much of what follows to be lamentably misguided. I can do no more to help or answer them. Readers who are persuaded about biblicism's impossibility yet who do not believe its problems can be surmounted within an evangelical framework may find this chapter interesting but inadequate. But readers who are persuaded of biblicism's impossibility and who wish to re-address scripture in a way that may in fact be more truly evangelical should read on.

I do not believe that American evangelical biblicists are currently in a particularly good position to simply identify and adopt some comprehensive and complete set of principles that will set their approach to scripture aright. Better—given the power of the biblicist heritage and the risk of adopting flawed alternatives—to take the time and care needed to rethink these issues well. A lot of historical water has gone under the bridge, shaping established habits and tendencies of evangelical thought and practice, and this necessitates careful reconsideration. Certain other related contemporary disagreements—between evangelical conservatives, postconservatives, emergents, postmoderns, and other types of evangelicals—create challenges that also affect our discussion here. Biblicism, I have said, is impossible. But there are other approaches—including outright liberalism—that I think are even worse.

American evangelicals in this discussion need to resist their natural historical tendencies toward entrepreneurial, activist, pragmatic, immediate problem solving and instead spend the time needed to think matters through carefully, creatively, and in interaction with the larger, longer Christian tradition. Furthermore, success in this matter would seem to require an open, civil, collective discussion leading to something more like an eventual near-consensus, rather than some convicted party launching off into a high-visibility program or movement that leaves most of the others behind. The last thing American evangelicalism needs is more autonomously impulsive reformist action and more organizational and identity fragmentation. In any case, the kingdom of God is not going to shift into neutral until American evangelicals get their approach to the Bible straight. So evangelicals might as well take their time to engage the matter openly, carefully, honestly, civilly, and thoroughly. Better to have been patient and actually gotten somewhere good twenty years from now than to jump to immediate problem solving and end up getting nowhere.

The thinking for the kind of constructive process I offer in the following pages contributes only one set of limited, partial, and fallible ideas. I want to underscore the word "toward" in the part title for this section of the book. The purpose of what follows is not to resolve all of the problems. It is rather to point to what I think are some promising ways forward, beyond biblicism. My hope is that thoughtful evangelicals would be ready, willing, and able to consider them, and possibly embrace them, and then contribute to a larger critical and constructive discussion.

The ideas in the following pages do not offer a fixed package of solutions to the problems raised in previous chapters. To repeat, I do not have a comprehensive program to rehabilitate biblicist evangelical Bible reading. Some of what follows I am quite confident about, but I am more tentative about other parts and welcome continued conversations. I am more than happy to see where I am wrong and to be persuaded of better alternatives. Some of the following ideas will seem obvious to many readers. Others will seem more challenging.

To reiterate, the guiding purpose in the remainder of the book is to contribute *toward* theorizing a nonbiblicist yet definitely evangelical approach to scriptural authority that particularly addresses the specific problem of pervasive interpretive pluralism. I am not trying here to develop a full-fledged theory of all theologically relevant aspects of the Bible—such as inspiration or infallibility—a task well beyond both my scholarly competence and the scope of this book. At the same time, any attempt to rethink scripture and address pervasive interpretive pluralism will inevitably raise other related matters of concern. I will not hesitate to develop broader ideas as necessary to pursue this goal. But I will always try to bring the discussion around to this book's core concern, which is how the Bible can function as an authority even if biblicism is impossible.

## The Centrality of Jesus Christ

The purpose, center, and interpretive key to scripture is Jesus Christ. It is embarrassing to have to write this, for it should be obvious to all Christians. But I am afraid this is not always so obvious in practice in biblicist circles. At least the profound *implications* of this fact *for reading scripture* are not always obvious to many evangelicals. Truly believing that Jesus Christ is the real purpose, center, and interpretive key to scripture causes one to read the Bible in a way that is very different than believing the Bible to be an instruction manual containing universally applicable divine oracles concerning every possible subject it seems to address.

For one thing, seeing Christ as central compels us to always try to make sense of everything we read in *any* part of scripture in light of our larger knowledge of who God is in Jesus Christ. We do not then read scripture devotionally to try to find tidbits there that are "meaningful to" or that "speak to" us, wherever we are in our personal subjective spiritual experiences. We do not read scripture as detached historians trying to judge its technical accuracy in recounting events. We do not read scripture as a vast collection of infallible propositions whose meanings and implications can be understood on their own particular terms. We only, always, and everywhere read scripture in view of its real subject matter: Jesus Christ. This means that we always read scripture Christocentrically, christologically, and christotelically,[2] as those who *really* believe what the Nicene and Chalcedonian creeds say. That is, for Christians, Christ is the center, the inner reason, and the end of all of scripture. From the Bible's account of the creation of the world in Genesis to its final consummation in Revelation, it is all and only about the work of God in time and space in the person of Jesus Christ for the redemption of the world. "The [Old Testament] law is only a shadow of the good things that are coming—not the realities themselves" (Heb. 10:1). The reality is the sacrificial cross of Jesus Christ. Thus, the great Baptist preacher Charles Spurgeon (1834–92) wrote, "O you who open your Bibles and want to understand a text, the way to get into the meaning of a text is through the door, Christ."[3]

This also means that we always read the Bible as committed trinitarians, as those who do not merely "believe in God," but who actually believe in God in particular as Father, Son, and Holy Spirit. Furthermore, and crucially, we understand whatever we understand about the Father through Jesus Christ. And we understand whatever we understand about the Holy Spirit through Jesus Christ. Jesus Christ, God incarnate, God with us and for us, the only "image of the invisible God" in human form (Col. 1:15; John 1:1–18), is how we know God and know about what God is doing in history and our lives. The Bible seems to know about this itself. "No one has ever seen God, but God the One and Only, who is at the Father's side, has made him known" (John 1:18). "No one knows who the Father is except the Son and those to whom the Son chooses to reveal him" (Luke 10:22).

"You diligently study the Scriptures because you think that by them you possess eternal life," Jesus said, but "these are the Scriptures that testify about *me*" (John 5:39). Therefore, when Jesus "opened the Scriptures" to his unrecognizing companions on the road to Emmaus, which caused their hearts to "burn within" them, "he explained to them what was said in all the Scriptures concerning *himself*" (Luke 24:25–32). And when Jesus appeared to his own disciples after the resurrection, on what did he focus pertaining to learning from scripture?

> "This is what I told you while I was still with you: Everything must be fulfilled that is written about me in the Law of Moses, the Prophets and the Psalms." Then he opened their minds so they could understand the Scriptures. He told them, "This is what is written: The Christ will suffer and rise from the dead on the third day, and repentance and forgiveness of sins will be preached in his name to all nations, beginning at Jerusalem. You are witnesses of these things." (Luke 24:44–48)

In short, Jesus opened the disciples' minds to truly understand the scriptures precisely so that they would see the *evangelion* of the gospel of Jesus Christ behind, in, and through all of scripture. If believers today want to rightly understand scripture, every narrative, every prayer, every proverb, every law, every Epistle needs likewise to be read and understood always and only in light of Jesus Christ and God reconciling the world to himself through him.

This does not mean trying to detect Christ in every piece of scripture or forcing every verse in the Bible to somehow be directly about the gospel. That itself would be bad prooftexting. Rather, every part of scripture and scripture as a whole—which obviously has background and foreground material, a center and a periphery—is read in light of the centrally defining reality of Jesus Christ. As Keith Ward notes, "For a Christian, every part of the Bible must in some way point to Christ, to the living person of Jesus who is the Christ, and to the unlimited, liberating love of God which is revealed in Christ. To put it bluntly, it is not the words of the Bible that are 'the way, the truth, and the life.' It is the person of Christ, to whom the Bible witnesses."[4] And as Bonhoeffer says of scripture, "In its entirety and in all its parts it is nothing but this witness of Christ, his life, his death, and his resurrection."[5]

Another way to say that we must read the Bible christologically and as committed trinitarians is to state clearly that any doctrine of revelation, scripture, or inspiration must, in any larger theological system, be properly located within the doctrine of God and *not* as a foundational prolegomenon or epistemological preface. Unfortunately, the latter is what typically happens in biblicist evangelical theology: "Christian theological talk of revelation migrates to the beginning of the dogmatic corpus, and has to take on the job of furnishing the epistemological warrant for Christian claims."[6] This "absorption of revelation into foundations," John Webster rightly notes, is, however, a "mislocation and . . . reassignment to undertake duties which it was not intended to perform."[7] Placing revelation at the start of theology also isolates doctrines of revelation and scripture materially from the rest of any substantive theological exposition.

There is a better way. Rather than using a doctrine of inspired revelation as a prologue to real theologizing in order to provide a foundationalist "defense of the viability of Christian talk . . . before the tribunal of [allegedly] impartial reason,"[8] Webster insists on locating all understanding of revelation and scripture within an epistemologically prior trinitarian doctrine of God:

> The doctrinal under-determination and mislocation of the idea of revelation can only be overcome by its reintegration into the comprehensive structure of Christian doctrine, and most especially the Christian doctrine of God. . . . Revelation [thus understood] is the self-presentation of the triune God, the free work of sovereign mercy in which God wills, establishes, and perfects saving fellowship with himself in which humanity comes to know, love, and fear him above all things. . . . As the gracious presence of God, revelation is itself the establishment of fellowship. It is not so much an action in which God informs us of other acts of his through which we are reconciled to him; rather, revelation is a way of indicating the communicative force of God's saving, fellowship-creating presence.[9]

Webster continues:

> The proper location for talk of revelation is the Christian doctrine of the Trinity, and, in particular, the outgoing, communicative mercy of

the triune God in the economy of salvation. Revelation is the corollary
of trinitarian theology and soteriology. . . . What Christian theology
has to say about revelation is not simply deployed as a means of dealing
with epistemological questions, or primarily as an answer to questions
of the sources and norms of church and theological discourse. It may
address these concerns, but it does so as an application or extension
of its material content, which is the sovereign goodness of Father,
Son, and Spirit in willing, realizing, and perfecting saving fellowship.[10]

Thus, a Christocentric and trinitarian approach to the Bible does
more than just help believers to read it better. It also provides a clue
for revising our larger theological mentality and method in a way that
places the Triune God, not modern standards of warranted knowledge, at the center.

The view commended here is a decidedly and unapologetically
Christ-centered approach to scripture. It tells us, among other things,
that if the Bible embodies an internal unity or harmony that helps
point the way toward a common Christian mind about what scripture
teaches, that unity centers on the living Christ. This Christocentric
approach does not begin with a theory of the Bible that tells us deductively that scripture *must not* contain any serious internal tensions
or contradictions since it reflects the mind of a perfect God. Such
a view reflects a particular philosophical way of reasoning, not a
Christocentric theological one. Peter Enns strikes the right note here:

Can Christians speak of a unity to the Bible? Yes, but it is not a superficial unity based on the surface content of the words of passages taken
in isolation. The unity of the Bible is more subtle but at the same time
deeper. It is a unity that should ultimately be sought in Christ himself,
the living word. . . . We believe not only that the *Bible* is the word of
God, but that *Christ* himself is the word. . . . The written word bears
witness to the incarnate word, Christ. . . . The Bible bears witness
to Christ *by Christ's design*. He is over the Bible, beyond it, separate
from it, even though the Bible is *his* word and thus bears witness to
him. Christ is supreme, and it is in him, the embodied word, that the
written word ultimately finds its unity. Christ is the final destiny of
Israel's story, and it is to him that the Bible as a whole bears witness.[11]

Of course, unless we are anticanonical hermeneutical nihil-
ists, we must believe in *some* kind of internal biblical coherence or

unity—despite the Bible having been written by many different authors who lived in highly divergent historical and cultural circumstances across thousands of years. But by this Christocentric account, the internal harmony that scripture embodies does not stem from all of its propositions and narrative accounts fitting together perfectly like a neat jigsaw puzzle.

Scripture's internal unity or harmony, rather, derives from its central purpose in divine revelation of telling us about Jesus Christ. It prepares us for the coming of Christ. It witnesses to the incarnate person and work of Christ. It offers apostolic theological reflections on Christ for the church and the world. It shows the difference that Christ made in human life during the earliest years of the church. It tells us who and what we really are in light of Christ. And it sends us on a mission in life in response to the good news of Christ. Biblical unity comes not from an empirically observable, perfect noncontradiction evident among all of its many texts. Biblical unity comes instead from the real and living God/Man Jesus Christ who stands at scripture's center. Everything revolves around him and draws its significance from him. It is Jesus Christ who runs as the consistently present thread more or less explicitly through its sometimes-meandering story.[12]

Reading the Bible Christocentrically does *not* mean dividing reality up into two realms—into "religious and faith" matters, on the one hand, versus purportedly "not religious" topics on the other hand—and then claiming that the Bible really concerns itself authoritatively only with the former. Some problematic versions of the position of noninerrantist biblical infallibility suggest that kind of approach, namely, that the Bible is only about "faith and Christian morals" but not about anything else in life. Inerrantists are right, in my view, to object to that dichotomy—though they usually do not object for the right reasons, in the end. It is true, as inerrantists say, that the strict division between the religious and not religious is artificial and impossible in practice to apply with any precision. Christocentrism naturally agrees that all of reality belongs to God and is subject to Christ's authority and judgment. No allegedly "nonreligious" topic or issue in the entire world may then be set aside as not relevant to the Bible's concerns, as if we lived in a dualistic reality.

But a Christocentric hermeneutic does not conclude from those objections that the Bible contains perfect and explicit instructions on

every imaginable topic it seems to address, as well as indirectly to literally every possible topic, through the application of its "worldview."
A Christocentric reading of the Bible instead simply says that all topics both addressed in the Bible and not must be read and considered
through the logic of the gospel of Jesus Christ. Thus, no part of life
is cut off from Christ. But neither is any part of life allowed to be
understood through any lens other than Jesus Christ.

I hardly stand alone in making this larger suggestion about Christ
as the Bible's hermeneutical key, of course; a number of solid evangelical theologians have argued the same idea. The evangelical giant,
John Stott, for instance, is perfectly clear on this point. In his book
*Understanding the Bible*, Stott begins by asking, "How can the Bible
. . . possibly be said to have a 'purpose'?"[13] His reply?

> The Bible is primarily a book neither of science, nor of literature, nor
> of philosophy, but of salvation. . . . The salvation for which the Bible
> instructs us is available "through faith in Christ Jesus." Therefore, since
> scripture concerns salvation and salvation is through Christ, Scripture
> is full of Christ. Jesus himself thus understood the nature and func-
> tion of the Bible. "The Scriptures," he said, "testify about me." . . .
> Our savior Jesus Christ himself (in terms of promise and fulfillment)
> is Scripture's unifying theme.[14]

Stott spends many pages demonstrating that Bible readers need primarily to seek to "appropriate by faith the riches of Christ which are
disclosed to us in Scripture." He then concludes: "There is a great
diversity of content, style, and purpose among the books of the Bible,
and in some of them the witness to Christ is indirect, even oblique. . . .
[But] the conclusion is simple. Whenever we read the Bible, we must
look for Christ. And we must go on looking until we see and until
we believe."[15]

The evangelical Dutch Reformed theologian G. C. Berkouwer
(1903–96) was also emphatic about the Christ-centered nature of
the Bible, arguing that

> the significance [of scripture] can never be isolated from the redemptive-
> historical work of Christ. . . . Think of the description of the signs of
> Jesus focused on a concrete goal: "But these are written that you may
> believe that Jesus is the Christ, the Son of God, and that believing you

may have life in his name" (John 20:31). That which is written is like
an arrow shot to hit a man's heart. . . . The theological purpose of
Scripture [is] that we might know God unto salvation.[16]

Repeatedly, Berkouwer underscored the fact that the Bible has a single
"center" in Jesus Christ. "Scripture is not composed of a number of
isolated words, theses, and truths expressed," he notes, "but a centered
witness." Again, he writes, "In Scripture itself, attention is emphati-
cally drawn to its nature as witness. We recall Christ's words about
Scripture testifying to him. . . . It witnesses of Christ."[17] He goes on:

> The purpose of the God-breathed Scripture is not at all to provide a
> scientific *gnosis* in order to convey and increase human knowledge and
> wisdom, but to witness of the salvation of God unto faith. This does
> not mean to separate faith and knowledge. But the knowledge that is
> the unmistakable aim of Scripture is the knowledge of faith, which
> does not increase human wisdom, but is life eternal (John 17:3).[18]

On this basis, Berkouwer calls readers of scripture to be "conscious
of this centralization, mindful of that word of Paul which clearly
indicated the center: 'For I decided to know nothing among you except Jesus Christ and him crucified'" (1 Cor. 2:2). This means, he
says, paying "concentrated attention to the very words, *to the Word
in the midst of the words*, to its intent and purpose." Berkouwer
questions rhetorically: "How shall the God-breathed Scripture ever
be understood without focusing on the one concentrated mystery of
the Spirit of Christ?" Of course, he admits that reading the Bible with
an eye always to Christ the center is "not a simple matter. But," he
adds in the strongest of terms, "fear of this idea of *scopus* [the center
or target bull's-eye] is fruitless, for *Scripture disintegrates into many
words without the goal*, and its God-breathed character is thereby
neglected."[19]

Berkouwer therefore warns against biblicist readings of the Bible
as a "flat" text: "The perspective of this centeredness of Scripture is
easily endangered by a leveling process whereby the God-breathed
Scripture is primarily approached in isolation. . . . Then the attention
for contours and centralization fades. There is no room for emphasis and centralization when there is a leveling of the many words of
Scripture." Again, in the strongest words, Berkouwer calls the Bible

"meaningless" when it is not read Christocentrically: "Believing in Scripture does not mean staring at a holy and mysterious book, but hearing the witness concerning Christ. . . . Every word about the God-breathed character of Scripture is *meaningless* if Holy Scripture is not understood as the witness concerning Christ."[20]

Another important example is elaborated by Geoffrey Bromiley. In his fantastic little book, *The Unity and Disunity of the Church*, Bromiley addresses the ways in which the Bible itself may be a source of unity rather than disunity among Christians—precisely the concern of the present book. Bromiley insists that the Bible can serve as a means of Christian unity only when Jesus Christ is placed at its center. "In the first place we must remember," he says, "that the Bible is not to be abstracted from Christ and made a center of unity in its own right. . . . Unity is grounded in Christ himself, and . . . it is served by the Bible when the Bible is understood in clear relationship to Christ as the authoritative prophetic and apostolic testimony."

Bromiley continues: "We may go to the Bible with very different views of what it is and how it is to be understood or applied. But if we go primarily to see Christ (John 5:39), i.e., to learn what the Bible has to tell us about Him, and our new life in Him, we shall be brought together at the one true center of the church and its unity." The Bible, Bromiley insists, will only "unify as it is used for the purpose for which it was given, namely, as an instrument of ministering Christ to the people. . . . It will not be a means or focus of unity merely in virtue of the fact that we are all trying to present biblical truth. But it will certainly be this as we are all trying to present Christ Himself as the Truth attested in the Bible." Bromiley concludes: "The Bible should always be seen in this relationship to Christ Himself and the given unity which there is in Him. Otherwise it can only be a center of division." Truly spoken.[21]

The evangelical theologian Donald Bloesch likewise writes, "The biblical text is entirely truthful when it is seen in relation to its divine center, God's self-revelation in Jesus Christ. When separated from this center, the text is not perceived in its proper context. . . . The truth of the Bible is available to us only when we strive to see the text in relation to the New Testament Gospel."[22] Citing Hebrews 1:10, Bloesch continues: "The true or comprehensive picture of God's dealing with humanity is hidden from us until the text becomes for us a window to the light of the glory of God in Jesus Christ. . . . The object of our faith is not the church or the scriptures, not even our experience of Jesus Christ. It is Jesus Christ himself, but Christ testified to in Scripture and proclaimed in the church."[23] On that basis, Bloesch peppers his theology of the Bible with statements reinforcing this key point: "The Bible comes alive when it is read in light of the cross of Christ"; "the text does not yield its full meaning until we see it in its theological relation to the wider context—the sacred history of the Bible culminating in Jesus Christ"; "the salvific content of Scripture is God's self-revelation in Jesus Christ. What makes Scripture authoritative is that it focuses on Christ"; and "while fully acknowledging both cultural and theological diversity within Scripture, the Reformers held to its overarching unity. One of their key principles was that 'the whole of Scripture presents Christ everywhere.'"[24]

Bloesch also points out that this Christocentric view of scripture was a hallmark of Martin Luther's approach to the Bible. Luther insisted that "the source" of scripture is "the cross of Christ," to which, when the reader is led, "then he will surely strike the center." Bloesch notes that Luther also spoke of certain biblical passages as hard nuts whose shells had to be cracked by throwing them against the rock of Christ, which would then produce their "delicious kernel."[25] According to Luther, "Christ is the Lord of Scripture." And again, "Scripture is to be understood . . . for Christ. Hence it must either be referred to him, or it must not be held to be true Scripture." Yet again, Luther declared: "The whole scripture is about Christ alone everywhere, if we look to its inner meaning, though superficially it may sound different."[26]

For a final evangelical witness to the need to read the Bible Christocentrically, I cite Kevin Vanhoozer of the Wheaton College Graduate School: "The ground of Scripture's indispensible role in the economy of the gospel is ultimately Christological. The Bible—not only the Gospels but all of Scripture—is the (divinely) authorized version of the gospel, the necessary framework for understanding what God was doing in Jesus Christ. Scripture is the voice of God that articulates the Word of God: Jesus Christ."[27] Throughout his theology, Vanhoozer hammers away on this Christocentric theme: "Jesus Christ is the content of the Scriptural witness, the one who interprets the Old Testament witness, and the one who commissions the New Testament witness. Accordingly, Jesus is both the material and the formal principle of the canon: its substance and its hermeneutic"; "Jesus Christ, the Word/Act of God, is the internal meaning of the canon, and the canon is the literary form that normative witness to Christ now takes";[28] and "Jesus Christ is the Christian's ultimate ethic."[29] Vanhoozer could not be more clear:

> The biblical stories, commands, promises, songs, prophecies, and didactic discourse all mediate God's communicative action, but not all in the same way. What they share, however, is the same basic orientation. The canon is a unique compass that points not to the north but to the church's North Star: Jesus Christ.[30]

The answer, then, to what holds scripture together is *Jesus Christ*. The key response to how to sort through the diversity and seemingly different viewpoints expressed in scripture is Jesus Christ. It is only Jesus Christ—the real, living Lord, the Creator of all things, the source of any evangelical good news at all, the man who is God-with-us, the one person who shows and tells us what a real human is—who is the one in the light of whom anything and everything in scripture makes any sense, as anything other than quaint historical records. What holds scripture together is not simply accurate information or inerrant propositions about God, life, and the world. What holds it together is the reality of Christ himself, the living, eternal Son through whom God reconciles the world to himself in love.

The centrality of the gospel of Jesus Christ not only guides the right interpretation of scripture, originally, in the early church, it also actually helped determine what texts were accepted as scriptural canon itself. Before there was a commonly recognized canon, "the rule of faith," as the church called it, stood above the specifics of any written or oral tradition. The rule of faith was an essential summary of gospel Christian truth—of core "apostolic teaching," "tradition," "sound doctrine," and "the faith," as various New Testament writings put it—at the center of which stood the birth, life, death, and resurrection of Jesus Christ:[31]

> The church in the first couple of centuries spoke more of the "canon of truth" or the "rule of faith" than the canon of scripture. This, rather than scripture itself, was the ultimate "canon" according to which all teaching had to be assessed. . . . [It was] a framework within which

> both Scripture and church teaching must be heard and assimilated, and
> against which both may be judged. This "rule" or "canon" provides
> a very basic outline of Christian doctrine, as we would call it, and
> underlies rather than is identical with any particular formulations. . . .
> If we are speaking of *authority* for Christians, it lies with such a rule
> rather than with Scripture itself; for scripture is capable of being read
> in many different ways.[32]

This Christ-centered "rule of faith" was so central an authority in
the early church before the scriptural canon was universally defined
that early church leaders relied on it to help discern which of the possible texts being considered for inclusion in the scriptural canon were
scriptural and which were not.[33] That is, even early Christian writings
that were eventually included in the canon of the New Testament (as
well as those which were excluded) were subject to the authority of
this christological rule of faith. In short, it was in part this evangelical
rule of faith that helped determine what the New Testament even *is*
by guiding the selection process.[34]

Happily, the germ of this Christocentric insight concerning scripture is actually already present in some official statements and declarations of American evangelicals who may otherwise tend to lean toward
biblicism. The "2000 Baptist Faith and Message" of the Southern
Baptist Convention, for instance, affirms that "all Scripture is a testimony to Christ, who is Himself the focus of divine revelation." And
the "Essentials of Our Faith" statement of the Evangelical Presbyterian
Church states that "the infallible Word of God, the sixty-six books
of the Old and New Testaments, is a complete and unified witness to
God's redemptive acts culminating in the incarnation of the Living
Word, the Lord Jesus Christ."

Christocentrism also shows up in evangelical books on occasion.
John Armstrong, for example, has written against human-interest-
driven "topical preaching," arguing that "preaching on marriage,
family, or finance without the word of the Cross at the center is a
new form of legalism. It is a modern moralism without Christ and
the Cross. It is not, *fundamentally*, evangelical."[35] And J. I. Packer
and Thomas Oden write that "all that is in the Bible fits together
as a single Christ-centered message of grace to sinners."[36] So the
present Christocentric proposal is not alien to all evangelicals.[37] It is
already present in places as a potential theological resource that many

evangelicals can appropriate and more clearly emphasize in order to move beyond biblicism.

Yet such short, isolated Christocentric statements are rarely if ever strong enough to counter the implications of the many other declarations about complete coverage, the handbook model, and so on, which tend to lead to a flat, centerless, biblicist reading of scripture. The reality is that it is not possible to take fully seriously a Christocentric hermeneutic of scripture and to hold to biblicism. One or the other must give. In most cases to date, the biblicist tendencies overwhelm Christocentric gestures and intuitions. Nobody ends up explicitly denying that Christ is the purpose, center, meaning, and key to understanding scripture. But in actual practice Christ gets sidelined by the interest in defending every proposition and account as inerrant, universally applicable, contemporarily applicable, and so on, in ways that try to make the faith "relevant" for everyday concerns.

Vern Poythress's book on "symphonic theology" provides an interesting case in point, demonstrating how easy it is for an initial focus on a Christ-centered, rule-of-faith approach to scripture to slip into trying to offer "biblical" teachings on every dimension of human life imaginable. "There is," Poythress argues, "a single dominant perspective in the Bible. That is, the Bible teaches us a particular view of God, ourselves, and the world." This statement suggests strong assumptions about scripture's internal consistency, univocity, complete coverage, and universal applicability. But then Poythress's summary of that "view" in the next sentence nicely echoes the kind of authoritative rule of faith noted above: "According to the Bible, there is one God, there are three persons of the Godhead, humans were created good but fell into sin, Christ came to save us, died for us, was raised bodily from the dead, sits at God's right hand, and will come again to renew us and the world and to condemn the wicked."[38] Almost sounds like the Apostles' Creed. Perhaps Poythress will be evangelically Christocentric after all?

Right away, however, the purpose of scripture begins to open wider: "In short, the Bible provides us with a world view. It explains the origins and purpose of everything, tells us who we are, tells us how to deal with sins, and shows us our basic responsibilities toward God and toward our neighbors." It is true that, viewed through a christological lens, scripture can tell us these things. But then the argument immediately slips into underwriting a biblicist comprehensive "hand-book model": "These teachings and other central doctrines of the Bible are intended to provide us with a basic framework for serving God in every area of life—in our Bible study certainly, but also in our study of science, our use of money, our activity in government, and *every other area*. The Bible, then, provides us with a Christian world view, or a Christian perspective, *on everything*."[39] Somehow, in the space of four contiguous sentences, Poythress's biblical concern with the gospel of salvation transformed into a worldview telling us how to live in "every" area of life and providing a Christian perspective on "everything." The initial, apparently Christ-centered vision easily slips out of focus, so that the Bible once again effectively becomes a handbook or instruction manual for living in all areas of life. With this kind of theology in the background, is anyone then surprised to see Christian publishers selling books about biblical cancer cures, financial prosperity, cooking, business operations, alternative medicine, feminine rites of passage, science facts, marital intimacy, leadership communication, racism, stress management, understanding the weather, and so on, ad nauseum? I'm not.

If my argument so far is correct, then the weight of interpretive gravity needs to shift decisively and irreversibly in the hermeneutically Christocentric direction. The centrality of Jesus Christ and the gospel of reconciliation make sense of all of scripture. But we must also consider the meaning and relevance of various parts of scripture that do not clearly fit its gospel message centered on Jesus Christ—such as, for example, New Testament passages that assume and grant the legitimacy of human slavery or say nasty things about Cretans. Goldingay suggests some of the helpful interpretive implications of this approach:

> Paul . . . values the Torah and the Prophets primarily as witness rather than command, and his own letters, even when issuing imperatives, may be seen as [a] more fundamentally reflective witness to Christ than a body of commands. . . . [This] enables us to give some account of the fact that the contents of such parts of scripture do not always seem permanently valid or relevant in the way one might expect. This material witnesses to what God was doing in the life of Israel and of the early church as they sought to reshape their lives in the light of God's involvement with them. The . . . Epistles record the solutions

that early Christian groups reached to the questions facing them, and we understand those solutions in relation to their specific problems as part of their witness. We do not have to assume that these solutions are always universalizable and directly binding on us. They are part of the witnessing tradition.[40]

Unfortunately for some evangelical authors and publishers, once this Christocentric hermeneutic is grasped and embraced, more than a few of the popular books they write and publish will become sadly inappropriate and embarrassingly misguided. The Bible is not about offering things like a biblical view of dating—but rather about how God the Father offered his Son, Jesus Christ, to death to redeem a rebellious world from the slavery and damnation of sin. The Bible is not about conveying divine principles for starting and managing a Christian business—but is instead about Christ on the cross triumphing over all principalities and powers and so radically transforming everything we consider to be our business. Scripture, this view helps us to see, is not about guiding Christian emotions management and conquering our anger problems—but is rather about Jesus Christ being guided by his unity with the Father to absorb the wrath of God against sin in his death and conquering the power of sin in his resurrection. Scripture then ceases to be about teaching about biblical manhood and womanhood or biblical motherhood and fatherhood—and becomes instead the story of how a covenant-making and promise-keeping God took on full human personhood in Jesus Christ in order to reconcile this alienated and wrecked world to the eternally gracious Father.

That is not to say that evangelical Christians will never have theologically informed moral and practical views of dating and romance, business dealings, emotions, gender identities and relations, and parenting. They may and will. But the significance and content of all such views will be defined completely in terms of thinking about them in view of the larger facts of Jesus Christ and the gospel—not primarily by gathering and arranging pieces of scriptural texts that seem to be relevant to such topics in order to pinpoint "the biblical view" on them. Those are two very different kinds of theological exercises that can lead to very different outcomes.

Real evangelicals will think about the issues and problems they confront in life not by searching a holy handbook for instructions and information but by passing them through the perceptual and mind-transforming "lens" of the fact of the living Jesus Christ and of God's reconciling the world to himself in Christ. Therefore, for instance, "The central function of the Old Testament may not be there to 'tell us what to do.' It may be more a part of a larger story that God brings to an end many hundreds of years later in Christ. And this story, which ends with the incarnation of God's Son, had an incarnational dimension from the start."[41]

I have in my argument been criticizing popular biblicist teachings on cooking, dating, parenting, gardening, marital intimacy, dressing, career development, voting, aging, finance and business management, medicine, science facts, organizational leadership, stress management, and so on. But those are easy targets. Let me now take the Christocentric argument one step further, though more tentatively. It may be not only that God, in giving us the Bible, does not intend through it to inform us about topics like biblical cooking and stress management. It also may be that God does not even intend the Bible to provide us with *direct*, *specific*, "*nonnegotiable*" instructions about things like church polity and government, the "end times," the ethics of war, divine fore-knowledge, the "scientific" aspects of the Genesis creation, the correct modes of baptism, proper elements of correct Christian worship, the exact nature of sanctification, or the destiny of the unevangelized.

Perhaps those are simply not scripture's central point. Perhaps at least some of those are what the church has long called "matters of indifference," *adiaphora*. Perhaps others of them are subjects about which we are simply not completely informed. Perhaps by *making* the Bible provide us specific, definite answers to such matters we are forcing the Bible to be something quite other than what it intends to be: a witness to Jesus Christ and the gospel of salvation from sin. Perhaps, if and once people have really grasped the good news of Jesus Christ—what *really* matters, in light of which anything else must make sense—God is happy to let his people work their lives out in different forms of church government and using different modes of baptism, for example. Perhaps some diversity in such matters is okay. And perhaps God has no interest in providing to us all of the specific information people so often desire about the "end times," divine foreknowledge, and the destiny of the unevangelized.

Further, perhaps God wants *us* to figure out how Christians should think well about things like war, wealth, and sanctification, by thinking *christologically* about them, more than by simply piecing together this and that verse of scripture into an allegedly coherent puzzle picture. Perhaps a major error of biblicism has been to try to extinguish the large sphere of "things indifferent," what for Christians truly are *adiaphora*. Perhaps evangelicals today could recover a truly valid and defensible understanding of how scripture really is authoritative and definitive by first focusing christologically on the scripture's center as the definitive and nonnegotiable truth and then greatly expanding the boundaries of much of what is left to "things indifferent," to *adiaphora*—and then actually behaving as if they really are *adiaphora*. There seems to be biblical warrant for such an approach (Rom. 14; 1 Cor. 8; 10:31; Col. 3:17). It would seem to lead to a more genuine Christian unity-in-diversity. And it would certainly help to dissolve much of the problem of pervasive interpretive pluralism. At the very least, I suggest that such an approach is well worth evangelicals considering seriously.

The standard biblicist response to such a suggestion, I am well aware, is that such an approach places the Bible interpreter in the position of having to make *judgments*, of having to *decide* what is central and what, by contrast, allows for different understandings and practices (consider again, for example, the charge of "precarious subjectivism" made by G. K. Beale against noninerrantists,[42] noted in chapter 3).

My reply? Making judgments and decisions? Of course! That is the world in which we have *always* lived. That is the situation we *always* find ourselves in, whether we admit it or not. That is a task and responsibility we humans simply cannot escape. It is much better for us to "own" that task and to take responsibility for our active role as interpreters of scripture, always drawing on historical Christian tradition, than to pretend that everything in the Bible—not just the gospel of Jesus Christ, but everything else it says as well—is self-evident, self-interpreting, and perfectly self-consistent, so that we merely need to passively absorb and obey it.

The standard objection asks, if humans have to actively interpret and make judgments, *who will decide* and *how can we be certain that they will not decide wrongly*? Very good questions. But asking those questions does not make the inescapable need to discern, judge, and decide go away. *Every* reader of the Bible in one way or another ends up actively interpreting, discerning, judging, and deciding all sorts of matters in scripture. The only question is how honest or in denial about that fact we all are. Biblicism is a strategy that pushes us toward denial. I am here suggesting that we accept honesty and responsibility. "But," the standard objection still presses, "does not this Christocentric and *adiaphora* approach cast us into 'subjectivism'? Do not humans then subjectively decide what matters and what doesn't?"

Well, yes and no. The hermeneutical approach I am suggesting entails "subjectivism" only to the extent that it acknowledges that all good Bible readers are active *subjects* seeking to understand the truth, with the Spirit's help, and that our own minds and spirits necessarily play an active role in that process. That is true about every human scripture reader (and reader of any other text), whether they realize and admit it or not.

However, what I am suggesting here does *not* need to become "subjectivism" in the sense of the reading subject acting as the sole arbiter of truth, as if the Bible itself simply becomes putty in the reader's hands to be molded as the reader wishes. That of course *can* happen and sometimes does happen—including among biblicists. But simply denying the active interpretive role of the Bible reader as involved subject does nothing to prevent the inescapable and legitimate kind of "subjectivism" to which nobody can or should object. How *else* could humans possibly know truth, other than to involve themselves as personal subjects in the discerning and understanding of it? Of course that can become "precarious," as Beale warns. But what *else* is new about life, even redeemed life, as finite humans in this broken world?

Biblicism does nothing to eliminate our precarious positions—it merely hides the precarious from us and, in so doing, often makes our positions even more precarious. The bottom line, then: standard biblicist objections to Christocentric biblical hermeneutics—in which human scripture readers actively interpret texts using discernment and judgment about what is central and what are "things indifferent"—simply do not hold water. They are red herrings. There are no other alternatives in reality, and we should not pretend otherwise.

Having said that, I now return from engaging the standard objections to further developing my main line of argument in this larger section. Such a Christocentric approach to scripture has implications not only for Bible reading but also for biblical preaching. Four days before I wrote this very sentence I heard a sermon preached on a passage from the book of James at a good evangelical church. The sermon was a fine exposition of the text and was well crafted and delivered. At one level it was impressive and edifying, and I am glad to have heard it. Unfortunately, however, that sermon could also have just as well been preached nearly word-for-word at any Unitarian or Mormon meeting. With a slight bit of editing, it might also have been shared after a dinner banquet at any secular humanist association. To be sure, the sermon—which was essentially about being good and our need to do better—was, strictly speaking, "biblical." But it said almost nothing about Jesus Christ and nothing at all about the gospel story as context for even thinking about "being good." It did not talk about Christian behavior in light of the overridingly important, cosmos-defining reality of the amazing news of an absolutely gracious God reconciling the world to himself in Jesus Christ. It was about the damage our wrongdoing can wreak and our need to apply James's words to try harder to avoid living wrongly. The sermon's "text" consisted of good, straightforward, expository preaching. But its subtext told us essentially that Christianity is moralism and the Christian life consists of trying to do better.[43]

The subtext of that sermon is flat wrong—a travesty, actually. Yet it is the fruit of biblicist tendencies. Without a clear commitment to Jesus Christ as the sole purpose, center, and interpretive key to all of scripture—and all the implications thereof for all of our hermeneutical practices concerning scripture—that is exactly the kind of "good" sermon that can, and I suspect does, get preached on a regular basis at many "biblical" evangelical churches. The homiletic result is all too often what Goldingay calls the "three-point 'thoughts that have occurred to me and that I am prepared to attribute to the Spirit and inflict on you,' which can be the fare of the pulpit."[44] A Christocentric understanding of scripture, however, points us in a different direction.

What does this do to address the problem of pervasive interpretive pluralism? It gives us a crucial hermeneutical principle: read everything in scripture, however unrelated it may seem to be, in relation to Jesus Christ. To accept this Christocentric hermeneutical principle is to admit that all the texts in the Bible cannot be read as if each of their words, sentences, paragraphs, and even books as a whole are equally significant for one's larger theological understanding. The fact is inescapable (nor should we wish to escape it) that "certain parts of scripture which are [believed] to be central tend to condition their reading of the rest."[45]

It is inevitable to have a "canon within a canon." But our canon-defining canon must only and always be Jesus Christ. Anything else abuses the Bible for purposes other than that for which God gave scripture to us through Israel and the church. This is true even for the Old Testament: "Christ is the goal of the Old Testament story, meaning that he is the ultimate focus of Christian interpretation. Not every verse or passage is about him in a superficial sense. Rather, Christ is the deeper sense of the Old Testament—at times more obvious than others—in whom the Old Testament drama as a whole finds its ultimate goal or *telos*. . . . This is something we seek after. A christotelic coherence."[46] What, I ask, could be more evangelical?

We must be clear: a resolutely Christocentric approach to scripture in and of itself will not resolve all the problems of pervasive interpretive pluralism. But this hermeneutic is a necessary and crucial first step in moving in that direction. By choosing decisively to read all of scripture only and always in the light of Jesus Christ, we knock off the table a number of other interpretive instincts and tendencies that tend toward biblicism and foster pervasive interpretive pluralism. A Christocentric reading of the Bible, then, is a crucially helpful step in the right direction.

## Jesus Christ: The True and Final Word

Jesus Christ is the true and final Word of God, in relation to whom scripture is God's secondary, written word of witness and testimony. This line of reasoning carries the prior point one important step further. Biblicists are often so insistent that the Bible is God's only complete, sufficient, and final word that they can easily forget in practice that before and above the Bible as God's written word stands Jesus Christ, who is God's living Word and ultimate and final self-revelation. "In the beginning was the Word and the Word was with God and the Word was God. He was with God in the beginning. . . . The Word became flesh and made his dwelling among us" (John 1:1, 14).

American evangelical biblicists often fall into the trap of talking and acting as if the Bible is God's highest self-revelation. They have done this for various understandable reasons. One has been to exclude other forms of revelation, such as private prophetic revelations. Another has been to undercut perceived Catholic claims to extrabiblical teaching authority. Yet another has been to protect the Bible from the corrosions of modernist and liberal views of scripture.

But talking and acting as if the Bible is God's only and highest self-revelation is completely "unbiblical," even when considered in biblicist terms. God's truest, highest, most important, most authoritative, and most compelling self-revelation is the God/Man Jesus Christ. It is Jesus Christ—and not the Bible—who is "the image of the invisible God" (Col. 1:15). It was in Jesus Christ that "God was pleased to have all of his fullness dwell" (Col. 1:19). As C. S. Lewis wrote, "It is Christ Himself, not the Bible, who is the true Word of God. The Bible, read in the right spirit, and with the guidance of good teachers, will bring us to Him."[47]

Such a view of scripture is rooted in the earliest church. For instance, the first-century church father Ignatius of Antioch, in answering those who said they can believe about the gospel only what they can find in the Old Testament scriptures, claimed in response that the "records" that really matter are not written texts but "Jesus Christ. For me, the sacrosanct records are the cross and death and resurrection of Jesus Christ, and the faith that comes through him."[48] If we want to know anything authentic about who and what God is, that is revealed to us in Jesus Christ. If we want to know the message that God truly and reliably speaks to us, we need to look to Jesus Christ. The *evangelion*, the gospel, is not simply some cognitive information gleaned from the Bible to which we have to give intellectual assent. Jesus Christ himself *is* the gospel.[49] And Christ is not simply a figure who once lived in Palestine and has left us alone on earth with nothing but a written historical record of the past, which we are to believe. Jesus Christ is the living Lord who is present in and to his church through his Spirit, the sacraments, right preaching, and the written word of scripture.

The Bible is of course crucial for the Christian church and life. But it does not trump Jesus Christ as the true and final Word of God. The Bible is a secondary, subsidiary, functional, written word of God, the primary purpose of which is to mediate, to point us to, to give true testimony about the living Jesus Christ. Jesus Christ did, could, and will live and reign and make his home with us without the Bible as we know it. The Bible did not and could not exist or have any meaning without the higher, truer, more final Word of God, Jesus Christ. The Bible points. Jesus Christ *is the amazing person* to whom the Bible points. Scripture mediates God's revelation. Jesus Christ *is* the fullness of revelation, which scripture helps mediate. The Bible is passing.[50] Jesus Christ is eternal. The Bible points us to the truth, proclaims God's truth; Jesus Christ himself *is* that Truth.

Biblicism borders on idolatry when it fails to maintain this perspective. The living reality of the resurrected, victorious Jesus Christ at the Father's right hand and throughout the world in the Holy Spirit is God's ultimate Word to and for us. Scripture too is God's word, but a secondary, subsidiary, penultimate, written, pointing, mediating, testifying word. The same is true of biblical preaching, except that preaching is a tertiary form of God's word—subsidiary and accountable to scripture, though, like scripture, always and entirely oriented toward pointing to the living reality of Jesus Christ. Therefore, "Faith does not rest simply on texts, but—also and more—on persons and events. Faith stands or falls not with the status of a holy text . . . but with the knowledge and meaning of these persons and events, which can be mediated by the text."[51] The important person and event here, of course, is Jesus Christ.

Some biblicists may be tempted at this point to label this thinking "liberal." That would be an ill-informed mistake best to avoid. Theological liberalism is all about rethinking Christianity from an anthropological perspective, making it essentially about *human* consciousness and experience and progress. The view just elaborated—in which everything is all about its definition and existence in relation to the reality of Jesus Christ—offers the starkest contrast to liberalism imaginable. Liberalism wants to reconfigure Christian faith and doctrine in the terms of modern, human categories and concerns. The view just elaborated says that every category, concern, idea, and identity must itself be reconceived in light of the ultimate fact of Jesus Christ. Liberalism wants to "demythologize" Christian stories and beliefs in view of "modern" scientific knowledge and plausibility systems. But the view elaborated here tells us that every knowledge system—including, if not especially, modern epistemologies—is literally lost and needing to be rescued and reoriented by the living person of Jesus Christ.

Liberalism gives prior authorization to some or other human philosophical or political system. The view elaborated here acknowledges that all authority has been given to the living Lord, Jesus Christ (Matt. 28:18; John 17:2; Eph. 1:17–21; 1 Cor. 15:24). To label such a Christ-centered understanding of the word of God as "liberal" would betray an ignorance of what theological liberalism is. It would also reveal a motivation to use the "liberal" label defensively to police sacred cows rather than to engage in helpful, constructive, theological discussions. And those kinds of responses are below the best of a thoughtful, informed evangelicalism.

Biblicists may reply that Christ is, of course, the ultimate Word of God, but nevertheless object that the only way anybody actually knows about him is the Bible—and so all anyone is left with today for knowledge of God and Christ is scripture. This claim has a grain of truth in it, but it is overstated when put that way.

Of course the Bible as described above is the primary testifying, mediating witness to Jesus Christ. Of course the Bible comes to the church in writing and therefore enjoys a durability and some level of material objectivity over time (leaving aside the problems of copying and translating). But something is nevertheless wrong with the idea that all presence, communication, fellowship, exchange, and commerce between God and humans always and only transpire somehow through the paper and ink of the Bible. That is an overly rationalistic, modern approach to faith and life. John Webster rightly notes, "Accounts of scriptural inspiration are not infrequently curiously *deistic*, in so far as the biblical text can itself become a revelatory agent by virtue of an act of divine inspiration in the *past*."[52]

But what does the Bible itself say? Jesus Christ is present to his people in the church in the bread and the wine. Jesus Christ is personally present with the believer, who in baptism dies with Christ and is raised in Christ to new life—and so to those already baptized who baptize others as well. Jesus Christ is made present through the Holy Spirit to all people who hear him in the faithful preaching of the gospel. Jesus Christ is the mystical head of the church body in which all his people are united to him. Jesus Christ is present, as promised, with any two or three of his own who gather in his name.

Jesus Christ is present to the church generally in the Holy Spirit, who is sent to call, teach, lead, enlighten, comfort, and heal. Jesus Christ is present to the believer in prayer. Jesus Christ is present to the believer in the form of his or her needy neighbor. So the Bible is a crucial but not an isolated nor a sufficient mediating means of knowing, living with, and sharing in the life of Jesus Christ. To argue that our only lifeline to God is the Bible is way off base. It also fails to recognize the many ways we know about and simply know Jesus Christ. It fails to explain how the Christian church for its first three hundred and fifty years—when it did not possess the defined biblical canon as we now know it—managed to know Christ. "The Christian faith," Craig Allert rightly observes, "did not grow in response to a book but as a response to God's interaction with the community of faith."[53]

Again, what does this recognition—that Jesus Christ is the primary, true, and final Word of God to whom scripture as written word only secondarily testifies—do to address the problem of pervasive interpretive pluralism? For starters, it prevents us from turning the Bible into an idol. It removes from us the temptation to turn the printed book into the way, the truth, and the life. It reminds us that the Bible is only a means, a testimony, a pointer. What really matters is Jesus Christ as the end, the object of the testimony, the one to whom we are urgently pointed. That helps to keep the Bible in its proper place in the economy of salvation.[54]

This approach also provides an interpretive center to guide our scripture reading. The Bible is not about offering tips for living a good life. It is about Jesus Christ who is our only good and our only life. By ceasing to look to the Bible to answer inerrantly all of life's questions, we thus remove from the table the temptation to take definitive moral and theological stands on a number of issues that the Bible does not exist to address. Such a view forces us to back up and approach some of those questions within a very different framework of inquiry—a gospel-centered, not a biblicist, framework.

When done well, this can have the salutary effect of taking some "biblical" ammunition out of people's hands that ought not to be there in the first place, fostering greater humility and openness in areas of disagreement, and providing a more coherent Christ-centered framework for engaging in deliberations on matters about which scripture seems to be multivocal. The ultimate reference of authority in sorting out such matters becomes, then, not variously collected pieces of biblical texts but rather the real and living person and work of Jesus Christ, in relation to whom every and any scripture text makes any sense. The written and reproduced text becomes subordinate to and ordered toward the living and life-giving Christ.

This essentially repositions Bible readers in a way that addresses the problem of pervasive interpretive pluralism. It does that not so much by somehow hammering out definitive answers to which all must consent, but by *dissolving* many of the original differences and problems that create the intractable logjams in the first place, and then reconstituting them to be addressed with a different frame of mind—one that thinks of everything in life in terms of what God has done and is doing to and in the world through Jesus Christ. Such a perspective, again, does not automatically resolve every problem of pervasive interpretive pluralism. Instead, it reorients our approach to scripture in a more truly evangelical direction that promises to change the grounds upon which we approach differences in understandings about Christian faith and practice.

## Learning from Karl Barth's *Church Dogmatics*

At the risk of being redundant, I here underscore the above two points in a more theologically pointed way. American evangelicals have generally given Karl Barth a very poor reception during the last eighty years. This is unfortunate, in my view, and unfair, because Barth offers a very powerful, sophisticated, biblically grounded, antiliberal, evangelical vindication of historically orthodox Christianity that is essentially committed to Reformation principles yet equipped to smartly address and engage modern biblical and theological scholarship. Many American evangelicals consider Barth a liberal, but that is sadly erroneous. Barth was one of European Christianity's strongest critics of theological liberalism and advocated for evangelical faith during the middle of the twentieth century.

It is obvious from reading American evangelical critiques of Barth that many if not most evangelicals who criticized him have not actually read him—or at least have not read him seriously enough to truly understand his theological program. I all too often see Barth written off by evangelical writers as merely part of a "neo-orthodox" or "dialectical theology" fad of the early twentieth century, which has thankfully gone out of fashion. That is unfortunate and misguided. It would be very good for American evangelicalism today if that mentality were to change.

The poor reception given Barth on this side of the Atlantic is actually understandable for sociological and psychological reasons. In the 1930s and '40s, American neo-evangelicalism pulled itself up out of the wreckage of the largely failed fundamentalist-modernist battles of the 1900s to 1920s. Those battles had been intense and traumatizing, and the fundamentalists did not fare well in them.[55] I believe that most of the neo-evangelicals who personally lived through those battles, or who through socialization received the evangelical heritage shaped by them, suffered something like what we now call "postcombat stress reaction" or "post-traumatic stress disorder." What I mean by this is that I think at least two generations of evangelicals living after the fundamentalist-modernist battles and comprising the evangelical subculture continued in various ways to suffer at a primal level something like ongoing, collective, negative, cognitive-emotional effects as a result of that traumatic experience. American evangelicalism as a developing subculture simply had difficulty shaking various analogous forms of flashbacks, anger, hypervigilance, and unwarranted fear of ideas and people associated with the trauma. It was all too easy to suspect new liberal threats lurking around every corner, especially since some serious liberal threats, in fact, were lurking.

But Barth was not one of them. Unfortunately, the writings of Karl Barth came to America in the 1930s and '40s, which was probably the worst possible time for battle-traumatized US evangelicals to consider a bracing yet unusual voice like Barth's seriously and with a receptive mind. Barth's theological orthodoxy was not a brand of orthodoxy conceived from a biblicist perspective and so it was easily labeled "liberal."[56]

Cornelius Van Til's misguided but highly influential early book on Barth played a huge role here in poisoning the American well for Barth.[57] That problem was compounded by the fact that the "early Barth" that hit America first—his *Letter to the Romans*—was by his own admission less well formed, coherent, and mature than the "later Barth" of the *Church Dogmatics*. It also had something of a Kierkegaardian existentialist tone that receded in the later Barth, after many evangelicals had already made up their minds about him. Many in those years simply dismissed the first Barth that they had read or heard of, failing to consider all of the Barth that followed in the next decades.

These problems were no doubt also greatly compounded by the fact that Barth is not easily read and understood, at least until a great deal of work has been invested into really "getting" his approach. His theological writings are a challenge to get into, take real effort to understand, and ultimately demand of most American evangelicals a kind of paradigm shift in thought and sensibility to grasp as a whole. It was (and is) too easy for the uninitiated and skeptical to give Barth a quick try, find him inscrutable, and set him aside as unhelpful.

Many American evangelical criticisms of Barth that I have read amount to little more, frankly, than misinformed, quick, cheap "potshots."[58] Others, perhaps by not reading the *Dogmatics* in their entirety, simply fail to understand certain key aspects of Barth's thought—such as the nature of time and eternity, for instance—and consequently fundamentally misunderstand and mischaracterize other arguments that rely on those (misunderstood) ideas.[59] But all of that was and is American evangelicalism's great loss. Even if he is "foreign" in certain ways, Barth is not a stealthy enemy but rather a good friend and valuable ally of genuine evangelicalism.

Karl Barth is relevant for this book because he provides an immensely promising way out of the cul-de-sac of biblicism. Here I can do little more than offer a few suggestive ideas how and why that is so. Barth takes the Bible with the utmost seriousness as God's true and authoritative, even if not always strictly inerrant, word. Serious readers find that Barth's *Church Dogmatics* abounds with thousands of pages of careful exegetical wrestling with scripture as the basis of all his theological contributions. Barth engages liberal, humanistic, and modernist readings of scripture and usually smartly dashes them to the ground for their fundamental failings, which he was so deft at showing. Barth made two crucial moves with regard to scripture that overcome biblicist problems—both of which I have already addressed above. Precisely because they reframe understandings in key ways, they both can help American evangelicals but also can make some uncomfortable. As we seek a way out of the biblicist mind-set, however, some discomfort will be unavoidable.

The first of Barth's moves concerning the Bible is to properly affirm scripture as God's word, written within the larger context of
God's true Word in Jesus Christ and God's word spoken in church
proclamation. Revelation, Barth helps us to see, is threefold. The highest, truest, most real and authoritative divine revelation to humanity
is the Word of God, Jesus Christ, the second person of the Trinity
(John 1:1–18). Jesus Christ is God's absolutely authentic revelation,
the truth to which persons are drawn. The Bible, Barth says, is also
God's word, his word written. But Jesus Christ is the highest, most
final, most real word of God. The Bible is God's word written, which
exists as a *witness* and *testimony* to the Word of God, Jesus Christ.
Finally, God's word also consists of truthful church proclamation,
right preaching, and teaching in the voice of the church.

The Bible is thus affirmed as a divine word of revelation spoken by
God through and to humans, the key authority for coming to know
the truth. Scripture thus speaks a real truth that mediates knowledge
of the Real Truth. But the Bible is not God's only revelation, or onto-
logically the highest and most authentic. Jesus Christ—the object and
purpose of scripture itself—is that. Scripture is thus removed from
the vulnerable position of encouraging an "idolatry of the book," of
which biblicism is sometimes, if not often, guilty.

Scripture is not worshiped. It is not in scripture that we place
our hope. It is not on scripture that we stake our lives. All of that is
reserved for Jesus Christ alone. Scripture, rather, is God's true word
written—as faithful church proclamation is likewise God's true word
spoken—both of which attest to, bear witness about, and give testimony of the Word of God, Jesus Christ.

The second crucial move Barth makes concerning scripture follows
naturally from the first: that all of scripture must be read through
a strongly christological lens, just as I argued above. The Bible is
given to tell us about Jesus Christ, about God's reconciling the world
to himself through Christ. The Bible must therefore be read with a
strong Christocentric hermeneutical perspective as a guide by which
to make sense of its message, given scripture's multivocality and polysemy.[60] It is simply misguided to read the Bible as a jack-of-all-trades
handbook for life or an owner's manual that answers every question
about nearly everything. Biblicism falls prey to what Barth unmasks
as the idolatrous quest to find an absolute foundation of truth and

knowledge that we can hold in our hands, manipulate and control in our minds, and promulgate in our textbooks.

Biblicism often slides into reading the Bible as a "flat" and "centerless" book, as if every one of its verses and words and ideas and propositions—or at least the ones needed to make a particular point of concern at a particular time—was as equally central, important, meaningful, and instructive as every other.[61] Barth helps us to refocus on the purpose, point, and meaning of all of scripture: Jesus Christ. Scripture then must consistently be read christologically. The Old Testament, for instance, must be read retrospectively, through the subsequently revealed knowledge of Christ as the Word. Helpful hints for living or scientific facts with which to battle secular humanists are not what matters in the Bible. What matters about the Bible is knowledge of Jesus Christ, first, foremost, and finally. This strongly christological—and therefore trinitarian—crux of all scripture is what enables believers together, the church, to discern God's truth amid the rich, often complicated, sometimes confusing, abundantly polysemous, and occasionally even strange and boring pages of the Bible.

American evangelical biblicists would do well to study and consider making these moves regarding scripture. They resolve many of the problems inherent to biblicism in a way that remains firmly committed to a high view of scripture, centers Jesus Christ theologically as the point of the Bible, and provides the proper hermeneutical guide to better biblical interpretation. To remain Protestant and yet to refuse to make these moves is, among other problems, to invite a bad outcome. In the words of the Scottish Presbyterian theologian T. F. Torrance, "The effect . . . is to give an infallible Bible and a set of rigid evangelical beliefs primacy over God's self-revelation [in Christ] which is mediated through the Bible. This effect is reinforced by the regular fundamentalist identification of biblical statements about the truth with the Truth itself to which they refer. . . . The living reality of God's self-revelation through Jesus Christ and in the Spirit is in point of fact made secondary to the Scriptures."[62]

In short, biblicism confuses a true and reliable testimony about reality with that reality itself. It naturally replaces that reality with a written book whose sole mediating purpose is to point us to and bring us into the presence of *not* the book itself but of the *real* reality, the Word of God, Jesus Christ, the true image of the invisible God

(Col. 1:15). In biblicism, the Bible becomes the thing itself to which Christians become devoted, what they call "holy," the basis upon which they build their faith.

It starts early: "The B-I-B-L-E, yes that's the book for me. *I stand alone on the word of God*. The B-I-B-L-E." It becomes easier than many would like to imagine to begin to cling to the Bible and forget about Christ—in fact, perhaps, sometimes to use the Bible precisely to avoid a real encounter with Christ. At worst, the Bible becomes an idol that literally confuses the scriptures with their rightful subject matter. Slightly less perilously, the Bible becomes a preoccupation ironically distracting believers from attending to the living, trinitarian God. Though not inevitable, these very strong tendencies are inherent in biblicism, and they are outcomes hardly worthy of true evangelical faith. Karl Barth helps us greatly to avoid them.[63]

# 6

# Accepting Complexity and Ambiguity

The previous chapter emphasized a Christocentric approach to reading scripture as a step toward overcoming biblicism through a more genuinely evangelical reading of the Bible. This chapter continues with more proposals focused on the need to learn to live with more complexity and ambiguity than biblicism allows.

## Embracing the Bible for What It Obviously Is

We ought in humble submission to accept the real scriptures that God has provided us as they are, rather than ungratefully and stubbornly forcing scripture to be something that it is not because of a theory we hold about what it must and should be. One of the strangest things about the biblicist mentality is its evident refusal to take the Bible at face value. Ironically, while biblicists claim to take the Bible with utmost seriousness for what it obviously teaches, their *theory about* the Bible drives them to try to make it something that it evidently is not. Presumably God knew what he was doing in providing his covenant people, through inspiration, with the written testimony of his redemptive work in history. Presumably God is confident—to speak in quite human terms—that the actual scriptural texts he has given his church are sufficient for communicating well the message of the gospel.

To the extent that the critique of this present book is valid, however, biblicism forces a gap between what the Bible actually is and what its theory demands that the Bible be. Thus, it is hard to conclude otherwise than that biblicists are shamefully untrusting and ungrateful when it comes to receiving God's written word as God has chosen to confer it. In effect, biblicists throw the Bible as it is back in God's face, declaring that *they* know what scripture has to be like and that *they* will make sure that the scriptural texts that God gave us are treated and used not as what they are but as the biblicists insist they must be. Regardless of the actual Bible that God has given his church, biblicists *want* a Bible that is different. They want a Bible that answers all their questions, that tells them how to have marital intimacy, that gives principles for economics and medicine and science and cooking—and does so inerrantly. They essentially demand—in God's name, yet actually based on a faulty modern philosophy of language and knowledge—a sacred text that will make them certain and secure, even though that is not actually the kind of text that God gave.

By contrast, we should "confess *at the outset*, along with the historic Christian church, that the Bible *is* the word of God [written]. That is our starting point, a confession of faith, not creating a standard of what the Bible *should* look like and then assessing the Bible on the basis of that standard. . . . Once we confess *that* the Bible is God's word, we can look at *how* it is God' word."[1] Goldingay likewise observes: "The *fact* that the Bible is inspired provides our thinking with a starting point. The *nature* of the Bible's inspiration we must learn from scripture itself."[2]

If American evangelical biblicists are to learn to move beyond biblicism, they must step back from biblicism's highly demanding theory and move toward a humble, trusting acceptance of the Bible as it actually is, as God actually saw fit to deliver it to his church. They will have to learn to start with the scriptures that they actually hold in their hands, however marked as they are by the fully human (as well as divinely inspired) process that brought them into being.

Rather than saying, "Here is what God must have given us in the Bible, so let us make it so," a better approach would say, "Here are the scriptures that God in his wisdom has delivered to us. Bless his name. How ought we best to read and understand them?" Such an approach follows the lead of Peter Enns, who writes, "I have found again and again that listening to how the Bible itself behaves and suspending preconceived notions (as much as that is possible) about how we think the Bible ought to behave is refreshing, creative, exciting, and spiritually rewarding. . . . One must observe how scripture *does* behave and draw conclusions from that. . . . We are to place our trust in God who gave us Scripture, not in our own conceptions of how Scripture ought to be."[3] Here is how Gordon Fee puts it:

> God did not choose to give us a series of timeless, non-culture-bound theological propositions to be believed and imperatives to be obeyed. Rather, he chose to speak his eternal word *this* way, in historically particular circumstances and in every kind of literary genre. By the very way God gave us this Word, he locked in the ambiguity. One should not fight God and insist that he give us his Word in another way or, as we are more apt to do, rework his Word along theological or cultural prejudgments that turn it into a minefield of principles, propositions or imperatives but denude it of its ad hoc character as truly human. The ambiguity is part of what God did in giving us the Word in *this* way.[4]

Related to this trusting perspective is the merit of evangelicals embracing a time-honored view of God's revelation as "accommodating" human limitations.[5] The idea of divine accommodation, or condescension, concerning scripture refers to God's adoption of his human audience's finite and even fallen perspectives in his communicating work of inspiring scripture. Accommodation takes seriously the qualitative difference between created, fallen humanity and the absolutely transcendent God—acknowledging that such a God necessarily must accommodate himself to the limits of human perception, cognition, and understanding. It suggests that, in the process of divine inspiration, God did not correct every incomplete or mistaken viewpoint of the biblical authors in order to communicate through them with their readers. That would have been distracting. The point of the inspired scripture was to communicate its central point, not to straighten out every kink and dent in the views of all the people involved in biblical inscripturation and reception along the way.

Many church fathers and theologians across history have taught a few different versions of divine accommodation in scripture, as a means to help make sense of apparent confusions and errors in the Bible. These include Origen of Alexandria, Justin, Athanasius,

Gregory of Nyssa, Basil the Great, Gregory of Nazianzus, John Chry-
sostom, Augustine of Hippo, and John Calvin—last but not least for
many American evangelicals. "Calvin," for instance, "likens this divine
'descent' to the way a nurse will speak to a child, condescending to
our 'ignorance' and thus 'prattling to us in Scripture in a rough and
popular style.'"[6]

Contemporary advocates of divine accommodation include Kenton Sparks, Nicholas Wolterstorff, and Peter Enns.[7] D. A. Carson
too has written that the sixteenth-century reformers "developed
a nuanced doctrine of 'accommodation' to enable them to think
through how the God who is described as transcendent, personal,
and noncorporeal could be thought to speak in human words, and a
contemporary restatement of that doctrine would be salutary today."[8]
Certain high-profile conservative evangelicals (e.g., Wayne Grudem,
Carl F. H. Henry) oppose the doctrine of accommodation, believing
that it necessarily attributes error, if not lies, to God. Kenton Sparks
very effectively shows those objections to be misguided. Evangelicals today struggling toward a postbiblicist world will benefit from
incorporating the notion of divine accommodation into their understanding of scripture.

Accepting the scriptures that God has actually provided us as they
are—rather than ungratefully and stubbornly forcing scripture to be
something that it is not because of a theory we hold about what it
must and should be—is, if anything, the properly "inductive" way of
approaching scripture as an authority. This is the kind of believing,
trusting attitude toward the Bible that the church has long said proper
understanding requires. If we then come across accounts, propositions,
or passages of scripture that do not match our deductive theoretical
expectations of what the Bible must be like, we are not thrown for a
loop, and we do not push back and revolt against what is real. Instead,
we take it seriously for whatever it is, give thanks to God for speaking
to us through it, and humbly learn what the Holy Spirit might teach.

How is taking the Bible for what it is relevant for our present
concerns? Such a receptive approach is more likely to allow different
Christians, through reading, discussing, and living the scriptures, to
better live with some of the ambiguity about what the Bible seems
to teach, to work to de-escalate rather than to reinforce pervasive
interpretive pluralism.

## Living with Scriptural Ambiguities

Scripture is sometimes confusing, ambiguous, and incomplete—we have to admit and deal with that fact. Biblicism insists that the Bible as the word of God is clear, accessible, understandable, coherent, and complete as the revelation of God's will and ways for humanity. But this is simply not true. Scripture can be very confusing. It can be indefinite. The Bible can lack information and answers that we want it to have. To say such things seems, from a biblicist perspective, to insult God, scripture's divine author. But that is, again, because biblicism starts off with wrong presuppositions about how the Bible ought to work.

There is no reason whatsoever not to openly acknowledge the sometimes confusing, ambiguous, and seemingly incomplete nature of scripture. We do not need to be able to explain everything all the time. It is fine sometimes simply to say, "I have no idea" and "We really just don't know." Even the Bible itself on occasion acknowledges the difficulties in understanding scripture. In Acts 8, for example, Philip encounters an Ethiopian eunuch who was reading a passage from Isaiah (53:7–8) but who simply could not understand it. "How can I," he reasonably asked, "unless someone explains it to me?" (Acts 8:31). (Note too that it was only by Christocentrically pointing this man to "the good news about Jesus" that the Isaiah passage came to make any sense to him.) Similarly, the author of 2 Peter admits about Paul's writings that, "his letters contain some things that are hard to understand" (3:16).

Many theologians across church history (of the sort that American evangelicals respect) have also easily acknowledged the confusions, ambiguity, and "incompleteness" of scripture. Take Augustine and Luther, for example. Augustine wrote about the "problems and ambiguities of many kinds" in scripture that cause some readers to find "no meaning at all, even falsely, so thick is the fog created by some obscure phrases." Regarding this, he said, "I have no doubt that this is all divinely predetermined, so that the pride may be subdued by hard work, and intellects which tend to despise things that are easily discovered may be rescued from boredom and reinvigorated. . . . It is a wonderful and beneficial thing that the Holy Spirit organized the holy scripture so as to . . . remove the boredom by means of its obscure [passages]."[9] Regarding Luther, the Christian ethicist Brian

Brock points out that, while working on lectures on the psalms during the years 1513–15, Luther admitted "that he cannot possibly have fully understood Scripture. . . . Luther believes that the desire for comprehensiveness is futile. . . . Says Luther, 'I openly admit that I do not know whether I have accurately interpreted the psalms or not,' a posture he maintained for the rest of his career. Despite his becoming even more sure of his material, he claims only the certainty of familiarity, not comprehensiveness."[10] Many assume that Luther's doctrine of scriptural perspicuity entails a refusal to admit confusions, ambiguity, and unevenness in the Bible. But here a distinction between scripture itself and the "matter" of scripture is crucial:

> When Luther insists against Erasmus [in their 1525 debate] that the Bible is *not* obscure or dark but plain and clear, it is important to notice that he does not mean by "the Bible" or "Scripture" exactly what Erasmus meant: this long and complex text, with so many obviously obscure passages. Indeed, he does not precisely say that "Scripture" is clear. He says that *res scripturae*, the "matter" of scripture, is clear, and he glosses this as follows: "What kind of deep secret can still be hidden in the scripture, now that the seals have been opened, the stone rolled away from the grave, and the deepest secret of all revealed: that Christ, the only Son of God, has become man, that there is one eternal God in three persons, that Christ has died for us, and that he reigns for ever in heaven?" What is clear, we may say, is not exactly "scripture" but "the gospel"—"the rule of faith," as we may recall it was sometimes called in the early church.[11]

Once again, what comes to the fore as key is not everything conceivable that the Bible apparently speaks to, but the gospel of Jesus Christ. *All* of scripture is not clear, nor does it need to be. But the real *matter* of scripture is clear, "the deepest secret of all," that God in Christ has come to earth, lived, taught, healed, died, and risen to new life, so that we too can rise to life in him. On that, the Bible is clear. But to try to claim a plenary clarity, consistency, and completeness of information for all passages of all of scripture is futile. There are parts of scripture that we do not understand and probably never will understand. We might as well admit that fact. On some issues of biblical interpretation, as Keith Ward says, "We can afford to be agnostic."[12] To acknowledge some ambiguities does not undermine the proper authority of scripture with regard to what scripture is actually about. For, as Berkouwer points out, "the confession of perspicuity is not a statement in general concerning the human language of Scripture, but a confession concerning the perspicuity of the gospel *in* Scripture."[13]

## Dropping the Compulsion to Harmonize

Where scripture is sometimes internally at odds with itself, even apparently self-contradictory, we would do better to let stand the tensions and inconsistencies than to force them into an artificial harmony. Evangelical biblicists have had to become expert harmonizers in order to rescue their approach from the apparent inconsistencies in the Bible. Harold Lindsell, for instance, famously argued in his *Battle for the Bible* that Peter denied Christ *six* times before the cock crowed on two separate occasions. This was to overcome the differences between Matthew 26:34 and 73–74, Mark 14:30 and 72, Luke 22:34 and 60–61, and John 13:38 and 18:27 about how many times Jesus said Peter would deny him, how many times the cock would and did crow, and the order of those events. Allert rightly notes, however, that "rather than demonstrate the accuracy and truthfulness of the gospel, Lindsell has actually shown that none of the Gospels give an accurate account of how many denials there were."[14] To undermine the Gospels in order to force harmony does not seem to be a helpful move.

Vern Poythress, by comparison, offers a more sophisticated approach to harmonizing apparent differences in scripture, by distinguishing between the multiple perspectives, models, metaphors, analogies, interests, and expressions in the Bible versus "*the* [singular] biblical world view." "Different perspectives," he writes, "though they start from different strands of biblical revelation, are in principle harmonizable with one another."[15] Some of Poythress's insights are helpful and I think impressive, especially for having been formulated in the mid-1980s before "perspectivalism" hit full-force in the academy. But in the end, because scriptural "perspectives" do not present the same magnitude of problem as the reality of biblical multivocality described in chapter 2 does, Poythress underestimates some of the differences he hopes to harmonize and so papers over the larger challenges with the promise of his "symphonic theology." His analysis, that is, because it is set within a particular theoretical framework of a certain view of inspiration, truth, and worldviews, has not grasped the fullness of the difficulties involved in avoiding interpretive pluralism. I fear that his case, despite being somewhat more sophisticated than many, may merely perpetuate the persistently unhelpful temptation in evangelicalism to harmonize.

In some cases, to be sure, harmonizations of biblical accounts may actually be right. Events in life can be strange or unlikely enough in any given situation, and multiple reports of them can be truthful but incomplete enough, that such harmonizations can at times actually best represent after the fact what actually happened. But that does not mean that we need or ought to allow a particular, preconceived, deductive biblicist theory about the Bible to force us to address all apparent discrepancies in the Bible through such harmonizing exercises. Many times they are obviously forced and implausible. The harmonizer ends up twisting rather than respecting what the Bible says.

Harmonizing is also usually not necessary. A postbiblicist, genuinely evangelical approach to the Bible can be content simply to let the apparent tensions and inconsistencies in scripture stand as they are.[16] God is not shaken from heaven. Christ is not stripped of authority. The gates of hell do not prevail against the church. The Bible, understood as what it actually is, still speaks to us with a divine authority, which we need not question but which rather powerfully calls *us* and our lives into question. Meanwhile, if God did not feel the need to provide us, his church, with a fully harmonized version of biblical accounts, then we ought not to feel the need to impose one ourselves.

### Distinguishing Dogma, Doctrine, and Opinion

Evangelical Christians need to much better distinguish dogma from doctrine and both of those from opinion, in a way that demands much greater humility, discernment, and readiness to extend the fellowship of communion to those who understand scripture differently. The common confusion of dogma with doctrine, and of dogma and doctrine with opinion, is both a cause of pervasive interpretive pluralism and one of the difficulties that it creates for those who are serious about biblical authority. These three distinguishing terms—dogma, doctrine, and opinion—were highlighted by the Truett Seminary evangelical theology professor Roger Olson,[17] but they point to a truth that has informed the thinking of the Christian church from the beginning—that not every belief held by Christians is of equal centrality, sureness, and importance as every other belief.

Some Christian beliefs are nonnegotiable for any believer—such as the dogmas of the Trinity and Nicene Christology. Other beliefs are those to which groups of Christians adhere with firm conviction but also disagree over with other kinds of Christians—such as Calvinist or Wesleyan systems of theology. Still others are beliefs that some Christians hold, sometimes with strong feelings, but that are far from being central, sure, and most important in the larger scheme of Christian belief and life. Examples of the latter include a preference for baptism by immersion rather than sprinkling, the commitment to homeschooling children versus sending them to Christian or public school, and so on. The most central, sure, and important of these beliefs we may call "dogmas." Those occupying the middle range of centrality, sureness, and importance are in this scheme called "doctrines." Those which are the least of these let us call "opinions."

The problem is that Christians have an extremely strong tendency to inflate the centrality, sureness, and importance of their doctrines so as to turn them into dogmas. They also tend to do the same thing with their opinions by elevating them to the level of doctrine. In addition, Christians also tend to demote the beliefs of those others with whom they disagree to a level lower than they claim for their equivalent belief in the disagreement.

For example, many evangelicals have the tendency to push the "penal satisfaction doctrine of atonement" up to the level of dogma, thereby suggesting that others who do not believe in it in just the way that they do deny a nonnegotiable of all Christian faith and so put themselves out of the bounds of orthodoxy. Or again, some charismatics and Pentecostals believe that having an experience of a "second baptism of the Holy Spirit" stands at the same level of importance as salvation by grace through faith, and so marginalize those who do not share that belief as questionable, second-class Christians. An even smaller group of Pentecostals do the same thing—based on what seems to be, at least for biblicists, the clear teaching of Mark 16:17–18 as illustrated by Acts 28:5—with their belief in the practice of handling snakes and drinking poison. Similarly, some Christians in the American conservative Protestant tradition not too long ago insisted that playing cards, shooting billiards, wearing makeup, and dancing socially were sinful and unacceptable for any "real" Christian. Like hot air, in these ways, the significance, certainty, and salience of various such beliefs tend to rise higher. Meanwhile, like cold air, the urgency, reliability, and value of the beliefs of those with whom one disagrees sink, as they are dismissed, discounted, ridiculed, or ignored.

This is not all about pure theological conviction only, either. Both tendencies clearly follow a well-known and established fact in social psychology: namely, that people predictably tend to inflate the goodness, importance, and credibility of anything associated with the social groups to which they belong (their "in-groups") beyond what is objectively real and justified; and they predictably tend to depreciate the goodness, importance, and credibility of anything associated with groups that are socially different and to which they do not belong ("out-groups"). It is all unfortunately part of "normal" social-psychological personal and group identity construction and maintenance. But that does not make it right, good, or helpful when it comes to Christian theology and church unity.

What I am suggesting here, then, is this: Christians, including evangelicals, need to learn better, first, how to put and keep their dogmas, doctrines, and opinions in their proper places, and then, second, to stop excluding, dismissing, discounting, and ignoring other Christians who do not deserve that kind of treatment. Everyone needs to take a hard look at their own rankings of their own beliefs and work on pulling down to their proper levels the doctrines that they tend to treat as dogmas and opinions that they tend to treat as doctrines or dogmas.

It should be possible for all sorts of Christians, if they really grasp the difference and importance of these three distinctions, to agree on a short list of beliefs that genuinely belong at the level of dogma, that are dogmatic (in fact, the church already did this very many centuries ago). Then, every Christian should happily extend the right hand of fellowship and communion with every other Christian who professes those dogmatic beliefs. Such an attitude of mutual embrace as fellow believers in the Christian faith by virtue of commonly affirmed dogma—however much they might disagree and debate at the level of doctrine—ought then to come to pervade the subtle attitudes, speech habits, and interpersonal relationships among different types and groups of believers. Such an embrace of fellow believers would go a long way toward overcoming the sin of disunity that currently besets the Christian church today. It would also create a different atmosphere in which Christians who disagree about what the Bible teaches could constructively address those disagreements, perhaps toward overcoming pervasive interpretive pluralism.

Note, however, how evangelical biblicism inherently works against what I suggest here. The logic of biblicism sets up scripture readers to assume that once they have decided what the Bible appears to teach, they will then have come into the possession of absolutely definite, divinely authorized, universally valid, indubitable truth. And that truth will be equally valid and certain for every subject about which scripture appears to speak, whether it be the divinity of Jesus or how to engage in "biblical dating." Because biblicism interprets the ideas of the plenary inspiration, perspicuity, and inerrancy of scripture (among other beliefs) as it does, it is difficult if not impossible within its terms to prioritize the centrality, sureness, and importance of what scripture teaches—once one has decided what (one thinks) scripture in fact teaches. It is difficult under those conditions to hold a biblical belief tentatively, to acknowledge that one's interpretation might be wrong, to recognize that alternative interpretations are plausible too, and to admit that something one thinks one read in the Bible is not a faith-defining or communion-breaking issue.

Biblicists sometimes and maybe often do make such concessions about their beliefs, but not because biblicism coherently justifies doing so. They do so rather because the logic of nonbiblicist Christian truths overwhelms the logic of biblicism and pushes biblicism's adherents in better directions, despite their rigid and poorly discriminating theoretical tendencies. And those concessions are another way in which biblicism is impossible. In this way it also simply cannot be carried out consistently on its own terms.

I suggested in chapter 1 that a biblicist reply to my critique that simply reasserted the adage, "In essentials, unity; in nonessentials, liberty; in everything, charity," was inadequate for addressing the problem of pervasive interpretive pluralism. Yet that adage sounds something like what I advocate here about maintaining the proper distinctions between dogma, doctrine, and opinion. What gives? The difference is that I do not think this proposal by itself can do much to counter the problems of biblicism. If it serves that purpose, it will have to do so while acting along with most or all of the other proposals advanced in this chapter and probably some other ones as well. Furthermore, my proposal in this book pushes much harder than the standard adage tends to do on Christians actively agreeing on a short list of dogma, actively building bonds of Christian communion across their doctrinal differences, and deflating the importance of many of their own beliefs to the levels at which they appropriately belong.

I am not entirely persuaded by the rule of St. Vincent of Lérins (AD 434) that the catholic faith is defined as that set of things "which has been believed everywhere, at all times, by all." Very little turns out to qualify as catholic Christianity by those criteria. But I do think it provides a helpful rule of thumb for positioning our own beliefs. Five-point Calvinists have to pause and seriously consider that the majority of Christians throughout history and today believe that they are wrong when it comes to double predestination.[18] Anabaptists have to take seriously the reality that the majority of Christians throughout history and today do not believe that nonviolence, nonresistance, and pacifism are essential elements of the Christian gospel itself. The same applies to every other Christian group, including the charismatic church's second baptism of the Holy Spirit, the fundamentalists' purity sectarianism, and so on.

The point is not that every particular Christian group and tradition needs to strip itself of all its distinctives. The point, rather, is in right humility to put those distinctives into proper theological and pastoral perspective, to not make any of them more theologically significant than they are, and to do everything possible to prevent them from serving as unnecessary obstacles to peace and unity. Of course, nobody wants to back down or give up on the things for which their group has long fought, seemingly with biblical warrant, with great conviction—and perhaps even killed and have had one's people killed over.[19] It can take a lot of swallowing of pride to be able to extend the right hand of Christian fellowship and communion, even to those with whom one shares belief in dogma, when one strongly disagrees about doctrine. Yet such matters of group identity, pride, distinctiveness, and so on are radically relativized in the kingdom of God. And it is possible to enjoy the fellowship of Christian communion with those with whom one profoundly disagrees about not-insignificant matters.

Those kinds of moves of humility, unity, and realistic perspective will be necessary if American evangelical biblicists, among others, are, with God's help, to pull themselves out of the hole of pervasive interpretive pluralism into which they have dug themselves and that undermines the authority of scripture in practice.

## Not Everything Must Be Replicated

It is also important for contemporary Bible readers to understand that just because some of God's covenant people did or obeyed something in their time and place does not mean that it is God's command for us to do and obey the same things. Biblicists are often unclear about the normative implications for contemporary scripture readers of Bible passages that recount what God's people did or said in their own day. Sometimes it is believed that God's people today should do whatever God's people did millennia ago, precisely because they did it. At other times, however, such cases are dismissed as pertaining only to people in the past. Rarely do biblicists have any explanation for which should be when and why. Some, for example, argue that Christians today should baptize by full immersion because that is what early Christians did (John 3:23; Acts 8:38–39).[20] By this logic, baptizing by merely sprinkling is positively unbiblical. Others likewise claim that women today should not have teaching authority in churches because the apostle Paul did not allow women even to speak in church, "as in all the congregations of the saints" (1 Cor. 14:33–34). Biblicists may well argue that because these practices and others like them can be observed in scripture, they must be "biblical" and therefore universally normative.

Yet most early churches during the apostolic era met in houses (e.g., Rom. 16:5; 1 Cor. 16:19; Col. 4:15). Should Christians today meet in houses? The earliest church in Jerusalem practiced a kind of communal sharing of material goods (Acts 2:44–45). Should Christians today do the same? Paul tells the believers in Corinth that men should not cover their heads while praying but that women should always cover their heads—indeed, "the churches of God," he says, "have no other practice" (1 Cor. 11:13–16). Should Christians today imitate the universal female head covering among Christians of Paul's day? Celebrations of the Lord's Supper during the apostolic era often took the form of the church eating a full meal together (1 Cor. 11:18–22). Ought Christians in the twenty-first century follow that practice? Or what does it mean if the actions of the early church in Acts 6:1–7, in selecting men to "wait on tables," is normative to contemporary believers? Does it mean all "biblical" churches today should have "deacons"? Or rather that church leaders and members are authorized, by example, to create and "ordain" new positions in the church to fill whatever functional needs arise in various times and places? And, if they do so, what, if any, are the limits? Or do the actions described in Acts 6:1–7 not really teach anything specific for Christians today? The issue of following by "biblical example," we see, can be knotty.

Complicating this point is what one might mean by "God's people." Do real historical and sociological differences between the patriarchs, the ancient Israelites, the Jews in captivity, Jesus's twelve disciples, Jesus's much larger following of disciples, the apostles, believers in Jerusalem, and pagan converts across the Roman Empire—all God's covenant people—matter for instructing contemporary Christians about what practices they should follow? Which practices that different ones of them followed in their day "apply" to Christians today, which do not, and why exactly? Is the default that all former practices apply unless they are explicitly nullified? Or that none are obligatory unless positively commanded as applying to all of God's people in all places and times? Why is one or the other of these the default? Scripture itself hardly tells us.

My point here is not to drive readers into skeptical despair about learning anything from the Bible about how to live faithfully today. My point, rather, is to undermine simplistic and divisive interpretive habits of some biblicists who easily point to this or that practice of God's people recorded in the Bible and pronounce that the same practice is binding on Christians today because it is clearly "biblical." If we are more intelligently and consistently to sort through scriptural practices in order to learn how to live today, we will need a stronger, more coherent hermeneutical guide to foster discernment. Many of the points discussed in the second half of this book can contribute toward the formation of that guide. I cannot here develop specific criteria for making sense of the possible contemporary relevance of the practices and obedience of God's people of former ages. As I said at the start of this chapter, my arguments here are limited and partial.

Obviously much more work needs to be done to better address these issues. Toward that end, these words of Peter Enns seem relevant:

> Although the Bible is clear on central matters of the faith, it is flexible in many matters that pertain to the day-to-day. To put it more positively, the Bible sets trajectories, not rules, for a good many issues that confront the church. . . . Different [people] in different contexts will enter into these trajectories in different ways and, therefore, express their commitment to Christ differently. This flexibility of application is precisely what is modeled for us in the pages of Scripture itself.[21]

With this point I would emphasize the relevance of the apostle Paul's teaching on Christian freedom: "Therefore do not let anyone judge you by what you eat or drink, or with regard to a religious festival, a New Moon celebration or a Sabbath day. These are a shadow of the things that were to come; the reality, however, is found in Christ" (Col. 2:16–17, in the context of vv. 13–23; also see 1 Cor. 8:1–13; 10:23–33; 2 Cor. 3:16–18; Gal. 5:1).

### Living on a Need-to-Know Basis

God deals with us on a "need to know" basis and we ought to be content with that, rather than insisting on having "certain" knowledge built on scant evidence that God has actually not made very clear.[22] Humans generally tend to prefer to know about the things they are interested in than to not know. Being left in the dark is no fun. Academics and intellectuals, perhaps especially evangelical biblicist ones, are particularly keen on getting answers to their questions, providing research findings, figuring out the systems, nailing down the loose ends, getting all the pieces on the table and put together. I myself am like this.

The "problem" is, God often does not cooperate with us. In his wisdom, God has chosen to reveal some of his will, plan, and work, but clearly not all of it. To the extent that the Bible tells us about matters of Christian faith and life, it clearly does not tell us everything. It certainly does not tell us everything we often want to know. There are many areas of belief, knowledge, doctrine, and ethics about which scripture is not entirely clear, complete, or definitive. If we do not like that, then it's too bad for us. God is not obligated to answer all our questions, to fill us in on all his plans, to provide us with all the information needed to develop our intellectual and moral systems. In fact, during his life on earth, there were parts of God the Father's plan that Jesus himself did not know (Mark 13:32). As for us, God tells us what we need to know and instructs us to get on with living in light of what he does tell.

If we had any spiritual maturity, we would be content with that situation. But often many of us are not. Christians want to squeeze out of the Bible definite and reliable knowledge that simply is not there. For some, this concerns God's "will for their lives." For others it concerns the "end times." Some Christians want the Bible to tell them how to raise their children rightly. Others want answers about counseling people with various kinds of problems and illnesses. Of course scripture does not leave us hanging on every question. It certainly does not leave us in the dark about its purpose, center, and key: Jesus Christ. But often the Bible does not provide the information and answers that people demand from it. It just doesn't. The logic of biblicism nevertheless tends to encourage Bible readers to search the scriptures to find whatever shreds of evidence and tidbits of possibly relevant information might be pieced together to come up with "biblical" answers to their questions and problems. Then when others disagree, pervasive interpretive pluralism is born. In short, the church suffers from pervasive interpretive pluralism in part because too many people insist on the Bible giving clear and complete information, answers, and directions, which the Bible simply does not give. All sorts of "biblical" teachings are extracted from scripture and promoted for validation, but they rely on the flimsiest of textual evidence, and lead to disagreement among believers.

In light of these tendencies, Christians would do well to simply accept and live contentedly with the fact that they are being informed about the big picture on a "need to know" basis. This means believing that if God has not made something completely clear in scripture, then it is probably best not to try to speculate it into something too significant. Let the ambiguous remain ambiguous. Focus first instead on what is clear and direct. What is actually amazing in all of this is how wrapped up believers can become in what is incomplete and uncertain, while they nearly completely ignore the most obvious truths and commands that stare them in the face.

Sometimes it seems as if believers—myself included—distract themselves with the more obscure, speculative, and cryptic issues related to scripture *precisely in order to avoid having to face and act on the parts that are very clear and directive.* Why address the main issues when one can mess around with peripheral details? It is like a kid fixating all day on exactly how much to shut his bedroom closet door to obscure the mess in his room that his mother told him in no uncertain terms to clean. Wanting and trying to know what we evidently don't need to know is a great way to avoid having to deal with other, more basic things that we already quite clearly know but prefer to avoid, delay, or ignore. Jesus had a word for this: "Whoever can be trusted with very little can also be trusted with much, and whoever is dishonest with very little will also be dishonest with much" (Luke 16:10). Why should God trust us with "advanced" things if we are not even faithful in acting upon basic things? Saint James too had something to say here: "Do not merely listen to the word, and so deceive yourselves. Do what it says. . . . The man who looks intently into the perfect law that gives freedom, and continues to do this, not forgetting what he has heard, but doing it—he will be blessed in what he does" (James 1:22, 25).

Notice too how Jesus, just before his ascension, turns his disciples' attention away from don't-need-to-know knowledge and instead turns their gaze on the specific task that he made quite clear to them: "It is not for you to know the times or dates the Father has set by his own authority. But you will receive power when the Holy Spirit comes on you; and you will be my witnesses in Jerusalem, and in all Judea and Samaria, and to the ends of the earth" (Acts 1:7). Oftentimes, I am afraid that we have our hands full with the basics that have already been made perfectly clear to us, but rather than getting down to business with that, we prefer to chase around after relatively peripheral and speculative matters that God has chosen to not make clear to us.

Do not all Christians have more than enough to learn and to do simply to obey the two clear commands upon which hang "all the Law and the Prophets": "'Love the Lord your God with all your heart and with all your soul and with all your mind.' This is the first and greatest commandment. And the second is like it: 'Love your neighbor as yourself'" (Matt. 22:37–40)? But why spend time and energy on such "simple" matters when we can instead beat the Bible's bushes to come up with answers to our questions about supralapsarianism versus infralapsarianism, premillennialism versus amillennialism, human perfectibility or not, double predestination or not, a literal six-day creation or not, speaking in tongues or not, and so on?

Let me sharpen the point of this stick here before moving on by raising a topic of personal concern as merely one example of the larger problem. Christians generally and evangelical biblicists specifically are badly divided about a host of biblical and theological matters that clearly do not qualify as dogma and that often genuinely consist of nonessential peripherals of the faith. Meanwhile, the vast majority of American Christians ignore one of the most pervasive, clear, straightforward, obvious, and simple commandments in scripture: to give away their money generously. I have in another book well documented this fact.[23] The vast majority of American Christians—who in fact are the wealthiest believers in all of history and the world today—give away relatively little of their money to the church or other worthy causes. Some give nothing at all. Yet the Bible simply could not be more persistently clear and forceful in teaching that what we do with our money and possessions is of major spiritual significance, that God commands his people to give and share their money and possessions generously, and that those who are selfish and stingy with their money and possessions will be judged by God. Giving money away is not rocket science. Nearly all ordinary people can do it. Yet only a minority of American Christians does so faithfully.

Why then do so many Christians get so invested in figuring out the intricacies of various biblical and theological matters about which the Bible is not entirely clear when they already don't and won't obey scripture on the very clear and simple matter of being generous with money and possessions? How are such believers to expect God to work to deepen their faith and knowledge of spiritual matters when they simply refuse to do what scripture has already made painfully plain and necessary? Jesus in Luke 16 says: "If you have not been trustworthy in handling worldly wealth, who will trust you with true riches? And if you have not been trustworthy with someone else's property, who will give you property of your own?" (vv. 11–12).

To be clear, I do not wish to encourage legalism in these matters. Far from it. The real thrust here runs in the opposite direction of legalism. It is all about humbly obeying what has already been clearly commanded as nothing more than faithful servants. I also do not mean to promote anti-intellectualism; I love the work of scholarly inquiry and the life of the mind as much as anyone. But scholarship and the life of the mind are also not all that Christian life is about. I say this tremblingly, since, if anything, evangelicals have historically been eager to jump into pragmatic, faith-driven activism of various sorts, at the expense of patient and careful thought.[24] The problem I am addressing here, however, does not concern careful thought, but rather undisciplined, speculative, irresponsible thought when it comes to reading and making claims from scripture. Even as those of us who love scholarship and the life of the mind engage in "faith seeking understanding," we must also remember that none of it is worth anything if we first and foremost do not attend to our clear calling to love God with our whole beings and really and truly to love our neighbors as ourselves (1 Cor. 13).

This insight creates an opportunity for American evangelicals not merely to admit and accept but to relish the mysteries of faith. "Mystery" is not a word much used by American evangelical biblicists, because they think their readings of the Bible dispel mysteries and reveal everything we want to know. By comparison, Catholics, the Orthodox, and Anglicans are much more comfortable with the word "mystery" when it comes to God, faith, the sacraments, and theology generally—which itself may also help to explain why many evangelicals avoid the term, precisely in order to distance themselves from these groups. "Mystery" may also evoke for evangelicals an association with premodern mystery religions, which they rightly wish to avoid. Still, concerning God as a transcendent mystery, St. Augustine even said, "If you understand it, it is not God."[25] Evangelicals today cut themselves off from a relevant and important vocabulary—which, when properly used, often describes well Christian faith and life—when they expunge from their theological vocabulary the category of mystery. They also in so doing perpetuate the problematic tendency in much of evangelicalism toward a dry, know-it-all rationalism in the form of a systematic cognitive covering of all intellectual bases—which ultimately has more to do with modern Enlightenment than scripture.[26]

To recognize and speak about the mysteries of faith does not need to mean problematic forms of subjectivism, mysticism, or obscurantism. It means readily embracing the awesome, sometimes partially understood, often known-yet-still-inscrutable story and reality of God's work in history and the cosmos through Jesus Christ. Being willing and able to think and speak in terms of mystery will reduce the pressure on former biblicists to know it all, to explain everything, to wrap it all up in a comprehensible package with an inerrant bow. On an awful lot of matters concerning Christianity, we remain partially or totally in the dark—provided a reliable enough knowledge but not filled in on all the details. That is fine. It can be exciting. It is no doubt good for us. Let the mysteries stand. Live despite, in, through, and because of them.

One likely implication of this point is that it is better to err on the side of a minimalist view of what is essential to Christian faith and life than a maximalist view. This proposal continues my previous line of thinking in this book. The more baggage that passengers of a train load into their carriage, the less room there is for other people to accompany them. The more Christians insist on making long lists of theological "essentials" that real or true Christians ought to believe in order to be recognized as within the bounds of the true faith and deserving the fellowship of communion, the more the body of Christ becomes conflicted, divided, and disunified—and the more the credibility of its witness is compromised. Many different Christian traditions—American evangelical biblicism included—tend to proliferate beliefs they consider important, if not essential. But often this comes at a major cost to the unity and proper focus of the church. In other words, believers need to work hard not to turn (what in fact are only) their preferences into doctrines and especially (what in fact are only) doctrines into dogma.

From a sociological perspective, when different groups elevate particular, distinctive beliefs to increasingly higher levels of importance, that serves functionally to establish group identity differentiation and security. And when such differences become matters of disagreement and conflict, which they normally do, that tends to increase members' commitments to and investment in their own groups—on the general sociological principle that "out-group conflict increases in-group solidarity." So, sociologically understood, from the perspective of each distinct group, elaborating a maximalist view of essential Christian beliefs serves the purpose of reinforcing their distinctive identity, solidifying member commitment, and maintaining and increasing inflows of resources—all things that organizational leaders like. But that does not make it good or right. Indeed, oftentimes what is sociologically effective in a broken world is anything but good or right. What matters more than the in-group strength of various divided Christian groups is the faithfulness and unity of the body of Christ as a whole. My suggestion here, then, is that movement toward a more minimalist rather than a maximalist view of essential Christian beliefs will both serve the higher interests of the church of Christ and contribute toward overcoming the problem of pervasive interpretive pluralism.

Let me try to say this using a different image. When my children were young, we often played with Legos and Duplos on the family room floor, constructing towers and other sorts of buildings. We owned a couple of large bins of building blocks and a lot of miscellaneous people, animal characters, and fancy ornamental building pieces that could be snapped into our works of art. One of our goals most of the time was to build a single structure that used every single piece of building material we owned. That could be quite a challenge, given the volume and diversity of pieces in our possession. Our final products were always embellished with fancy decorative and ornamental pieces snapped onto and spiring up from the main structure—simply because we owned all the pieces and were determined to make them attach somehow. A plastic tiger piece here, a radar antenna there, a smiley face block somewhere else, fifty pieces stacked straight up into a thin tower, horizontal terraces and extensions and arches in the middle, and so on. Often our insistence on using all the pieces meant we ended up building structures that were structurally weak and top-heavy. In all cases, my children found them fun to knock down.

Sometimes it seems that biblicists take the same approach to scripture in the course of building up their theological and moral systems. They do not want to "waste" even one bit of possible biblical evidence by not using it somehow to make a statement or take some "biblical" position. The intrinsic logic of biblicism encourages such a "thrifty" approach to Bible passages. It wants to squeeze as much meaning out of every text as possible. There is, of course, merit in not missing real meanings that scriptural texts contain. But the danger of this approach is to unwisely overbuild a theological structure with so much detail, complexity, and ornamentation that it ends up suffering from structural weaknesses, detracts from the "main event," and invites others to knock it down. Better to proceed with more modest but solid systems of belief that affirm what most other Christians across time and space also believe and have long believed. Better to focus primarily on the well-established, core substance of the Christian faith for thinking about and communicating the gospel and for considering how best to live in any given sociocultural context.

Again, this is not to put the kibosh on all sophisticated theological inquiry in the name of "back to basics." Nor does it say that some kind of least-common-denominator theology needs to be imposed on all churches that will wipe out their theological and cultural particulars. Sophisticated theological inquiry and some kinds of church distinctives are, of course, legitimate and even important. But these must be kept in proper perspective in the life of the church, lest Christians end up "majoring in the minors," stirring up tempests in teapots, and failing to really work out the one, holy, catholic, and apostolic faith that all believers share. The latter, of course, should be challenging enough to keep us busy without having to pile on a lot of nonessential and controversial particulars.

The sixteenth-century Anglican divine Richard Hooker put this well when he said about the Bible, "We must . . . take great heed, lest, in attributing unto scripture more than it can have, the incredibility of that do cause even those things which indeed it hath most abundantly, to be less reverently esteemed."[27] In other words, the more we try to make the Bible say allegedly important things that are in fact subsidiary, nonbinding, or perhaps not even clearly taught, the more we risk detracting from the crucial, central message of the Bible about God reconciling the world to himself in Jesus Christ.

# 7

# Rethinking Human Knowledge, Authority, and Understanding

Here we will pick up where the last chapter left off, thinking toward a postbiblicist evangelical world. This chapter focuses especially on the need to reconsider how we think about human knowledge, the authority of texts, and what it means as human beings to understand anything, as means to move toward a more truly evangelical reading of scripture.

## Breaking from Modern Epistomology

A more evangelical reading of scripture also requires Christians to break from modern epistemological foundationalism once and for all, but without sliding into a problematic postmodernism. Much of the motive to use biblicism to domesticate and control scripture and the gospel, rather than to open ourselves to be shaken and altered by its message, comes directly from a modern outlook, from modernity and the Enlightenment. This is ironic, given American evangelicalism's modernity-resisting self-identity. Evangelicals have for many generations now understood themselves to be standing for a gospel of eternal truth against the corrosive ideological forces of modernity. Since the late nineteenth century, evangelical identity has been formed in opposition to theological modernism and modern religious liberalism and secularism.

But there is more than one way to be shaped by modernity. Evangelicals have also themselves drunk deeply from some of the wells of modernity and the Enlightenment, yet in ways they often seem to fail to notice. By focusing especially on certain problematic aspects of modernity that they oppose—naturalism, materialism, liberalism, relativism, and secularism—many evangelicals have not realized other crucial aspects of modernity and Enlightenment that they have bought into, lock, stock, and barrel.

For present purposes, epistemological foundationalism is the most important of these aspects of modernity that needs exposing. Epistemological foundationalism is a conviction that rational humans can and must identify a common foundation of knowledge directly up from and upon which every reasonable thinker can and ought to build a body of completely reliable knowledge and understanding. Such a foundation upon which all knowledge is to be built must stand indubitably against all challenges, must be universally accessible to all rational people, and must unfailingly produce the kind of reliable knowledge sought after. When such a foundation is secured, then the resultant knowledge that will be built from and upon it will be for all rational people absolutely certain, completely truthful, and universally binding.

The modern epistemological foundationalist project thus promised and pursued the kind of certainty, universality, and security that people not only often yearn for generally, but also were particularly lacking in the early modern era—as a result of the fracturing of Christendom, religious and civil wars, political instabilities, unsettling new world discoveries, and more. Different modern thinkers took foundationalism in different directions. Some, following René Descartes, sought the foundation in the mind. Others, such as David Hume, attempted to find the foundation in empirical observation of external data. Neither strategy has proven successful. The entire epistemological foundationalist project has of late hit a philosophical dead end and largely collapsed.

In retrospect, however, we see that evangelicalism itself actually bought into foundationalism whole hog—only instead of it founding universal, indubitable truth on rationalism or empiricism, evangelicalism simply argued that the right foundation for indubitable knowledge is the text of the Bible and the Bible alone. The Christian tradition's correct earlier beliefs—from the patristic era through the end of the medieval age—about scripture's truthfulness and reliability were then projected by these modern Christians on to the modern foundationalist agenda. In due time, belief in the Bible as God's true word became strangely equated with defending the entire modern foundationalist project on its own terms. Rather than the Bible challenging rational and universal foundationalism as a misguided project, the Bible itself started to be defended on the very grounds that it successfully met the independent foundationalist criteria for reliable truth, based on theories of its plenary inspiration and inerrancy. Without realizing it, evangelicals embraced a view of scripture that was more driven by Cartesian and generally modern preoccupations with epistemic certainty than by scripture itself and a long Christian tradition of scriptural interpretation. A clearly modern standard that was derived independent of and indeed against scripture—the modern philosophy of epistemological foundationalism—came to be the legitimizing basis upon which the authority of scripture was championed.

Because of the taken-for-granted dominance of foundationalism until recently, few evangelicals even noticed that this move was self-defeating, since biblicism requires that scripture's authority be validated by scripture alone and not a secular modern philosophy of knowledge. In short, ironically, a great deal of evangelical biblicism came to the point where it was (and often still is) driven not by gospel concerns and scriptural self-attestation but by modern preoccupations with the certainty of knowledge, which was intellectually doomed from the start to fail. The longer biblicists continue to hitch their wagon to that failed—and frequently idolatrous and self-divinizing—epistemological agenda, the longer scripture will be misused and the gospel poorly expressed, as a result of modern philosophical illusions and distortions.

The right response to all this is not to jump into radical postmodern relativism. Many who defend versions of biblicism have that (mostly legitimate) fear and so stick to their biblicist guns as the only way they can imagine not to capitulate to postmodernism. But there are alternatives. Simply because epistemological foundationalism was erroneous does not mean that the only other possible option is radical postmodernism's historical and cultural relativism—the need to "unmask" all claims to truth as mere exercises of power, loss of faith in authorial intent, the ultimate legitimacy of local knowledge, the fluidity of all identities, the need to transgress established boundaries, and so on. Foundationalism and postmodernism are both seriously problematic extremes.

The more adequate alternative to serve as the provisional metatheory to help organize our expectations and understandings in our inquiry is the third-way philosophy of critical realism. This is not the place to elaborate the view of critical realism.[1] Suffice it for present purposes to say that it provides a coherent account of reality and knowledge that abandons foundationalist illusions, acknowledges the conceptually mediated and fallible nature of all human knowledge, accounts for the influence of historical and cultural context, and (unlike positivism and much of biblicism) recognizes the inescapably hermeneutical, cultural-historical, and interpretive character of all knowledge—while maintaining against postmodernism an insistence on the objectivity of reality, the oftentimes object-referencing nature of language, and an "alethic"[2] theory of truth that calls knowing agents to pursue truth as it is and not to pursue their subjective constructions of truth as they wish it to be.

The current arguments between conservative biblicist evangelicals and postmodern evangelicals embody certain limited truths expressed on both sides. Yet it is a debate that can never be settled adequately as long as the argument is drawn up in those dichotomous terms. So, the binary debate itself mostly serves to reinforce and entrench the views of the polarized sides. Critical realism breaks the stalemate and enables both sides to move forward, while holding on to what is best and most true about their original positions, but also conceding what is legitimate in the positions they originally opposed.

Returning to the more pressing matter of biblicism and pervasive interpretive pluralism, critical realism—in helping us to avoid both "positivist" (biblicist) and postmodern biblical hermeneutics—can orient thoughtful evangelicals to an awareness that will tend to reduce division and lead toward increased convergence in biblical interpretations. Critical realism brings to the table a number of crucial metatheoretical understandings about reality and knowledge that tend to foster openness and humility in inquiry, criteria for sorting through more and less compelling interpretations of evidence, and truly personal (not merely abstract cognitive) involvement in the process of pursuing truth without falling into individualistic subjectivism. In my view, if evangelicals hope to constructively address the problem of pervasive interpretive pluralism, they will need to absorb the intellectual resources of critical realism as a provisional background context for their thinking and the way out of the morass of modern epistemological foundationalism and its failures.

## Not Starting with a Theory of Inspiration

Evangelical biblicism gets itself into trouble when it *starts* its reflections on scripture's authority by elaborating a deductive theory of biblical inspiration. The Bible itself, of course, does not instruct its readers to do that. That is a human theological move that came to prominence only after the Reformation.[3]

The doctrine of inspiration came to play an especially important role in conservative American Protestantism in the nineteenth century, in response to the same threats to religious authority—higher criticism, modernism, and so on—that prompted Catholicism to promulgate the doctrine of papal infallibility. Yet today, beginning with a doctrine of inspiration has become a common move in mainstream evangelical theology, especially in currents influenced by Old Princeton's Charles Hodge and Benjamin Warfield. The usual logic is that (1) all scripture is in the biblical canon because it is inspired by God (per 2 Tim. 3:16–17); (2) "inspiration" definitely means "plenary verbal" inspiration (every word and grammatical form is divinely inspired); (3) since God does not err, tell falsehoods, or say useless things, everything in the Bible is not only inerrant but also meant to communicate divine truth, which readers must learn;[4] and, therefore, (4) in every statement the Bible, most often read in its "plainest" sense, communicates binding theological and moral truth.[5]

My proposal here is not that such an approach to inspiration is wrong so much as it is simply not the most helpful place to start. Again, the Bible itself does not say to start thinking about its authority by developing a theory of inspiration, so even biblicists are not obliged to do that. As Goldingay observes, "In scripture itself . . . models such as authority, inspiration, and revelation are little used to describe scripture."[6] In fact, in the one and only place in the Bible that uses the word "inspiration" (2 Tim. 3:16–17), the point of the text is not to define a theory of inspiration—which it does not—but to emphasize the *pastoral usefulness* of scripture.[7]

Instead of approaching questions about the authority of the Bible with a deductive theory of inspiration, then, I suggest some alternatives. One, which should be natural for biblicists, is to begin with the content of the texts themselves, unprejudiced (as much as possible) by a preconceived theory of inspiration. What do they say? What do different texts appear to teach about apparently similar issues? How much do they agree on those issues? And what does what we learn from that tell us about the nature and function of scripture's authority?

Another alternative is to learn about how the texts that comprise the New Testament canon came to be there in the first place.[8] What was the actual history? Many biblicists will be surprised to learn that, while most of the texts that eventually ended up in the New Testament canon had been written by the late first century, few Christian communities possessed all of them, and the specific content of the canon itself was not decided upon until the late *fourth* century. Moreover, some texts that many Christian communities considered scriptural were not included in the canon, and some texts that some Christian communities considered not scriptural were eventually included in the canon. The old theories of canonical formation championed by Theodor Zahn and Adolf von Harnack in the nineteenth and early twentieth centuries argued that the canon was already in place by the end of the first century or "closed" in the second century. Though evangelicals have tended to endorse such theories, they have since simply been discredited by better, more recent historical evidence and analysis.[9] This means that the early Christian church lived without "the Bible" as we know it canonically for nearly four hundred years, even if many churches possessed copies of many of the documents that eventually went into the New Testament. That has big implications for the role of the church, the Holy Spirit, and the "rule of faith" in the function of scriptural authority for Christians.

A third alternative to starting with a theory of inspiration is to begin by paying close attention to ways that the church has interpreted scripture for the last two thousand years. This means getting out of the present[10] and away from the local by stretching back across time and space. A "tradition of antitraditionalism" has unfortunately been a strong feature of American evangelicalism historically, although that appears somewhat to be changing recently.[11] To ignore what can be learned by attending to scriptural interpretation for most of church history—including, if not especially, by broadly orthodox Christians who were not American evangelicals—is foolish and arrogant. One need not be bound to accept every biblical interpretation rendered in every age of the church to nonetheless benefit enormously from the long experience and possible insights of Bible-reading, theologically reflecting believers across two millennia. We can learn from possible mistakes made as well as insights gained. A world of nonbiblicist possibilities opens up for those who learn from historical church sources, including, if not especially, prior to modernity and the Reformation.

Furthermore, instead of beginning to read the Bible with a certain abstract theory of inspiration in their heads, American evangelicals should pay much greater attention to how Christian believers read and interpret scripture in other parts of the world, across space, particularly perhaps in the Global South. "The church today must be open to listening to how other Christians from other cultures read Scripture and live it out in their daily lives."[12] American evangelicals have already learned and can still learn a great deal from Christian believers outside their subculture and normal social networks. Even "outside" scholars from as close as the United Kingdom and other parts of Europe—including Geoffrey Bromiley, J. I. Packer, Miroslav Volf, Colin Brown, and T. F. Torrance—have made very valuable contributions to the thinking and understanding of American evangelicalism. In retrospect, American evangelicalism has sometimes hurt itself by refusing to be open to learning from non-American evangelical-leaning scholars—such as, for example, the infamous case of Béla Vassady and Fuller Seminary in 1948–50.[13]

This is not to presuppose that non-American evangelical readings of scripture will always be better than more familiar readings. Sometimes they will, sometimes they won't. But listening to and learning from the interpretive approaches to scripture of other (but not necessarily only) evangelical Christians from very different parts of the world can help to reveal blind spots, challenge parochial views, offer insightful perspectives on the same texts, and suggest helpful ways to resolve differences of understanding within the American evangelical world. American evangelicals have no need to be biblically or ecclesially self-sufficient, much less superior to other believers around the world. By listening—critically but also appreciatively—to the voices of genuine others, evangelicals stand a chance of learning more and perhaps better about what the Bible is and how it can best be read and understood.

## Understanding Different Ways of Doing by Saying

In understanding God's communication as mediated through scripture, Christians need to distinguish between what philosophers call "locutionary" acts, "illocutionary" acts, and "perlocutionary" acts. There are different ways in which saying something is doing something. Biblicism often fails to understand and appreciate these differences and as a result finds itself in some difficult spots. It is helpful to distinguish three particular ways of doing something by saying something.[14] First, one can do something by saying something in *locutionary* acts. A locutionary act is simply the action of uttering or writing words, to voice or inscribe a meaningful utterance. To say, for instance, "Let him have it," as a meaningful utterance involving phonetics, grammar, syntax, and so on is to perform a locutionary act.

A second way to do something by saying something is by *illocutionary* acts. An illocutionary act is an action performed through or by way of a locutionary act. Illocutionary acts are actions such as commanding, promising, warning, asking, asserting, assuring, appealing, criticizing, offering, honoring, bequeathing, challenging, and so on. Thus, by performing the one locutionary act of uttering the particularly ordered four words, "Let him have it," one also performs another act, an illocutionary act, the act of commanding or suggesting. If we were to replace the period in that locution with a question mark, we would then be altering the illocutionary act from commanding to perhaps suggesting an answer to a question.

Finally, the third way of doing by saying is with *perlocutionary* acts. A perlocutionary act is the achieving of some effect on the hearer or reader, whether intended or not, by performing a locutionary act. Perlocutionary acts concern the "external" psychological consequences on or in the one who receives the oral or written utterance; they relate to the cognitive, affective, or volitional consequence realized in the "target" of communication. Examples of perlocutionary acts are motivating, surprising, impressing, inspiring, persuading, insulting, frightening, belittling, and so on. For example, by uttering the words, "Let him have it," one may be performing the perloctionary act of intentionally encouraging generosity in the one to whom the suggestion is being made, intentionally fostering the subordination of the one being commanded, or unintentionally achieving defeated resignation and apathy in the commanded person who does not want to "let him have it" (whatever "it" is) but who has no other option but to comply. Again, it depends upon the context, social roles, conventions, situation, and intentions of the parties involved.

In short, locutionary acts utter or inscribe words, illocutionary acts use uttered or inscribed words to perform communications concerning the purpose or disposition of the speaker or writer, and perlocutionary acts rely on uttered or inscribed words to accomplish a particular effect in the hearer or speaker. All of it concerns getting things done with speech. But the things gotten done are different in quality and "location," even when they are all gotten done by means of a single speech act, such as uttering the phrase, "Let him have it."

The point of distinguishing these three speech acts is to help us to recognize that the use of speech to communicate is not a simple matter of speakers intending to make clear propositional statements that, when properly interpreted, reproduce the original propositional meaning in the minds of those receiving the statements. It is more complicated than that. First, locutionary acts, as simple as they can be, succeed only when uttered or inscribed in appropriate linguistic contexts. When they are uttered or even translated in different contexts, significant problems of meaning can arise.

Second, individual locutionary acts can perform different illocutionary actions. The simple locution, "I will be there," for example, can achieve the illocutionary acts of informing, promising, threatening, reassuring, or honoring, among other possibilities. Exactly which of those it is in any given case depends upon understanding the particular context of actors, the conventions operative in their situation or story, the intentions of the speaker or writer, the particular perceptual and emotional framework of the hearer, and so on. Lacking that knowledge, the illocutionary force of any given locutionary act can be badly misunderstood.

Suppose, for example, a glamorous celebrity is heading to an award ceremony in order to be honored for her lifetime of artistic work, but she runs into someone who says to her with a sly smile and a knowing expression, "I will be there." In reality, the speaker is a hugely loyal fan who has spent all of his savings to buy the ticket to attend this award ceremony. The celebrity, however, mistakenly believes that the speaker is a mentally deranged stalker who harassed her the year before and who is now likely hostile and armed. So, in order not to be murdered, she smiles, hops into her limo, drives home, locks her doors, and skips the award ceremony. Lacking the necessary knowledge to interpret the proper illocutionary act "off of" the loyal fan's stated locutionary act, the celebrity misses her lifetime achievement award and disappoints her most loyal, now penniless fan. The moral of the story: no given locutionary act automatically determines one and only one possible meaning as an illocutionary act. Much room exists for misunderstanding and misinterpretation—with sometimes very unfortunate results. Therefore, "a distinction should always be made between what Scripture reports and includes and what it teaches or intends."[15]

Third, there are very many different ways in which a speaker or writer can achieve the same perlocutionary act as it affects the hearer or reader. Seemingly disparate and unconnected locutions, for instance, can all perform the same perlocutionary outcome of provoking repentance from sin, instilling faith in Jesus Christ as Lord and Savior, or strengthening human belief and hope in God's faithful love during difficult times. Indeed, one larger suggestion of the second half of this book is that a great variety of scriptural texts say very many different things indirectly, directly, cumulatively, and in different genres precisely in order to do with their various locutions only one thing illocutionarily: to confront all people with the reality of the living Jesus Christ. Why? So that they will understand God's love and forgiveness, repent of their sin, and live in the truth.

Secondarily, of course, the perlocutionary acts of scripture's locutions may also have to do with enlivening, comforting, healing, instructing, and so on. But those acts make no sense at all apart from the primary and central perlocutionary performance of motivating people to faith. If so—and assuming, as evangelicals do, that God purposed certain perlocutionary acts in providing scripture—then readers who project on to the inscribed utterances of scripture meanings and consequences that God did not intend completely misunderstand God's purposes. Suppose, for instance, that the perlocutionary act God performs in providing bodies of prophetic-apocalyptic literature in scripture—such as Daniel and Revelation—is to comfort his people during times of political persecution. If this were so, then to read those texts instead in order, let us further suppose, to determine the exact sequence of coming historical events in the "end times" would be to miss what God wants to do with his people. And that would reflect anything but holding a "high view" of the Bible.

Fourth, the meanings of terms such as "error," "mistaken," "inaccurate," and "fallible" become not entirely straightforward when speech acts are understood in this way. Of course, certain kinds of cases *can* be straightforward about descriptive truth or falsehood. If the illocutionary action of the locution, "Jesus went throughout Galilee," for example, is to inform hearers or readers about actual events in specific locations, then if Jesus had never been to Galilee, the locution would be in error and the related illocutionary act would be performed fallibly. In such cases of reporting mistakes, the readers or hearers would then have good reason to increase their distrust of the speaker or writer.

But many cases of speech communication are not that simple. Consider some of the illocutionary acts named above: commanding, promising, warning, asking, assuring, appealing, criticizing, offering, honoring, bequeathing, and challenging. What would it mean for them to be in error or mistaken? Is it even strictly possible? Can a command itself be inaccurate? No. Commands can be unauthorized or misguided but not inaccurate. Can an appeal be mistaken? Not really. Appeals can be hopeless or unnecessary but not mistaken. Can a promise itself be in error? Not exactly. A promise, by virtue of its own future orientation, may later prove to have been empty or untrustworthy. And present knowledge about the one making the promise may provide grounds to judge his or her promises as unlikely to be fulfilled. But promises as *promises per se* are not the sort of things that either entail errors or do not.[16]

Given the richness of the variety of kinds of speech acts that appear to be at work in the Bible, therefore, it seems quite inadequate to try to describe or defend scripture's truthfulness, reliability, authority, and whatever else we might say on its behalf with single, technical terms like "inerrancy." That particular term—a favorite of many evangelicals—tends to zero in on matters of accuracy in reporting on facts and events as a matter of correspondence between propositions and the real states to which those propositions refer. But that term tends not to capture the multitude of other ways in which the locutions of texts and their illocutionary and perlocutionary acts may or may not be reliable, authoritative, compelling, powerful, inviting, and so on.

Imagine, for instance, that you comfort someone in distress over her deep personal loss and then the next day have her thank you profusely for your being so precise or aesthetically stimulating. It would not compute. Those terms would simply not capture the quality of the merits of your comforting actions that deserve appreciation and gratitude. "Inerrancy" often works like that. Evangelical defenders of biblical inerrancy are used to the typical charge by more liberal critics that "inerrancy" is too strong, extreme, or demanding of a concept to accurately describe what the Bible is. What I am suggesting here is quite the opposite. "Inerrancy" is far too limited, narrow, restricted, flat, and weak a term to represent the many virtues of the Bible that are necessary to recognize, affirm, and commend the variety of speech acts performed in scripture. I suspect that most evangelicals, including biblicists, more or less intuitively know this. Nevertheless, lacking a richer and more appropriate vocabulary with which to work in thinking about and describing the Bible, far too many evangelicals—who understandably feel the need not to compromise on their "high view" of the Bible—stretch the technical term "inerrancy" to applications and meanings beyond its reasonable use value. But in the end it is not a helpful situation for enabling people to read, understand, and live from the Bible.

In sum, recognizing the distinctions between locutionary, illocutionary, and perlocutionary speech acts forces upon Bible interpreters a difficult set of questions. God may be doing quite different things by "saying" quite different things. So, we need to ask not only what the text appears to say in our English translations and what it as a locution apparently said in the linguistic context in which it was originally spoken or inscribed. We also need to consider what illocutionary and perlocutionary acts the writers and divine inspirer were performing in expressing their various locutions. They could often be any number of things. Insofar as the Bible is at once both a fully human and divinely inspired collection of texts, as evangelicals believe, we also need to ask whether the illocutionary acts of the human writer are the same as the illocutionary acts of God in inspiring them. Often perhaps it will be, but it need not necessarily be. For example, the intended illocutionary effect of the creation accounts of Genesis 1–2 could very well have been to convey to the reader the fact that the God who was to become known as Yahweh, the God of Israel, created a good world in sovereign power; modern biblicist readers may wrongly take the intended illocutionary effect of the same accounts to be providing literal scientific information about the exact method and time period involved in God's creation of the world.

Further, we need to attend to the best of our ability to the most likely perlocutionary acts that biblical texts seek to perform in and among readers. What written utterances intend to achieve in and among those to whom they are directed cannot always be obviously read off the "surface" words of texts. Many if not most of the interpretive mistakes in biblicism, I think, come in the form of texts having perlocutionary effects on biblicist readers that were not intended by the biblical authors or perhaps the God who inspired them. Following the example just given, the intended perlocutionary force of the Genesis 1–2 creation accounts could well be to banish rival pagan accounts of the world's origins and place the reader in awe and gratitude for the good world that Yahweh created, whereas the actual perlocutionary force on modern biblicist readers could mistakenly be to motivate them to mobilize a political movement to oppose the teaching of evolution in schools. Again, such a stance actually undermines scripture by disregarding the intentions of God and the human author of Genesis.

A listing of other examples of biblicist confusions about intended and actual perlocutionary effects could go on and on. The point of all of this is *not* to complicate scripture reading so much that we all collapse into exegetical despair, but rather to complicate the scripture reading of evangelical biblicists enough to provoke a shift away from their overconfident, simplistic readings of the Bible in problematic ways. It is never enough to argue, "Well, that's just what it says right there in black and white." If we believe that God wants to communicate to us through the mediation of the Bible, we have to ponder the various things God may be doing in, to, and among us through the locutions of scripture.

How might this help address the problem of pervasive interpretive pluralism? Most generally, it urges upon us caution about our own fallibility in understanding the Bible and God's speech acts in and through it. It also encourages openness to alternative readings of scripture. Both responses should foster spaces for discussions in which opposing views might find more common ground or move toward higher syntheses. To be more specific, the approach just elaborated undercuts a literalistic and presentist mind-set in reading the Bible, which may help address the problem of internal coherence and the larger purposes of scripture. It also sensitizes readers to possible differences between the Bible's written utterances as written locutions per se versus the illocutionary acts that God may be performing through those locutions and then again versus the perlocutionary acts that God may intend to perform in us as readers of the locutions and interpreters of the illocutions.

Scripture, in short, can be approached as something quite different from a holy life handbook, an error-free instruction manual, or a compendium of divine oracles about life's various and sundry issues and challenges. Instead of those "popular religion" approaches to the Bible, which are so often used for humanly driven, therapeutic purposes and so are inadequate to a truly evangelical approach, the view developed above puts us, the readers, back into the position of being acted upon by God through the words of scripture.

So much more than simply providing collections of error-free propositions with which to construct indubitably true systematic theologies; so much different from offering helpful tidbits for how to "biblically" dress, garden, cook, budget, parent, run a business, and everything else, this approach positions the living God in relation to scripture as one who through its humanly written utterances actively promises, confronts, beckons, comforts, invites, commands, explains, encourages, and much else in ways that personally address every reader. It therefore also positions readers before God through scripture as those who not only need to but also may and can—before and from God—know grace, understand mercy, receive love, embrace forgiveness, repent from sin, hear truth, renounce evil, receive the Spirit, and much more—all as driven and ordered by the fact that God in Jesus

Christ has reconciled and is reconciling the world to himself. Such a view, I suggest, and not biblicism, is an authentically evangelical approach to scripture.

## The Many Dimensions of "Biblical Authority"

The very notion of "biblical authority" itself needs to be considered as having multiple and qualitatively different dimensions. Evangelical biblicism tends to use the notion of "authority" when applied to the Bible as if it were a simple, straightforward, and obvious idea: whatever the Bible says on the face of it represents the very words of God; those are therefore absolutely true and without error; furthermore, those divine words, when put together rightly, provide an infallible system of doctrine; and, whenever apparently applicable to whatever sphere or activity of life, must be implemented or obeyed as stated. Again, such an approach might be somewhat relevant for a divine handbook or instruction manual, if that is what the Bible is. But it isn't. So such a notion of "authority" seems ill-fitted for the Bible we actually possess.

For one thing, only a minority of biblical texts are actually didactically instructive, whether about theology or moral behavior. Most of scripture is narrative. And a good deal of the rest of it is prophetic, liturgical, proverbial, poetic, and legal.[17] In what sense do those kinds of texts embody, reflect, or possess "authority"? If we take the texts themselves seriously, we are forced to complexify the notion of biblical authority. Yes, scripture can and does sometimes and in some places function authoritatively as didactic instruction of doctrinal belief and moral behavior. But, again, if we take the actual texts seriously, scripture must also somehow function authoritatively both doxologically and kerygmatically. That is, parts of scripture appear to communicate something about the means by which praise is or should be given to God, and about the means by which the gospel is well or rightly proclaimed.[18] Yet to be authoritative in those ways seems to require qualitatively different notions of what "authority" means.

Stepping back, we might ask: what is "authority" anyway? The word derives its etymological meaning from the notion of an author. Authors of texts have authority in relation to those texts by virtue of their status as authors. They make the texts what they are by authoring them and so have authority in those texts' determination and intended meaning. But that idea does not get us very far practically when it comes to the issue of "biblical authority." We can, of course, affirm that, in some mysterious duality of human-divine production, the human authors and God both had authority in determining the content of the Bible. But what does that mean in terms of scripture having authority in the church and in the lives of believers?

Some may wish to endorse meanings of biblical authority that convey a sense of government law-enforcement—as in the police being "the authorities" to turn to for order and legality in dangerous or illicit situations. In this case, the Bible is seen as giving us instructions, rules, and laws that we need to obey or be punished. But that seems to project a rather alien meaning, derived from social contexts involving modern nation-states, not one obviously native to the scriptures themselves.

A more sociological approach to authority, drawing especially on the theory of Max Weber, suggests that authority is essentially legitimate power. Weber viewed power as the ability to get actors to do things that they might otherwise not want to do.[19] Legitimacy is a collective belief that something is valid and lawful—even if it is undesired. Authority, then, is power that is potentially or actually exercised to get people to do things they might not want to do, which those people nevertheless recognize as valid or lawful, and so to which they generally comply. Most people do not want to pay taxes, for example, but they do so anyway because they believe in the government's *authority* to tax—that is, they not only see that the government has the power to make them pay, but also (perhaps begrudgingly) accept that the government has the valid and lawful right to extract taxes, given the larger constitutional system that presumably they also view as legitimate. If people want to pay fewer taxes, given the government's authority, then they have to pursue alternative *authorized* means for making that happen, such as making more charitable donations or electing officials who will lower tax rates. I find this notion of authority to be helpful in understanding much of human social life. But I am not convinced that it speaks well to the meaning of the authority of the Bible. Certainly the Bible is about more than issuing commands that readers must obey despite their not wanting to obey, simply because the Bible has some divine legitimacy.

A second sociological view of power may be more helpful. This view focuses not on the capacities some people have *over* others to make them do things they would rather not do ("power over"), but rather all people's normal capacities simply to "get things done" in the world ("power to"). Some sociologists call this "transformative capacity," that is, the ability as an agent to intervene in the world in some way that alters it.[20] For instance, in this sense, I have the power to rake my yard clean of leaves—and that has nothing to do with forcing someone else to do something that they do not want to do. I hope I also have the "power-to" capacity in writing this book to persuade readers where I am right and to help to clarify the issues where I may be wrong. And when this form of power is justified, valid, or legitimate, then we might think of it as having authority. I, for example, have the authority to rake my yard's leaves, but a total stranger does not. Perhaps in this sense we might rightly think of the Bible as having authority over and in our Christian lives, individually and collectively: it has the justified, valid, and legitimate power to "get things done" in our lives, to intervene with us to make a difference in outcomes. If so, this "power to" involved in the Bible's authority is a "transformative capacity," not merely to force the unwanted, but to change things in the world and our lives with a real justification and validity.[21]

Whether this definitional discussion of authority is helpful for present concerns, I will leave to readers to decide. If nothing else, this brief survey of a few approaches to the notion of authority should help to underscore the larger point that there are quite different meanings and applications of the word "authority," not all of which necessarily make sense when it comes to scripture. Evangelicals may do well to think more extensively about the various ways that the Bible does and does not and should and should not properly function as an authority in the lives of the church and believers. It is not as simple as it may look at first glance.[22]

## A Historically Growing Grasp of the Meaning of the Gospel

While the canon of scripture is closed (for all practical purposes[23]), the Christian church's historically progressive understanding and working out of the meaning and implications of the gospel as mediated to us through scripture has never in church history been complete and is not now complete. The authors of the New Testament did not understand and work out all the long-term implications of the gospel for theological knowledge, human life, and society. They just didn't, and there is no need for us to have to say that they did. The authors of the New Testament were among the first generation of Christian believers, many if not all of whom had personally known Jesus and lived during the time of his resurrection. Some of them were firsthand witnesses of it. They had a firm knowledge of core gospel truths from personal experience, the direct teachings of Jesus, oral transmission of important knowledge, and the enlightenment of the Holy Spirit after Pentecost—and they taught it with apostolic authority.

The authors of the New Testament texts, most evangelicals believe, laid down all that Christians needed to know as a theological starting point and sent subsequent generations of believers forward with that knowledge and direction. They also modeled the substantial beginnings of believers working out what the gospel means in a particular sociohistorical context. All of that is absolutely crucial. But it is not the same as their having understood and worked out all the long-term implications of the gospel for theological knowledge, human life, and society. That they began. But their work was continued and developed in new ways by generations of Christians after the New Testament era, up until today.[24]

What do I mean by this? For one thing, the authors of the New Testament did not fully work out precisely articulated doctrines of God and Christ. In fact, it took more than three hundred and fifty years after the death of the apostles to work out orthodox, catholic, christological, and trinitarian doctrines, which most evangelicals still affirm as theologically nonnegotiable today. That was done primarily at the ecumenical councils of Nicaea (AD 325), Constantinople (AD 381), Ephesus (AD 431), and Chalcedon (AD 451)—and, of course, in the theological wrangling that happened between those councils. The truths of the orthodox and catholic doctrines expressed in the decrees and creeds that resulted from those councils were located in the writings of the Bible. Scripture was a primary reference of the bishops and theologians who conducted the councils.

But—in the context of threatening misunderstandings and heresies in the early church—those biblical truths needed to be drawn out and very carefully formulated in doctrinal statements. What was embryonic in scripture needed to develop and grow into a more mature theological expression of what was there all along. New doctrines were not invented whole cloth. But new terms, definitions, and formulations needed to be worked out, precisely in order to give the most truthful and precise expression to the original biblical teachings themselves. Presumably the authors of the New Testament would have wholeheartedly endorsed the outcomes of the first four ecumenical councils. But when they were alive and writing, centuries earlier, they simply had not worked out the full implications of the truth that they knew, as later subsequent Christians needed to and did. That was a succeeding task laid upon orthodox, catholic church fathers of the first five centuries.

Take another example of the historical unfolding of the full meaning of the gospel for social relations: the authors of the New Testament did not understand and work out the clear moral implications of the gospel for the moral issue of slavery. They were, like all humans, limited in time, place, and range of vision. So for them, slavery was an unalterable fact of life and the gospel meant primarily that slaves should submit to their masters and masters should treat their slaves well (e.g., 1 Cor. 7:20–22; Eph. 6:5–9; 1 Tim. 6:1–2; Titus 2:9–10; 1 Pet. 2:18–19). At the same time, even during the apostolic era the gospel began to plant seeds of eventual emancipation, in the form of the then-radical idea that slaves and masters were equals and brothers in Christ (e.g., 1 Cor. 12:12–13; Gal. 3:28; Col. 3:11; Philem. 1:15–17), and indirectly through the theological equation of slavery with sin (e.g., John 8:34; Rom. 6:6; 7:14; 8:15; Gal. 4:3; 5:1).

But for those seeds to germinate and grow—that is, for believers to realize that the gospel, when elaborated, actually means the end of slavery—took a long time and a lot of struggle. It happened through a historical process of learning and seeing new things resulting from old truths[25] (think William Wilberforce, John Newton, Harriet Tubman, Harriet Beecher Stowe, etc.). As a result, we today, rightly I believe, better understand that a full grasp of the gospel and its implications inevitably work out into a condemnation of human slavery as a categorical moral evil requiring termination. That, again, was not an apostolic teaching found anywhere other than in the most embryonic form in the New Testament. But it is nevertheless a truth of the apostolically taught gospel found throughout the New Testament, which was grasped eventually by Christians working out the ramifications of the gospel in history.

Numerous other examples could be given of the Christian church across two millennia progressively realizing and working out the meaning and implications of the once-delivered gospel in ways that were not explicitly elaborated in the New Testament. These might include, for example, the centrality of mutual personal love in marriage relationships, the full humanity and dignity of women, and the inestimable worth of every human person culminating in the modern notion of universal human rights. All of these were revolutionary insights, viewed historically, that were prompted not primarily by natural human reason but by the power of the gospel working its way out over time in social life and relations.[26]

Entailed in this larger perspective are some key background beliefs. One is that the total *meaning* of the gospel did not land on the apostles' doorsteps the day after Pentecost, like a cognitive FedEx package containing everything the church would ever need to know, think, and believe until Jesus returns in glory. The apostles understood and preached the truth of salvation in Jesus Christ. But they did not know and teach the *fullness of the many implications of* that truth for doctrine, relationships, and society. That was a task given to subsequent generations of believers across church history. Another belief behind this interpretive perspective is that the Holy Spirit has led God's people into an ever-growing fullness of understanding of truth of the gospel—though not without some serious setbacks and diversions due to human sin, of course. The gospel has many ramifications for human life. And it has taken a long time in history for Christians to fully realize some of them. That Christians have realized any of them is entirely due to the continued work of the Holy Spirit in the life of the church—despite the church's many human frailties and sins—in ongoing history.

I am not suggesting that every new idea that any Christian has concocted is a valid implication of the gospel. That would be ludicrous. Some alleged "implications" of the gospel have been badly misguided. Still, there is no doubt that history is full of positive cultural and social transformations that have resulted from the slow but ultimately revolutionary leavening of the gospel in human life—changes that are not prescribed overtly by the New Testament but that nevertheless validly result from New Testament teachings.

Although such an approach clearly cannot and need not be biblically prooftexted—which would be an unnecessary but classic biblicist move—it is not entirely lacking scriptural anticipation either. Jesus himself talked of the kingdom of God as something that would develop and grow—using images of the kingdom as a growing field of wheat, a gradually growing tree, and as yeast spreading through rising dough (Matt. 13:24–33; Luke 13:18–21). Jesus also spoke about his disciples surpassing his own ministry in the world: "Anyone who has faith in me will do what I have been doing. He will do even greater things than these, because I am going to the Father" (John 14:12). Just before his death, Jesus told his disciples, "I have much more to say to you, more than you can now bear" (John 16:12). It would take time and learning, in other words, even after Jesus's ascension, for the disciples to understand all they needed to know of the gospel truth. Therefore, Jesus promised, "when he, the Spirit of truth, comes, he will guide you into all truth. He will not speak on his own; he will speak only what he hears, and he will tell you what is yet to come" (John 16:13). Thus, a greater fullness of truth after Jesus's ascension would need to be pursued under the guidance of the Spirit.

Furthermore, according to the apostle Paul, salvation needs to be progressively worked out over time in order to realize God's intentions in human life. Paul thus implored the believers in Philippi to "continue to work out your salvation with fear and trembling, for it is God who works in you to will and to act according to his good purpose" (Phil. 2:12–13). In his letter to the believers in Ephesus, Paul wrote about their need to increasingly with time grasp the meaning of the love of Christ ("I pray that you, being rooted and established in love, may have power, together with all the saints, to grasp how wide and long and high and deep is the love of Christ"); to increase in their understanding of knowledge and life in God ("to know this love that surpasses knowledge, that you may be filled to the measure of all the fullness of God"); and to grow in maturity in knowledge of Christ ("until we all reach unity in the faith and in the knowledge of the Son of God and become mature, attaining to the whole measure of the fullness of Christ") (Eph. 3:17–19; 4:13). American evangelicals typically read these as calls for "personal spiritual growth" of a particular kind. Perhaps. But I suggest that these (also) imply a bigger-picture need for believers to increasingly work out the ramifications and consequences of the gospel of God's saving love in Christ over time in new ways of perceiving, thinking, and acting, informed by the knowledge of Christian truth.

What does all this have to do with the problems of biblicism and pervasive interpretive pluralism? Just this: biblicism lacks the imagination and categories to understand the dynamic nature of the gospel and the church's understanding of truth under the guidance of the Holy Spirit described here. Biblicism's limited perspective on revelation and static view of knowledge suggest that not only the heart of the gospel but also all of the gospel's implications can and must be found only and explicitly in the Bible. It isn't so. To say that takes nothing away from the authority and power of scripture—quite the contrary. Biblicism, again, views the Bible as a kind of catalog or handbook in which complete information and instructions for right living can be found.

By contrast, the present view understands the Bible and the gospel it preaches as a dynamic, living, active force of truth in human life and history. It sees the gospel as often slowly but resolutely churning through history and all the societies it touches with an inexorable force of redemptive transformation. And it views Christians as not simply reproducing what was already fully known about the gospel in AD 34, but rather as possibly working out with every new generation of believers further insights and implications of what the gospel means for belief and life in the world. That, I suggest, is the real view of the Bible possessing authority and power. And that, I believe, is a view of scripture and the gospel that is precisely and thoroughly evangelical.

Furthermore, recognizing the Christian church's historical understanding of and working out of the meaning and implications of the gospel might also contribute to constructively addressing the current plague of pervasive interpretive pluralism. How so? For one thing, the change in the frame of mind that this view involves entails a deemphasizing of Bible passages as collections of complete and final teachings on every subject imaginable. The full meaning and work of the once-delivered gospel is instead viewed in more active, dynamic, and historically developing terms. That itself undermines biblicist prooftexting of the sort that leads to conflicting interpretations of particular sets of scriptural texts, which then lead to entrenched divisions. Had this view of scripture and the gospel that it mediates been widespread among American Christians prior to the civil war, for example, the proslavery party's mobilization of the Bible to defend its position may well have more quickly disintegrated—which might have led to very different, less tragic and destructive subsequent historical outcomes. Instead, the biblicist approach, which could not grasp the notion of a historically progressive understanding of gospel implications, readily supported the proslavery's biblical defense of slavery and so helped entrench the divisions that eventually led to civil war.

Likewise, the perspective advanced here could help to soften both sides of the contemporary debate about the Bible's teaching about the "role" of women in the church and home. While the implications clearly favor the egalitarian rather than the traditionalist's side, the present perspective would still force both sides to back away from some of their tightly wound arguments about the "biblical" authority of their incompatible views. The debate could then be set within a larger, better theologically and historically informed, and hopefully more constructive framework of discussion. And that might help to reduce some of the divisive conflict and move in the direction of a faithful resolution. Again, one wishes not to promise too much. The approach suggested here does not itself provide a panacea for all the problems under review. Still, combined with many other ideas suggested in this chapter, I think it promises to make a particular contribution to a more comprehensive and constructive consideration of a badly needed postbiblicist evangelical approach to reading and understanding the Bible.[27]

## Conclusion

Evangelicals need to find a way into a postbiblicist world—a way that reduces rather than exacerbates pervasive interpretive pluralism. And they need along the way to avoid the dead end of Protestant liberalism. Toward that goal, the simple but profound notion that I am suggesting is this: the most effective way for evangelicals to move into a faithful postbiblicist world is to become more thoroughly *evangelical* when it comes to the Bible. Because of some understandable particularities of American evangelical history—especially the regrettable effects of the traumatic modernist-fundamentalist battles of the early twentieth century—too many American evangelicals today still approach the Bible in a markedly nonevangelical way. They are stuck in biblicism.

A robust evangelicalism, however, can break free from biblicism's debilitating problems. The key will be to approach scripture with a consistent and resolute focus on the *evangelion*, the good news of Jesus Christ, as the Bible's interpretive focus, center, and purpose. Numerous other ideas, proposed in this and previous chapters, might also contribute to a more authentically evangelical reading of scripture, which then might help us to find a way into a postbiblicist world.

# Conclusion

Biblicism is impossible. It literally does not work as it claims that it does and should. Biblicism does not live up to its own promises to produce an authoritative biblical teaching by which Christians can believe and live. Instead, biblicism produces *myriad* "biblical" teachings on a host of peripheral and crucial theological issues. Together, those teachings lack coherence and are not infrequently contradictory. Biblicism does not add up. In this simple sense, it is self-defeating. The theoretical ideals of American evangelical biblicism collapse under the weight of the pervasive interpretive pluralism that biblicism itself generates.[1]

At the heart of biblicism's problem of impossibility and incoherence, I have suggested, is its failure to come to terms with the multivocality and polysemy of scripture that make pervasive interpretive pluralism possible and actual. Biblicism presupposes a text whose words and passages have single, specific, and readily identifiable meanings, implications, and instructions. Such an approach is based on a theory of language and meaning that is not only outdated but also flat wrong. Biblicism also presumes that the Bible speaks with one, clear, discernible voice on matters of relevance and interest in doctrine, practice, and morality. But this assumption is erroneous. If it was correct, we would not have anything like the disagreement, conflict, and division that we in fact do have in Christianity today—especially among evangelical biblicists.

Biblicism is thus not so much directly "proved wrong" as a theory, as it is simply never achieved in real life. It is therefore self-defeated in *relevance*.

Unfortunately, most practicing biblicists to date seem prepared to ignore these facts, to evangelicalism's discredit. Evangelicals should believe that pursuing truth and intellectual honesty under the governing authority of Jesus Christ is more important than protecting a particular, flawed, historically bound theory about the Bible. When lived experience shows the latter to be fatally flawed, evangelicals should be prepared to face the facts and find a better, more faithful way to read scripture. Instead, many simply equate biblicism as a theory with Christian faithfulness per se, and so end up having to defend a view that is impossible and dishonest.

Biblicists propose a theory about the Bible that claims that scripture alone can and must serve as a "final court of appeals" when it comes to matters of Christian doctrine, practice, and morals—and often also science, history, politics, education, health, and so on. But the obvious question is: how can the Bible function as a final court of appeals when the "judges" on that Scriptural Supreme Court end up rendering quite different judgments on most cases that come before it, at least as far as most of the plaintiffs and defendants are able to hear and understand? When their day in court is over, the various "litigants" involved in the different cases leave the courtroom having heard quite divergent judgments rendered. Each party is often sure that what it heard is the accurate and definitive judgment of the court. But the various final judgments that different litigants hear are conflicting and often incompatible.

In such a situation, it does little good for the bailiff or any other party involved to insist firmly and loudly that this court *really is* supreme and final, that its verdicts are truly just and binding, and that everyone must abide by its decisions. That is irrelevant, for few of the groups of people entering the court to take up and resolve a given case in question come away with a shared understanding of the decision rendered by the judges. Instead, what are rendered, as far as anyone involved can figure out, are a multiplicity of verdicts and decisions about the same cases.

If scripture is as authoritative and clear on essentials as biblicists say it is, then why can't the Christian church—or even only biblicist churches—get it together and stay together, theologically and ecclesiologically? Why are there thousands of Protestant denominations, conventions, associations, and splinter groups—often each claiming their own right to existence in virtue of their possessing the "biblical" truth? And if the Holy Spirit leads believers into revealed truth, then why is the Christian church fraught with such disagreements and divisions about that truth?

Biblicism discredits church proclamation by creating conditions that encourage massive disunity and fragmentation. Christian churches today—particularly biblicist churches—speak not about one Lord, one faith, one baptism. They speak rather with a cacophony of voices about many versions of faith, involving various approaches to baptism and concerning a God who by various accounts can end up sounding like quite different Lords.

Just before his arrest, Jesus prayed to the Father, "May [all who believe] be brought to *complete unity* to let the world know that you sent me and have loved them even as you have loved me" (John 17:23). Much of the world does not know or believe that the Father loves them and has sent his Son. Is anyone surprised?

Something is seriously wrong with the biblicist picture. And what is wrong is fatal, in the sense that it makes biblicism ultimately impossible. Biblicism thus proves to be both intellectually and practically bankrupt.

The actual multivocality and polysemy of scripture simply cannot be disavowed without living in serious denial. To continue to insist on biblicism therefore is an act of intellectual dishonesty and practical incongruity. And all of that deeply violates the spirit that animates evangelicalism and biblicism in the first place. But God does not need his people to live in denial in order to protect a particular theory of scripture, of fairly recent invention, from reality. Presumably, God's written revelation, in the nature and mode that it has actually taken, are perfectly adequate to achieve God's purposes.

Rather than insisting that God *must* have provided a revealed word of a sort that our preconceptions and historical social situations tell us *had* to be—and then bending over backward to defend that insistence in the face of good evidence to the contrary—we would do well to take the actual revelation that God has given us on its own terms and learn how to read and understand it well. If anything, biblicists should be shamed for refusing simply to accept—on what turn out to be faulty and outmoded philosophical grounds—the actual inspired scriptural writings that God has provided his people.

To be clear, yet again, what is problematic about biblicism as I have defined it is not its belief in inspiration. I have not in this essay questioned the doctrine of the divine inspiration of scripture. Nor have I directly and systematically taken on the questions of biblical inerrancy and infallibility. I do not recommend that evangelicals collapse into a typically liberal view of the Bible—please no. Nor am I arguing that the Bible should not be a central and trustworthy authority in Christian faith and practice—assuming that some of the problems noted above can be addressed by other means.

What is most problematic about biblicism are its assumptions about and beliefs in democratic perspicuity, internal harmony, commonsense hermeneutics, *solo scriptura*, inductive method, and the handbook model—as I have defined them in chapter 1. Along the way, my argument also calls into question the biblicist belief in universal applicability, if nothing else than by raising the problem of arbitrary determinations of cultural relativism. In short, if my case in this essay is sound, then much, though not every piece, of evangelical biblicism is in trouble.

One key to evangelicals moving into a postbiblicist world is to realize that nothing at all of the gospel of Jesus Christ needs to be lost in the rejection of biblicism. Quite the contrary, an appreciation for and reliance on that gospel will only be enhanced by rejecting biblicism. Stated differently, evangelicals can overcome the impossibility of biblicism not by losing the Christian *evangel* but by becoming even *more* evangelical when it comes to the Bible.

Evangelicals need to realize that the Bible is not a "how to" book. It is a "HERE IS WHO!" book. First and foremost it tells everyone: *Here is who Jesus Christ is and therefore here is who you are and need to become in relation to him.* The world is awash with "how to" books on every topic. The Bible is not simply another one of them that happens to be special because it is divinely inspired. Biblicism too often gets this matter confused.

The desire for this kind of "how to" book is a modern invention. It is related to the Kantian view of ethics as obeying imperatives, doing our rational duty. "Give me a rule to follow," it demands. But this view is alien to evangelical (in the best senses of the word) Christianity and ought to become alien to the subculture of American evangelical Christianity. It needs to be replaced with an approach that begins by asking: Who is God and what is God's relation to us, to the world, to me? And that *immediately* moves us to ask: Who is Jesus Christ and who am I in relation to him? That tells us the most important things we need to know to answer the questions: How do I stand in the world and the cosmos? What is my place? What is therefore good and right and true and worthy?

It is only first by getting answers to those questions—answers announced to us by the good news of the gospel—that we can begin to more specifically figure out what it means for our lives, our purpose, our relationships, our communities. The "how to" concerns the details that follow the much more central facts about "who is" and what that means for us.

Stated differently yet again: the indicative must precede and define the imperative.[2] What we need to do (the imperative) can only ever make sense in terms of the truth about reality (the indicative). The imperative must always be grounded on and operating from within the indicative. The indicative is the risen, living, and reigning Lord, Jesus Christ. Everything else, including imperatives, follows from there. Rather than looking to the Bible for answers to every human-interest imperative question we have, we should set them aside and focus on more seriously grasping the central truths about the indicative facts. Only then will any imperatives cohere and make sense.

Moving in a direction more promising than biblicism will require wielding a stronger hermeneutical lens and ecclesial teaching office than biblicism has ever provided, by which to sort out the best interpretations and understandings amid scripture's rich multivocality and polysemy.[3] I have tried in the second part of this book to offer some suggestions that I think move us in the right direction. I do not claim that they fit together into a neat package that definitely and sufficiently leads biblicists out of the quagmire of pervasive interpretive pluralism in which they are now stuck. The suggestions in the last three chapters are only possible partial contributions to what will have to be a larger reworking of biblicist evangelicals' approach to scripture. I will be the first to admit that perhaps I am wrong in some of the suggestions offered in those chapters. Any constructive argument for significant change of any sort risks the possibility of sometimes being wrong. If so, I will be glad to see and admit that.

Nevertheless, let it be clear that, even if some of the ideas elaborated above are off base, that does nothing to validate the biblicism described and critiqued in previous chapters. Biblicism is impossible. It cannot get "off the hook" simply by criticizing alternative proposals. Whatever may be the constructive merits of chapters 5–7, biblicism is in any case a major problem that evangelicals must learn to leave behind. In the process of figuring out how to do that well, participants in the discussion may express or encounter some ideas that also prove to be problematic. While that is nearly inevitable, it should never have the effect of legitimating biblicism. Whatever else may or may not be possible and worthwhile, biblicism as I have described it clearly is not.

Some of the needed changes in learned ways of reading the Bible may not be natural or comfortable, and may not come easy for American evangelical biblicists. My hope, however, is that, by becoming more genuinely evangelical with regard to the Bible, evangelicals might in time together find themselves living in a postbiblicist, Christ-centered, theologically orthodox world—a good and necessary thing all the way around.

# Notes

## Introduction

1. See Robert Woodberry and Christian Smith, "Fundamentalists, et al.," in *Annual Review of Sociology*, vol. 24, 1998, ed. John Hagan (Palo Alto, CA: Annual Reviews, 1998), 25–56; Christian Smith et al., *American Evangelicalism: Embattled and Thriving* (Chicago: University of Chicago Press, 1998). Biblicism may also be found in certain more conservative sectors of mainline Protestantism, e.g., in evangelical United Methodist congregations.

2. Although neither am I here developing a position on what exactly inspiration means and implies. For a discussion of the matter, see Craig Allert, *A High View of Scripture? The Authority of the Bible and the Formation of the New Testament Canon* (Grand Rapids: Baker Academic, 2007), 147–76.

3. J. Gresham Machen, *Christianity and Liberalism* (Grand Rapids: Eerdmans, 1923).

4. As Richard Lints observes, "The [evangelical] movement gained its theological unity as much from its common enemy as from a common theological heritage." Lints, *The Fabric of Theology: A Prolegomenon to Evangelical Theology* (Grand Rapids: Eerdmans, 1993), 40.

5. See, for example, http://www.borndigital.com/tcont.htm, http://www.infidels.org /library/modern/jim_meritt/bible-contradictions.html, and http://www.ffrf.org/books /lfif/?t=contra. Of course, some earnest Christians take the bait: http://www.bringyou.to /apologetics/bible.htm and http://contenderministries.org/discrepancies/contradictions.php.

6. Charles Hodge, *Systematic Theology* (1871–73; repr., Grand Rapids: Eerdmans, 1952), 1:184. Also see Benjamin Breckenridge Warfield, *The Inspiration and Authority of the Bible*, ed. Samuel Craig (1894; repr., Philadelphia: P&R, 1948), 107.

7. Alternatively, one can fall back on what Enns calls the "be patient" and "it's possible" approaches to difficult passages. Peter Enns, "Some Thoughts on Theological Exegesis of the Old Testament: Toward a Viable Model of Biblical Coherence and Relevance," *Reformation and Revival Journal* 14, no. 4 (2005): 81–104.

8. The evangelical biblical scholar Kenton Sparks, who I do not personally know and to whom my remark here does not refer, similarly observes that "many evangelical theologians and biblical scholars . . . recognize that their carefully considered, private scholarly

conclusions no longer fit into their old fundamentalistic wineskins demanded by their institutions." Sparks, *God's Word in Human Words* (Grand Rapids: Baker Academic, 2008), 369.

9. Of course the Catholic Church itself professes a very high view of scripture and must reckon with the same interpretive challenges outlined in the following chapters, although it arguably brings to that task a fuller toolbox of resources.

## Chapter 1  Biblicism and the Problem of Pervasive Interpretive Pluralism

1. John Frame, "In Defense of Something Close to Biblicism: Reflections on *Sola Scriptura* and Historical Theological Method," *Westminster Theological Journal* 59 (1997): 269–318. By biblicism, Frame means something even more objectionable than what I describe below.

2. J. I. Packer, e.g., defined the Reformation principle of *sola scriptura* in 1974 as "the view that Scripture, as the *only* Word of God in this world, is the *only* guide for conscience and the church, the *only* source of true knowledge of God and grace, and the *only qualified judge of the church's testimony and teaching, past and present.*" Packer, "'Sola Scriptura' in History and Today," in *God's Inerrant Word: An International Symposium on the Trustworthiness of Scripture*, ed. John Warwick Montgomery (Calgary: Canadian Institute for Law, Theology & Public Policy, 1974), 48, italics added for emphasis. A further note on Packer, for whom I have much respect, since I quote him repeatedly here: he is obviously no simple-minded biblicist; however, some of his writings over time lean in clearly biblicist directions. He is thus an ambiguous case concerning the present topic. The reader should not assume that because I am quoting him in this context I consider him to be a straight-out, hard-core biblicist.

3. Reformed theologian and apologetics professor Cornelius Van Til, for instance, claimed that the Bible "speaks to everything either directly or indirectly. It tells us not only of the Christ and his work but it also tells us who God is and whence the universe has come. It gives us a philosophy of history as well as history. Moreover, the information on these subjects is woven into an inextricable whole." Van Til, *The Defense of the Faith* (Philadelphia: P&R, 1963), 8. More recently, J. I. Packer has written, "So all [the Bible's] manifold contents—histories, prophecies, poems, songs, wisdom writings, sermons, statistics, letters, and whatever else—should be received as from God, and all that Bible writers teach should be revered as God's authoritative instruction. Christians should be grateful to God for the gift of his written Word, and conscientious in *basing their faith and life entirely and exclusively upon it.* Otherwise, we cannot ever honor or please him as he calls us to do." Packer, *Concise Theology* (Wheaton: Tyndale, 2001), 5, italics added for emphasis.

4. J. I. Packer, for instance, writes, "All Christians have a right and duty not only to learn from the church's heritage of faith but also to interpret Scripture for themselves. The church of Rome doubts this, alleging that individuals easily misinterpret the Scriptures. This is true; but the following rules, faithfully observed, will help prevent that from happening." The rules Packer then suggests include basic guides such as don't allegorize, pray, don't read meaning "on" to Scripture, etc. Packer, *Concise Theology*, 6. Three years later, Packer writes with Thomas Oden, "Anyone who engages seriously with the Bible, humbling asking God for light, will duly see . . . this great picture [of God and godliness] in all its divine glory." Packer and Oden, *One Faith: The Evangelical Consensus* (Downers Grove, IL: InterVarsity, 2004), 19.

5. I intentionally use the label *Solo* Scriptura, as distinct from *Sola* Scriptura, to distinguish a narrower view on the Bible associated with American biblicism from the arguably more sophisticated view of scripture developed by the original Protestant Reformers. See

Anthony Lane, "*Sola Scriptura*? Making Sense of a Post-Reformation Slogan," in *A Pathway into the Holy Scripture*, ed. Philip Satterthwaite and David Wright (Grand Rapids: Eerdmans, 1994), 297–327; and Craig Allert, "What Are We Trying to Conserve? Evangelicalism and Sola Scriptura," *The Evangelical Quarterly* 76, no. 4 (2004): 327–48. Note that some biblicists argue that creeds and confessions are not necessary but are nevertheless helpful for summarizing biblical truth. I could also have called this a belief in "nuda scriptura" or "*solitaria scriptura*," following James Callahan, "The Bible Says: Evangelical and Postliberal Biblicism," *Theology Today* 53, no. 4 (1997): 449–63. Among popular evangelical writers on the Internet, one can find explicit praisings of "nuda scriptura," as with this gem offered by "Christian Fellowship Devotionals" (self-described as "a personal outreach of Webservants Ministries. We are a group of individuals who want only to share the gospel with the lost and equip the body of Christ in growing and reaching a lost world for Jesus Christ"): "I am sure that the term Sola Scriptura is familiar to most Christians, and it is an important aspect of our faith. However, I came upon the term Nuda Scriptura this week. It really drives the point home even more clearly. We take the Scripture undressed, as it were, by itself, and without all the trappings that can sometimes accompany it. . . . The more we can look at Scripture naked, the more we can gain a fuller comprehension of its contents." http://www.cfdevotionals.org/devpg04/de041025.htm.

6. One of the common ways evangelicals view the Bible, according to Gary Meadors, Grand Rapids Theological Seminary professor of New Testament, is as "a reference manual for life in the sense that it is a book of codes that apply the same way throughout all time." Meadors, "Introduction," in *Four Views of Moving Beyond the Bible to Theology*, ed. Stanley Gundry and Gary Meadors (Grand Rapids: Zondervan, 2009), 13. I take Wayne Grudem's *Systematic Theology: An Introduction to Biblical Doctrine* (which already in its title immediately conflates "biblical" with "systematic theology") to be a good example of this bad view (Grand Rapids: Zondervan, 1995).

7. See, for example, Mark Noll, *America's God: From Jonathan Edwards to Abraham Lincoln* (New York: Oxford University Press, 2002); Nathan Hatch, *The Democratization of American Christianity* (New Haven: Yale University Press, 1991).

8. Information on the General Social Survey can be found at www.norc.uchicago.edu/GSS+Website.

9. On folk Christianity, see Roger Olson, *Questions to All Your Answers: The Journey from Folk Religion to Examined Faith* (Grand Rapids: Zondervan, 2007); 75–90 deal especially with the Bible.

10. http://www.godshandbooktolife.com.

11. http://www.musiclyric4christian.com/the-bible.html.

12. http://www.faithandfitness.net/node/89.

13. http://www.allsands.com/religious/bibleauthors_rkb_gn.htm.

14. John F. MacArthur Jr., "How Shall We Then Worship?" in *The Coming Evangelical Crisis: Current Challenges to the Authority of Scripture and the Gospel*, ed. John H. Armstrong (Chicago: Moody, 1996), 177.

15. Elmer Towns, *Bible Answers for Almost All Your Questions* (Nashville: Thomas Nelson, 2003); Patrice Tsauge, *Biblical Principles for Starting and Operating a Business* (Bloomington, IN: AuthorHouse, 2006); Alicia Walker, *100 Biblical Tips to Help You Live a More Peaceful and Prosperous Life* (Philadelphia: Xlibris, 2007); Anthony Chiffolo and Rayner Hesse, *Cooking with the Bible: Recipes for Biblical Meals* (Westport, CT: Greenwood, 2009); Don Colbert, *The Bible Cure for Cancer* (Lake Mary, FL: Siloam, 1999); Greg Johnson, *The World According to God: A Biblical View of Culture, Work, Science, Sex,*

*and Everything Else* (Downers Grove, IL: InterVarsity, 2002); Neil Anderson and Michael Jacobson, *The Biblical Guide to Alternative Medicine* (Ventura, CA: Regal Books, 2003); Clarence Blasier, *Bible Answers for Every Need* (Uhrichsville, OH: Barbour, 2006); Bruce Bickel and Stan Jantz, *Bible Prophecy 101: A Guide to End Times in Plain Language* (Eugene, OR: Harvest House, 2004); Nelson Reference, *What Does the Bible Say About . . . The Ultimate A to Z Resource to Contemporary Topics One Would Not Expect to Find in the Bible, Fully Illustrated—Discover What the Bible Says about 500 Real-Life Topics* (Nashville: Thomas Nelson, 2001); Kay Arthur, *How to Make Choices You Won't Regret—40 Minute Bible Studies* (Colorado Springs: WaterBrook, 2003); Ginger Garrett, *Queen Esther's Secrets of Womanhood: A Biblical Rite of Passage for Your Daughter* (Colorado Springs: NavPress, 2006); Charles Stanley, *Handbook for Christian Living: Biblical Answers to Life's Tough Questions* (Nashville: Thomas Nelson, 2008); Ray Comfort, *Scientific Facts in the Bible: 100 Reasons to Believe the Bible Is Supernatural in Origin* (Gainesville, FL: Bridge-Logos, 2001); Carol Lesser Baldwin, *Friendship Counseling: Biblical Foundations for Helping Others* (Grand Rapids: Zondervan, 1988); Troy Reiner, *Principles for Life: Using Biblical Principles to Bring Dynamic Psychological Healing* (Enumclaw, WA: Pleasant Word, 2005); Larry Burkett, *Business by the Book: Complete Guide of Biblical Principles for the Workplace* (Nashville: Thomas Nelson, 1998); James Steele, *Bible Solutions to Problems of Daily Living* (Upper Saddle River, NJ: Prentice Hall, 1983); Dennis Hurst, *The Biblical Connection to the Stars and Stripes: A Nation's Godly Principles Embodied in Its Flag* (Lincoln: iUniverse, 2006); Davil Jackson, *God's Blueprint for Building Marital Intimacy* (Lincoln: Writer's Club, 2000); Kathleen Madigan, *Crime and Community in Biblical Perspective* (Valley Forge, PA: Judson, 1980); Rachel Zohar Dulin, *A Crown of Glory: A Biblical View of Aging* (Mahwah, NJ: Paulist Press, 1988); Wilma Roberts James, *Gardening with Biblical Plants* (Chicago: Burnham, 1983); Oswald Chambers, *Biblical Psychology* (Grand Rapids: Discovery House, 1995); Ken Ham, Karl Wieland, and Don Batten, *One Blood: The Biblical Answer to Racism* (Green Forest, AR: Master Books, 1999); Richard Stoppe, *Leadership Communication: A Scriptural Perspective* (Cleveland: Pathway, 1987); Emmet Fox, *Diagrams for Living: The Bible Unveiled* (New York: HarperCollins, 1993); John MacArthur, *What the Bible Says about Parenting: Biblical Principles for Raising Godly Children* (Nashville: Thomas Nelson, 2000); Philip Wilson, *God Honoring Finances: What the Bible Tells You about Managing Money* (Lincoln: iUniverse, 2007); Vicki Caruana, *Success in School: Building on Biblical Principles* (Newburyport, MA: Focus, 1999); Samuele Bacchiocchi, *Christian Dress and Adornment—Biblical Perspectives* (Berrien Springs, MI: Biblical Perspectives, 1995); Barry Applewhite, *Feeling Good about Your Feelings: How to Express Your Emotions in Harmony with Biblical Principles* (Wheaton: Victor Books, 1980); Duke Clark, *Getting the Skinny on Prosperity: Biblical Principles That Work for Everyone* (Garden City, NY: Morgan James, 2006); Deborah Saathoff and Jane Jarrell, *Off to Work We Go: Teaching Careers with Biblical Principles* (Nashville: Broadman and Holman, 1999); Frederick C. Wootan, *Incoming: Listening for God's Messages—A Handbook for Life* (Charleston, SC: BookSurge, 2005); Dustin LaPorte and Anissa LaPorte, *Biblical Strategies to Financial Freedom* (Charleston, SC: BookSurge, 2006); Troy Reiner, *Revelations That Will Set You Free: The Biblical Roadmap for Spiritual and Psychological Growth* (Enumclaw, WA: Pleasant Word, 2005); Pat King, *Scripture Based Solutions for Handling Stress* (Liguori, MO: Liguori, 1990); Liz Curtis Higgs, *Bad Girls of the Bible and What We Can Learn from Them* (Colorado Springs: WaterBrook, 1999); Peter Hirsch, *Success by Design: Ten Biblical Secrets to Help You Achieve Your God-Given Potential* (Grand Rapids: Bethany House, 2002); Sandy Silverthorne, *The Awesome Book of Bible*

*Facts* (Eugene, OR: Harvest House, 1994); Chuck Missler, *Learn the Bible in 24 Hours* (Nashville: Thomas Nelson, 2002); Ben Lerner, *Body by God: The Owner's Manual for Maximized Living* (Nashville: Thomas Nelson, 2003); Wayne Grudem, *Biblical Foundations for Manhood and Womanhood* (Wheaton: Crossway Books, 2002); Jim Collins and John DiLemme, *Beyond Positive Thinking: Success and Motivation in the Scriptures* (Kirkwood, MO: Impact Christian Books, 2002); R. C. Sproul, *Biblical Economics: A Commonsense Guide to Our Daily Bread* (Dunnville, KY: Draught Horse, 2002); Richard Phillips and Sharon Phillips, *Holding Hands, Holding Hearts: Recovering a Biblical View of Christian Dating* (Phillipsburg, NJ: P&R, 2006); Dave Outar, *Politics and the Christian: A Scriptural Treatise* (Montgomery: E-BookTime, 2008); Toye Ademola, *Seven Secrets to Bible-Made Millionaires* (Bristol, TN: Selah, 2007); Chuck Missler, *Prophecy 20/20: Profiling the Future through the Lens of Scripture* (Nashville: Thomas Nelson, 2006); Donald DeYoung, *Weather and the Bible: 100 Questions and Answers* (Grand Rapids: Baker Books, 1992). The inclusion of these titles here does not imply that the author of every listed book is definitely biblicist as defined above; rather, my intent is to portray through this list of titles the larger biblicist culture that does in fact pervade American evangelicalism, including its book-publishing industry, in relation to which most if not all of the titles here make sense.

16. Mark Noll rightly notes, "If Catholic interpretation gives a preeminent place to religious authority, and if mainline or liberal Protestantism does the same for technical expertise, evangelical interpretation assigns first place to popular approval." Noll, *Between Faith and Criticism: Evangelicals, Scholarship, and the Bible in America* (New York: Harper and Row, 1986; Grand Rapids: Baker Academic, 1991; Vancouver: Regent College Publishing, 2004), 150–51. All citations are to the 2004 Regent edition.

17. http://www.examiner.com/x-4840–Orlando-Bible-Study-Examiner~y2009m7d3–Governor-Sanford-could-learn-from-King-David; http://www.cbsnews.com/stories/2009/06/26/politics/main5116912.shtml; http://tpmmuckraker.talkingpointsmemo.com/2009/06/sanford_king_david_didnt_resign_so_i_wont_either.php. This is reminiscent of Lancelot Andrewes (1555–1626) arguing that the British monarchy should be modeled on Old Testament passages: "We have to take our example from the Old Testament, seeing that there is none for us in the New," cited in Henning Graf Reventlow, *The Authority of Scripture and the Rise of the Modern World* (Philadelphia: Fortress, 1985), 139–40.

18. Both quoted in James Callahan, "The Bible Says: Evangelical and Postliberal Biblicism," *Theology Today* 53, no. 4 (1997): 455. Also see chapters by George Marsden ("Everyone One's Own Interpreter? The Bible, Science, and Authority in Mid-Nineteenth-Century America") and Nathan Hatch ("*Sola Scriptura* and *Novus Ordo Seclorum*") in Nathan Hatch and Mark Noll, *The Bible in America: Essays in Cultural History* (New York: Oxford University Press, 1982).

19. http://www.sbc.net/bfm/bfm2000.asp.

20. http://www.efca.org/about-efca/statement-faith.

21. http://www.tiu.edu/tiu/doctrine.

22. http://www.wheaton.edu/welcome/aboutus_mission.html.

23. http://www.moody.edu/edu_mainpage.aspx?id=930.

24. http://www.gordonconwell.edu/visitors/statement_faith, http://www.dts.edu/about/doctrinalstatement/, http://www.covenantseminary.edu/live/whatwebelieve/, http://www.talbot.edu/about/doctrinal_statement.cfm, http://www.csl.edu/about-us/why-were-here/, http://www.asburyseminary.edu/about/statement-of-faith. Anecdotal evidence from various personal sources also suggests, as I noted in the introduction, that more than a few faculty at different biblicist-oriented evangelical institutions actually personally do not subscribe to

biblical inerrancy and other elements of biblicism advanced by these institutions, yet will not "come out of the closet" with those private disbeliefs for fear of losing their jobs and endangering their careers—which means that sustaining biblicism requires some "emperor-has-no-clothes" fear and duplicity within the evangelical institutional system (although I cannot empirically validate that for the very reason of the fear and duplicity itself). Thus, formal statements of faith—which I am not against in principle—ultimately fail to guard against such private defections since, as John Barton puts it, "It is always possible to produce a formula which all will accept. This is because people all produce their own exegesis of it so as to accommodate what they really believe within its terms." Barton, *People of the Book? The Authority of the Bible in Christianity* (Louisville: Westminster John Knox, 1988), 80.

25. http://www.gutenberg.edu/about_gutenberg/doctrinal_statement.php.

26. "Affirmations and Denials Regarding Recent Issues," adopted by the Board of Trustees, Westminster Theological Seminary, Philadelphia, Pennsylvania, December 3, 2008, italics added for emphasis. This statement was generated in response to a book published by a Westminster Seminary professor of Old Testament, Peter Enns, which, despite significant faculty disagreements, Westminster Seminary as an institution found biblically heterodox and because of which Enns was pressured to resign.

27. That is, the *Westminster Confession of Faith*, the *Westminster Larger Catechism*, and the *Westminster Shorter Catechism*.

28. This kind of attitude is evident in most parts of American evangelicalism, as expressed, for instance, by the late Dr. D. James Kennedy of the Coral Ridge Presbyterian Church: "People . . . say, 'Well, the Bible is full of contradictions and errors.' I'm sure you have heard that many times. I would suggest a simple reply that I have used many times. I simply pull the New Testament out of my coat pocket and say to them, 'That is very interesting. I've been studying the Bible for years, and I haven't been able to find one. Would you be so kind as to show me where they are?' I'm still waiting to be shown. No, the Bible is not full of contradictions and errors; and the people that most facilely make the claim are usually those who know the least about what the Bible teaches." James Kennedy, *Truths That Transform: Christian Doctrines for Your Life Today* (Grand Rapids: Revell, 1996), 164–65.

29. Covenant Seminary, for instance, states concerning the Westminster Confession of Faith: "we hold firmly to the following doctrinal beliefs and standards."

30. http://www.bible-researcher.com/chicago1.html. Also see Carl F. H. Henry, *God, Revelation, and Authority*, vol. 4 (Waco: Word, 1979); Norman Geisler and William Nix, *A General Introduction to the Bible* (Chicago: Moody, 1986); R. C. Sproul, *Explaining Inerrancy: A Commentary* (Oakland: ICBI, 1980); Norman Geisler, ed., *Inerrancy* (Grand Rapids: Zondervan, 1980).

31. This kind of position has then generated a cottage industry of publications devoted to explaining away the very many "hard," "difficult," and "seemingly contradictory" passages of scripture, including, for instance, William Arndt, *Bible Difficulties and Seeming Contradictions* (St. Louis: Concordia, 1987); Norman Geisler and Thomas Howe, *The Big Book of Bible Difficulties: Clear and Concise Answers from Genesis to Revelation* (Grand Rapids: Baker Books, 2008); Gleason Archer, *The New International Encyclopedia of Bible Difficulties* (Grand Rapids: Zondervan, 2001); R. A. Torrey, *Difficulties in the Bible* (New Kensington, PA: Whitaker House, 2003); Gleason Archer, *Encyclopedia of Bible Difficulties* (Grand Rapids: Zondervan, 1982); Ralph Muncaster, *Are There Contradictions in the Bible?* (Eugene, OR: Harvest House, 2003); James Montgomery Boice, *Dealing with Bible Problems: Alleged Errors and Contradictions in the Bible* (Fort Washington, PA: Christian Literature Crusade, 2000); Ron Rhodes, *Commonly Misunderstood Bible Verses: Clear*

*Explanations for the Difficult Passages* (Eugene, OR: Harvest House, 2008); Joe Crews, *Answers to Difficult Bible Texts* (Roseville, CA: Amazing Facts, 2003); Peter Davids, *Hard Sayings of the Bible* (Downers Grove, IL: InterVarsity, 1996); Harold Lindsell, "Discrepancies in Scripture," chap. 9 in *The Battle for the Bible* (Grand Rapids: Zondervan, 1976); E. E. Dewitt, *Contradictions in the Bible—Examined! The God Who Loves Gave Us the Book We Can Trust* (Bloomington, IN: Wordclay, 2008); R. M. Dehaan II, *Studies in Contrasts: Resolving Alleged Contradictions in the Bible* (Grand Rapids: RBC Ministries, 1999).

32. http://www.ccci.org/about-us/ministry-profile/statement-of-faith.aspx.

33. http://www.promisekeepers.org/about/statementoffaith.

34. http://www.backtothebible.org/index.php/Statement-of-Faith.html.

35. http://www.gccweb.org/about/beliefs-values/statement-of-faith.

36. To assess the extent of biblicism in evangelical academic circles, I studied the textbooks, articles, and book chapters assigned in twenty-three introductory Bible and hermeneutics graduate courses taught at what are widely believed to be some of the top evangelical seminaries and divinity schools representing various theological traditions (Asbury Seminary, Bethel Seminary [St. Paul], Dallas Theological Seminary, Fuller Seminary School of Theology, Gordon Conwell Theological Seminary, Moody Bible Institute, Reformed Theological Seminary, Talbot Theological Seminary, Trinity Evangelical Divinity School, and Wheaton Graduate School of Theology). An examination of the most recent syllabi for those courses identified nineteen commonly assigned publications. A systematic review of those nineteen readings reveals a somewhat broad diversity of views concerning a variety of issues involved in biblical studies—ranging from very conservative and traditionalist approaches that emphasize the biblicist themes laid out above, to approaches that are much more moderate, sometimes ambiguous or equivocal, and occasionally engaged with new theoretical challenges, such as from speech-act theory and postmodernism. In several, though not all, readings, apparently biblicist ideas are nuanced or qualified by the recognition of relevant complexities. One or two of the readings even explicitly acknowledge the problem of pervasive interpretive pluralism on which this book focuses, although the answers they provide strike me as inadequate. The intellectual adversaries that many of these readings critically engage, either implicitly or explicitly, are the "neo-orthodoxy" of Karl Barth and Emil Brunner (though much of the criticism of Barth appears to me to be ill-informed) and the Catholic Church's teaching about authoritative tradition; other adversaries include skeptics about inerrancy, biblical higher critics, and postmodern relativists.

Taken as a whole, the evidence of these readings does *not* support the hypothesis that the kind of biblicism described above is being taught directly by most faculty at evangelical seminaries and divinity schools, at least through assigned readings by faculty who teach about the Bible—even when belief statements of those institutions seem to be more clearly biblicist (whether biblicist themes are taught by these faculty in class lectures and discussions or by other faculty at these institutions, I cannot say). At the same time, there is not much in most of the assigned readings that would clearly challenge students who are already predisposed to biblicism. In short, many of the relevant claims and arguments in the readings neither explicitly promote nor definitely oppose biblicism. That raises important empirical questions about the institutional sources of American evangelical biblicism, which are beyond the scope of this study to pursue. My own guess is that the evangelical book-publishing industry and a variety of popular pastors bear a lot of responsibility for sustaining the worst of biblicism. Suffice it to note here as a helpful empirical observation that biblicism in the evangelical subculture does not appear to be driven primarily by the assigned readings for pastors-in-training in Bible courses at evangelical seminaries and divinity schools.

The readings examined were: Millard Erickson, *Christian Theology* (Grand Rapids: Baker Academic, 1986); Kevin Vanhoozer, "Lost in Interpretation? Truth, Scripture, and Hermeneutics," *Journal of the Evangelical Theological Society* 48 (2005): 89–114; Kevin Vanhoozer, "The Semantics of Biblical Literature: Truth and Scripture's Diverse Literary Forms," in *Hermeneutics, Authority, and Canon*, ed. D. A. Carson and John Woodbridge (Grand Rapids: Baker Academic, 1986); D. A. Carson, *Exegetical Fallacies* (Grand Rapids: Baker Academic, 1996); D. A. Carson and Douglas Moo, *An Introduction to the New Testament* (Grand Rapids: Zondervan, 2005); D. A. Carson, "Recent Developments in the Doctrine of Scripture," in Carson and Woodbridge, eds., *Hermeneutics, Authority, and Canon*; Geoffrey Bromiley, "The Authority of Scripture in Karl Barth," in *Hermeneutics, Authority, and Canon*, ed. Carson and Woodbridge; Darrell Bock and Buist Fanning, eds., *Interpreting the NT Text: Introduction to the Art & Science of Exegesis* (Wheaton: Crossway, 2006); Francis Watson, *Paul and the Hermeneutics of Faith* (Edinburgh: T&T Clark, 2004); William Klein, Craig Blomberg, and Robert Hubbard, *Introduction to Biblical Interpretation* (Waco: Word, 2004); Joel Green, ed., *Hearing the New Testament: Strategies for Interpretation* (Grand Rapids: Eerdmans, 1995); A. K. M. Adam, Stephen Fowl, Kevin Vanhoozer, and Francis Watson, *Reading Scripture with the Church: Toward a Hermeneutic for Theological Interpretation* (Grand Rapids: Baker Academic, 2006); Stephen Harris, *The New Testament: A Student's Introduction* (New York: McGraw-Hill, 2009); J. I. Packer, *God Has Spoken* (Grand Rapids: Baker Books, 1994); J. I. Packer, *Concise Theology* (Carol Stream, IL: Tyndale, 2001); Ned Stonehouse and Paul Woolsey, eds., *The Infallible Word* (1946; repr., Philadelphia: P&R, 2003); Frank Thielman, *Theology of the New Testament: A Canonical and Synthetic Approach* (Grand Rapids: Zondervan, 2005); Jeannine Brown, *Scripture as Communication: Introducing Biblical Hermeneutics* (Grand Rapids: Baker Academic, 2007); David DeSilva, *An Introduction to the New Testament* (Downers Grove, IL: InterVarsity, 2004).

37. Joseph Lienhard, *The Bible, the Church, and Authority: The Canon and the Christian Bible in History and Theology* (Collegeville, MN: Michael Glazier, 1995), 78.

38. Robert K. Johnson, *Evangelicals at an Impasse: Biblical Authority in Practice* (Atlanta: John Knox, 1979), vii–viii. For a status update five years later, see Robert Price, "Inerrant the Wind: The Troubled House of North American Evangelicals," *Evangelical Quarterly* 55, no. 3 (July 1983): 129–44. For a strict biblicist critique of "liberal drift" evident in these debates from a fundamentalist perspective, see Donald McCune, *Promise Unfulfilled: The Failed Strategy of Modern Evangelicalism* (Greenville, SC: Embassador Emerald International, 2004), 157–94.

39. Johnson, *Evangelicals at an Impasse*, 6, 7.

40. Noll, *Between Faith and Criticism*, 166. In 1987, Westminster Theological Seminary professor of New Testament Moisés Silva likewise noted: "To say that the Scriptures are clear seems to fly in the face of the realities of contemporary church life. . . . Even those who share significant areas of doctrinal agreement find themselves at odds in the interpretation of important biblical passages. . . . If those who are wholeheartedly devoted to the authority of Scripture cannot agree on such questions, has the authority of the clarity of Scripture become meaningless?" Moisés Silva, *Has the Church Misread the Bible?* (Grand Rapids: Zondervan, 1987), 79.

41. N. T. Wright, "How Can the Bible Be Authoritative?" *Vox Evangelica* 21 (1991): 13.

42. Vanhoozer, "Lost in Interpretation?" 97. Also see I. Howard Marshall, *Beyond the Bible: Moving from Scripture to Theology* (Grand Rapids: Baker Academic, 2004), 28.

43. Carson, *Exegetical Fallacies*, 18. Also note the wrestling with these issues in David Wright, "Scripture and Evangelical Diversity with Special Reference to the Baptismal Divide," in *A Pathway into the Holy Scripture*, ed. Philip Satterthwaite and David Wright (Grand Rapids: Eerdmans, 1994), 257–75.

44. Geoffrey Bromiley, *The Unity and Disunity of the Church* (Grand Rapids: Eerdmans, 1958), 68–69, italics added for emphasis.

45. John W. Nevin, "The Sect System," *Mercersburg Review* 1 (1849): 482–507, quotes from 491–92.

46. Joseph Smith, *The Pearl of Great Price: Being a Choice Selection from the Revelations, Translations, and Narrations of Joseph Smith* (Salt Lake City: George Q. Cannon and Sons, 1891), 56–70, cited in Nathan Hatch, "*Sola Scriptura* and *Novus Ordo Seclorum*," in Hatch and Noll, eds., *The Bible in America*.

47. Richard McNemar, "The Mole's Little Pathway," ms. copy, Shaker Papers, Library of Congress, 1807, referenced in Mario De Pillis, "The Quest for Religious Authority and the Rise of Mormonism," *Dialogue: A Journal of Mormon Thought* 1 (1966): 75, quoted in Hatch, "*Sola Scriptura*," 73.

48. From "The Everlasting Gospel," lines 13–14, quoted in Lienhard, *The Bible, the Church, and Authority*, 3.

49. Quoted in Hatch, "*Sola Scriptura*," in Hatch and Noll, *The Bible in America*, 61. Also see Richard Popkin, *The History of Skepticism from Erasmus to Spinoza* (Notre Dame, IN: University of Notre Dame Press, 1979), esp. 1–17, 68–86.

50. Vincent of Lérins, *Commonitory* 2.5, in *Nicene and Post-Nicene Fathers of the Church*, Series 2, ed. Philip Schaff and Henry Wace (Grand Rapids: Eerdmans, 1983–87), 11:132 (originally published circa 434).

51. Tertullian, *The Prescription against Heretics* 3.16–19, in *The Ante-Nicene Fathers*, trans. Peter Holmes, http://www.earlychristianwritings.com/text/tertullian11.html.

52. Vern Poythress, *Symphonic Theology: The Validity of Multiple Perspectives in Theology* (1987; repr., Phillipsburg, NJ: P&R, 2001), 19, italics added for emphasis.

53. Michael Meiring rightly observes: "Many scholars have written on the subject of hermeneutics . . . and given us 'rules' for biblical interpretation. Reformed theologian Edward Gross cites three rules from Charles Hodge: 'Scripture is to be interpreted in its grammatical historical sense, Scripture must interpret Scripture and cannot contradict itself, and the guidance of the Holy Spirit must be sought to interpret Scripture.' . . . Gross concludes, 'If Christians would constantly unite a thorough investigation with these simple rules, *differences in interpretation would practically disappear.*' The problem with Gross's concluding statement should be obvious. Christians *have* engaged in thorough investigations, applying these three rules of hermeneutics, and yet have *still* come up with differences of interpretation." Michael Meiring, "Why There Is Disunity," in *Preserving Evangelical Unity*, ed. Michael Meiring (Eugene, OR: Wipf and Stock, 2009), 3–10, italics in original.

54. Gregory Boyd and Paul Eddy, *Across the Spectrum: Understanding Issues in Evangelical Theology*, 2nd ed. (Grand Rapids: Baker Academic, 2009). Thankfully, in the real world many of the positions tend to cluster around relatively coherent theological schools (e.g., Calvinism), significantly reducing the number of combinations actually believed, but the formal math on the different, unique, potential theological belief positions is: $2^{10} \times 3^4 \times 4^3 = 5,308,416$.

55. Craig Branch, "Unity and Purity in the Church," in *Preserving Evangelical Unity*, ed. Meiring, 28.

56. Kenton Sparks, *God's Word in Human Words* (Grand Rapids: Baker Academic, 2008), 257–58, 327.

57. Disagreeing Bible readers thus may continue to assert a shared "high view" of scripture, as in the case of Gary Meadors's introduction to his *Four Views on Moving Beyond the Bible to Theology*: "The proponents of the variety of views within evangelicalism hold a high view of Scripture as God's Word, although their views of *how* Scripture is relevant in the contemporary setting may vary widely. It is a mistake to assume that disagreement over how the Bible teaches signals a greater or lesser view of the authority of Scripture." Meadors, "Introduction," in *Four Views of Moving Beyond the Bible to Theology*, ed. Stanley Gundry and Gary Meadors (Grand Rapids: Zondervan, 2009), 14–15, italics in original. That may be well and good, but it fails to recognize the larger point here, namely, that, in the end, shared "high views" of scripture themselves cannot rescue the authority of scripture from being seriously undermined in *functional practice* by pervasive interpretive pluralism. Furthermore, Meadors reflects the highly *individualistic* principle of the right of individual "private judgment" in determining the truth of scripture and theology when he writes as the last sentence of his conclusion for this *Four Views* book that: "the remaining task is for each reader to determine when and how such an extension of the Bible [to theology] is appropriate" (347).

## Chapter 2  The Extent and Source of Pervasive Interpretive Pluralism

1. I am focusing many of my examples here on issues that often divide *biblicists*. Broadening the scope of the investigation to all Christian groups across church history, including those who do not embrace a strictly biblicist viewpoint but who still consider the scriptures to be divinely inspired revelation and a definitive authority in doctrine and practice, would deepen the problem of interpretive pluralism. We could begin, e.g., with the "Judaizer" enemies of the apostle Paul within the early church, who read the Law and the Prophets and perhaps the writings of the Old Testament—which were the *only* sacred scripture of Paul's day—as teaching the "biblical" need for Christians to continue observing the laws of the covenant, including circumcision. We could recall the many "biblical" arguments advanced by Arius and his numerous followers against the notion that the man Jesus of Nazareth could be fully God in nature. We might call to mind the "biblical" bases for the arguments of those who believed in christological "adoptionism." We could remember how the Bible was used to support both sides of the East-West struggle over iconography and papal supremacy. And so on.

2. On a related matter, illustrating how social context shapes biblical reading, George Thomas has shown how the massive shift in the dominant American Protestantism away from the predestinarian Calvinism of the eighteenth century to a more individualistic, revivalistic, freewill gospel in the nineteenth century was significantly caused by the spread and penetration of the national market, which made a rereading of scripture as actually teaching a gospel emphasizing autonomous individual choice more plausible and consistent with new social structures than the old Calvinism. George Thomas, *Revivalism and Social Change: Christianity, Nation Building, and the Market in Nineteenth-Century United States* (Chicago: University of Chicago Press, 1998).

3. Some Christian traditions (Lutheran and Catholic) believe that this is the third, not fourth, commandment, as most Orthodox, Reformed, Anglican, and other Christians by contrast believe.

4. Robert Miller, *They Both Prayed to the Same God: Religion and Faith in the American Civil War* (Lanham, MD: Lexington Books, 2007); John Daly, *When Slavery Was Called Freedom: Evangelicalism, Proslavery, and the Causes of the Civil War* (Lexington: University of Kentucky Press, 2004); Randall Miller, Harry Stout, and Charles Wilson, eds., *Religion and the American Civil War* (New York: Oxford University Press, 1998); Mason Howance, ed., *A House Divided: The Antebellum Slavery Debates in America, 1776–1865* (Princeton: Princeton University Press, 2003).

5. See, e.g., Molly Oshatz, "The Problem of Moral Progress: The Slavery Debates and the Development of Liberal Protestantism in the United States," *Modern Intellectual History 5* (2008): 225–50; Mark Noll, *America's God: From Jonathan Edwards to Abraham Lincoln* (New York: Oxford University Press, 2002), 417–21; Willard Swartley, *Slavery, Sabbath, Women, and War: Case Issues in Biblical Interpretation* (Scottdale, PA: Herald, 1983).

6. Mark Noll, *The Civil War as a Theological Crisis* (Chapel Hill: University of North Carolina Press, 2006).

7. Noll, *America's God*, 365.

8. This transformation was, of course, not entirely due to the moral failure of biblicism, but that still played a significant factor. See Christian Smith, *The Secular Revolution* (Berkeley: University of California Press, 2003); Louis Menand, *The Metaphysical Club: A Story of Ideas in America* (New York: Farrar, Straus, and Giroux, 2002). It was also set against the backdrop of the crisis of Christian authority in the West provoked by the Reformation and subsequent religious wars, as Jeffrey Stout rightly observes: "In the wake of the Reformation, theism ceased to provide a vocabulary in terms of which matters of public importance could be debated and decided by Christians of various persuasions without resort to violence." Stout, *The Flight from Authority: Religion, Morality, and the Quest for Autonomy* (Notre Dame, IN: University of Notre Dame Press, 1981), 13. Also see Richard Popkin, *The History of Skepticism from Erasmus to Spinoza* (Notre Dame, IN: University of Notre Dame Press, 1979), esp. 1–17, 68–86; Henning Graf Reventlow, *The Authority of the Bible and the Rise of the Modern World* (Philadelphia: Fortress, 1985).

9. I will spare readers the very long list of citations, although those interested can search Amazon.com on combinations of the keywords "biblical," "manhood," "woman," "church," and "feminism," keeping an eye out for names such as Wayne Grudem, Gilbert Bilezikian, John Piper, Stanley Grenz, Craig Keener, Aida Besancon Spencer, Stephen Clark, Bette Boersma, John Bristow, Alvera Mickelsen, Patricia Gundry, Elisabeth Elliot, Susan Foh, Peter Schemm, Loren Cunningham, Ronald Pierce, Rebecca Groothuis, Nancy DeMoss, Linda Belleville, Andreas Kostenberger, Bonnidell Clouse, Letha Scanzoni, Nancy Hardesty, and Stuart Scott, among others.

10. Ronald Sider, *Rich Christians in an Age of Hunger* (Downers Grove, IL: InterVarsity, 1977; Nashville: Thomas Nelson, 2005).

11. David Chilton, *Productive Christians in an Age of Guilt Manipulation: A Biblical Response to Ronald Sider* (Tyler, TX: Institute for Christian Economics, 1981).

12. Gregory Boyd and Paul Eddy, *Across the Spectrum: Understanding Issues in Evangelical Theology*, 2nd ed. (Grand Rapids: Baker Academic, 2009), 235–48; Wayne Grudem, Robert Saucy, Richard Gaffin, and Stanley Gundry, *Are Miraculous Gifts for Today?* (Grand Rapids: Zondervan, 1996).

13. The following draws on these, among other, works: Gustaf Aulén, *Christus Victor: An Historical Study of the Three Main Types of the Idea of the Atonement* (New York: Collier, 1969); Joel Green and Mark Baker, *Recovering the Scandal of the Cross:*

*Atonement in New Testament and Contemporary Contexts* (Downers Grove, IL: Inter-Varsity Press, 2000); James Beilby and Paul Eddy, *The Nature of the Atonement: Four Views* (Downers Grove, IL: InterVarsity Press, 2006); Stephen Holmes, *The Wondrous Cross: Atonement and Penal Substitution in the Bible and History* (London: Paternoster, 2007); Steve Chalke, Chris Wright, I. Howard Marshall, and Joel Green, *The Atonement Debate* (Grand Rapids: Zondervan, 2008); John Driver, *Understanding the Atonement for the Mission of the Church* (Scottdale, PA: Herald, 1986); Mark Baker, ed., *Proclaiming the Scandal of the Cross: Contemporary Images of Atonement* (Grand Rapids: Baker Academic, 2006); Stephen Finlan, *Options on Atonement in Christian Thought* (Collegeville, MN: Liturgical Press, 2007); Steve Jeffery, Micahel Ovey, and Andrew Sach, *Pierced for Our Transgressions: Recovering the Glory of Penal Substitution* (Wheaton: Crossway, 2007); J. Denny Weaver, *The Nonviolent Atonement* (Grand Rapids: Eerdmans, 2001); Stephen Finlan, *Problems with Atonement* (Collegeville, MN: Liturgical Press, 2005); Brad Jersak and Michael Hardin, eds., *Stricken by God? Nonviolent Identification and the Victory of Christ* (Grand Rapids: Eerdmans, 2007).

14. Among the large and contentious literature, see, e.g., John Piper, *The Future of Justification: A Response to N. T. Wright* (Wheaton: Crossway, 2007); N. T. Wright, *Justification: God's Plan and Paul's Vision* (Downers Grove, IL: IVP Academic, 2009).

15. John Barber, "Luther and Calvin on Music and Worship," *Reformed Perspectives Magazine* 8, no. 26 (2006): 1–16.

16. Such as the Reformed theologians John Murray and G. I. Williamson; see http://reformedonline.com/view/reformedonline/music.htm; http://reformedonline.com/view/reformedonline/sola.htm.

17. Such as Craig Carter, *Rethinking Christ and Culture* (Grand Rapids: Brazos, 2007); D. A. Carson, *Christ and Culture Revisited* (Grand Rapids: Eerdmans, 2008); Robert Webber, *The Secular Saint: The Role of the Christian in the Secular World* (Grand Rapids: Zondervan, 1979).

18. Mark Noll, *Between Faith and Criticism: Evangelicals, Scholarship, and the Bible in America* (Vancouver: Regent College Publishing, 2004), 166.

19. Nathan O. Hatch, "Response to Carl F. H. Henry," in *Evangelical Affirmations*, ed. Kenneth Kantzer and Carl Henry (Grand Rapids: Zondervan, 1990), 97–98.

20. See Donald Dayton and Robert K. Johnson, eds., *The Variety of American Evangelicalism* (Downers Grove, IL: InterVarsity, 1991); Robert Webber distinguishes fourteen branches of evangelicalism in *Common Roots: A Call to Evangelical Maturity* (Grand Rapids: Zondervan, 1978), 25–35; also see Iain Murray, *Evangelicalism Divided: A Record of Crucial Changes in the Years 1950 to 2000* (Carlisle, PA: Banner of Truth, 2000); Mark Ellingsen, *The Evangelical Movement: Growth, Impact, Controversy, Dialog* (Minneapolis: Augsburg, 1988).

21. J. I. Packer and Thomas Oden, *One Faith: The Evangelical Consensus* (Downers Grove, IL: InterVarsity, 2004), 14–15.

22. Rob Warner, pastor of Queen's Road Church, Wimbledon (UK), observes: "The fact that evangelicals have a high regard for truth brings with it a recurring danger. Our firmly held convictions can cause us to become highly fractious and prone to division. Of all the armies of the Christian church, the evangelicals have most often made a habit, or in some cases almost a virtue, of fighting one another. It has become a time-honoured evangelical custom to shoot ourselves in the foot." After reviewing a long list of "fracture points" mirroring those mentioned above, Warner concludes (writing in 1996): "There is enough explosive stored up in this catalogue of controversies to make the eagerly

anticipated fireworks display being planned to celebrate the year 2000 look like a bargain basement bonfire night. . . . [These are] thorny and irretractable [*sic*] differences . . . [tending toward] constant and destructive polarization. Any one of these fracture points has the potential to blow apart the evangelical movement." Warner, "Fracture Points," in *Together We Stand*, ed. Clive Calver and Rob Warner (London: Hodder and Stoughton, 1996), 60, 93.

23. Christian Smith et al., *American Evangelicalism: Embattled and Thriving* (Chicago: University of Chicago Press, 1998).

24. One example of this "we are right and everyone else is wrong" attitude is expressed by Westminster Theological Seminary New Testament professor Richard Gaffin in his critical response to an article published by John Franke in the previous issue of the *Westminster Theological Journal* ("Reforming Theology: Toward a Postmodern Reformed Dogmatics"), in which Gaffin follows B. B. Warfield's 1931 description of the Reformed theological tradition as a "perfectly developed representative" of Christianity by saying that the Reformed tradition is "the more perfectly developed representative" (adjusted by Gaffin to "put . . . less triumphalistically"). Gaffin approvingly quotes Warfield as saying that Calvinism, as mediated through the Westminster Standards, "is not merely the hope of true religion in the world; it *is* true religion in the world." He then adds his own commentary: "All sound religion is Reformed in its essence and implications. Reformed distinctives are truth held in trust for the other traditions, and Reformed theology . . . is not so much working together with those traditions out of a common theological orientation, as it is seeking to correct them." This, Gaffin (following Cornelius Van Til) notes, necessarily produces an "isolation" of Reformed theology, along with a "theological divide, with its resulting conflicts . . . with implications and not unimportant consequences for the faith, life, and mission of the church." He then interrogates his rival's perspective, asking, "How compatible are Franke's proposals with this stance? What about 'Reformed isolation' in his view?" Gaffin, "Response to John Franke," *Westminster Theological Journal* 65 (2003): 327–28.

25. Noetic means concerning the mind or intellect, from the Greek νοητικός "mental," from νοεῖν "to think," and from νοῦς "mind."

26. See, as one model perhaps, John Franke, *Manifold Witness: The Plurality of Truth* (Nashville: Abingdon, 2009).

27. D. A. Carson's 2003 book, *Exegetical Fallacies*, does not promise, but essentially implies, that most disagreement about what the Bible teaches among conservative Christians could be cleared up through better scriptural exegesis, stating, e.g., that "the importance of this sort of study cannot be overestimated if we are to move toward unanimity on those matters of interpretation that still divide us." Carson, *Exegetical Fallacies* (Grand Rapids: Baker Academic, 2003), see especially 17–20, quote at 18.

28. For a helpful historical examination of the role of scriptural perspicuity in Protestant hermeneutics, especially in the need for a theory of the full clarity of scripture to defend against the Catholic view of Christian authority, see James Callahan, "*Claritas Scripturae*: The Role of Perspicuity in Protestant Hermeneutics," *Journal of the Evangelical Theological Society* 39, no. 3 (1996): 353–72.

29. See http://www.bible-researcher.com/chicago1.html.

30. St. Augustine, for instance, wrote, "Sometimes not just one meaning but two meanings are perceived in the same words of Scripture. Even if the writer's meaning is obscure, there is no danger here, provided that it can be shown from other passages of the holy scriptures that each of these interpretations is consistent with the truth. . . .

Perhaps the author too saw that very [double] meaning in the words that we are trying to understand. Certainly, the Spirit of God who worked through the author foresaw without any doubt that it would present itself to a reader or listener, or rather planned that it should present itself, because it too is based on the truth. Could God have built into the divine eloquence a more generous or bountiful gift than the possibility of understanding the same words in several ways, all of them deriving confirmation from other no less divinely inspired passages? When one unearths an equivocal meaning which cannot be verified by unequivocal support from holy scriptures, it remains for the meaning to be brought into the open by a process of reasoning, even if the writer whose words we are seeking to understand perhaps did not perceive it. But this practice is dangerous; it is much safer to operate within the divine scriptures." Augustine, *On Christian Teaching* (Oxford: Oxford University Press, 1999), 86–87 (originally published circa AD 395–97). This matter is discussed further in chapter 3.

31. The distinguished literary critic Northrop Frye described the Bible as "a mosaic: a pattern of commandments, aphorisms, epigrams, proverbs, parables, riddles, pericopes, parallel couplets, formulaic phrases, folktales, oracles, epiphanies, *Gattungen*, *Logia*, bits of occasional verse, marginal glosses, legends, snippets from historical documents, laws, letters, sermons, hymns, ecstatic visions, rituals, fables, genealogical lists, and so on almost indefinitely." Frye, *The Great Code: The Bible and Literature* (New York: Harvest, 1982), 206.

32. Following Thomas Kuhn, *The Structure of Scientific Revolutions* (Chicago: University of Chicago Press, 1962).

33. Scot McKnight also uses this image in his book, *The Blue Parakeet: Rethinking How You Read the Bible* (Grand Rapids: Zondervan, 2008), 49–52.

34. Recall, for instance—as only one blatant among very many other, usually more subtle examples—Martin Luther's saying about the book of James—which he did not regard as an apostolic writing—that it "is really an epistle of straw, compared to [other New Testament books]; for it has nothing of the nature of the gospel in it." Martin Luther, *Works of Martin Luther—The Philadelphia Edition*, vol. 6, *Preface to the New Testament*, trans. C. M. Jacobs (Grand Rapids: Baker, 1982), 444. Luther also said of the book of Revelation, in a preface to his commentary on it, that he could "in no way detect that the Holy Spirit produced it. . . . Let everyone think of it as his own spirit leads him. My spirit cannot accommodate itself to this book." Martin Luther, "The 1522 'Preface to the Revelation of St. John,'" in *Luther's Works*, vol. 35, *Word and Sacrament I*, ed. E. Theodore Bachmann (Philadelphia: Fortress, 1960), 399.

35. Dispensational theology and Luther's discounting of the authority of the book of James are two among other possible examples of this.

36. On the particular modernness of expecting single meanings of all scriptural texts based on literal intentions of authors, see David Steinmetz, "The Superiority of Pre-Critical Exegesis," *Theology Today* 37, no. 1 (1980): 27–38.

37. John Barton, *People of the Book? The Authority of the Bible in Christianity* (Louisville: Westminster John Knox, 1988), 19.

38. Peter Enns, *Inspiration and Incarnation: Evangelicals and the Problem of the Old Testament* (Grand Rapids: Baker Academic, 2005), 71–112. At the same time, Enns insists that "diversity in no way implies chaos or error. . . . The presence of theological diversity does not mean that it lacks integrity or trustworthiness. It means that we must recognize that the data of Scripture lead us to conceive differently of how Scripture has integrity or is worthy of trust. Scripture may indeed 'lack integrity' [only] if we impose upon it standards that have little in common with how the Bible itself behaves" (80, 169).

39. A sampling of some scholarly works in biblical studies that attempt, more or less well, to address some of this diversity, include Paul Hanson, *The Diversity of Scripture: A Theological Interpretation* (Philadelphia: Fortress, 1982); John Goldingay, *Theological Diversity and the Authority of the Old Testament* (Grand Rapids: Eerdmans, 1987); John Goldingay, *Models for Interpretation of Scripture* (Grand Rapids: Eerdmans, 1995); Walter Brueggemann, *Theology of the Old Testament: Testimony, Dispute, Advocacy* (Minneapolis: Fortress, 1997); Timothy Ward, "The Diversity and Sufficiency of Scripture," in *The Trustworthiness of God: Perspectives on the Nature of Scripture*, ed. Paul Helm and Carl Trueman (Grand Rapids: Eerdmans, 2002), 192–218.

40. Paul Ricoeur, *Interpretation Theory: Discourse and the Surplus of Meaning* (Fort Worth: Texas Christian University Press, 1976); Paul Ricoeur, "Creativity in Language: Word, Polysemy, Metaphor," *Philosophy Today* 17 (1973): 79–111; Hans G. Gadamer, *Truth and Method* (New York: Crossroads, 1982).

41. Goldingay rightly observes that "texts, after all, cannot answer back ('No, I didn't mean that') as people can." Goldingay, *Models for Interpretation of Scripture*, 4.

42. Donald Bloesch, *Holy Scripture: Revelation, Inspiration, and Interpretation* (Downers Grove, IL: InterVarsity, 1994), 204.

43. John Goldingay, *Models for Scripture* (Toronto: Clements, 1994), 346.

44. P. B. Armstrong, *Conflicting Readings: Variety and Validity in Interpretation* (Chapel Hill: University of North Carolina Press, 1990).

45. David Wells, "Word and World: Biblical Authority and the Quandary of Modernity," in *Evangelical Affirmations*, ed. Kenneth Kantzer and Carl Henry (Grand Rapids: Zondervan, 1990), 161–62.

46. Kenton Sparks, *God's Word in Human Words* (Grand Rapids: Baker Academic, 2008), 121, 230, 244.

47. Christopher Wright, *Old Testament Ethics for the People of God* (Downers Grove, IL: InterVarsity, 2004), 444.

## Chapter 3  Some Relevant History, Sociology, and Psychology

1. See George Marsden, *Fundamentalism and American Culture* (New York: Oxford University Press, 1980), esp. 16–28; Sidney Ahlstrom, "The Scottish Philosophy and American Theology," *Church History* 24 (1955): 257–72; Gary Dorrien, "Scholastic Certainty: Princeton Realism as Reformed Orthodoxy," in *The Remaking of Evangelical Theology* (Louisville: Westminster John Knox, 1998), 24–28.

2. Kern Trembath, *Evangelical Theories of Biblical Inspiration* (New York: Oxford University Press, 1987), 19; also see Stanley Grenz, "Nurturing the Soul, Informing the Mind: The Genesis of the Evangelical Scripture Principle," in *Evangelicals and Scripture: Tradition, Authority, and Hermeneutics*, ed. Vincent Bacote, Laura Miguélez, and Dennis Okholm (Downers Grove, IL: InterVarsity, 2004), 21–41.

3. Thomas Reid, *Philosophical Works* (Hildesheim, Germany: Georg Olms Verlagsbuchhandlung, 1967), 1:440.

4. Charles Hodge, *Systematic Theology* (1871–73; repr., Grand Rapids: Eerdmans, 1977), 3, 11, 17.

5. Ibid., 183–84.

6. Mark Noll, *America's God: From Jonathan Edwards to Abraham Lincoln* (New York: Oxford University Press, 2002), 317.

7. Benjamin Breckenridge Warfield, *The Inspiration and Authority of the Bible*, ed. Samuel Craig (1894; repr., Philadelphia: P&R, 1948), 115.

8. Ibid., 118, 210.

9. See Mark Noll, "Charles Hodge as Expositer of the Spiritual Life," in *Charles Hodge Revisited*, ed. John Stewart and James Moorhead (Grand Rapids: Eerdmans, 2002), 181–216.

10. Wayne Grudem, *Systematic Theology: An Introduction to Biblical Doctrine* (Grand Rapids: Zondervan, 1994), 21, 23.

11. G. K. Beale, *The Erosion of Inerrancy in Evangelicalism: Responding to New Challenges to Biblical Authority* (Wheaton: Crossway, 2008), 220, though, to be clear, I repeat that my concern here is not with the inerrancy debate per se but the impossibility of avoiding active scriptural interpretation by the reader.

12. Carlos Bovell, *By Good and Necessary Consequence: A Preliminary Genealogy of Biblicist Foundationalism* (Eugene, OR: Wipf and Stock, 2009).

13. See, e.g., Christopher Scheitle and Amy Adamczyk, "It Takes Two: The Interplay of Individual and Group Theology on Social Embeddedness," *Journal for the Scientific Study of Religion* 48, no. 1 (2009): 16–29; Daniel Olson, "Fellowship Ties and the Transmission of Religious Identity," in *Beyond Establishment: Protestant Identity in a Post-Protestant Age*, ed. Jackson Carroll and W. Clark Roof (Louisville: Westminster, 1993), 32–53; William Bainbridge and Rodney Stark, "Friendship, Religion and the Occult: A Network Study," *Review of Religious Research* 22 (1981): 313–27; Larry Iannaccone, "A Formal Model of Church and Sect," *American Journal of Sociology* 94 (1988): 241–68; Christian Smith with Melinda Lundquist Denton, *Soul Searching: The Religious and Spiritual Lives of American Teenagers* (New York: Oxford University Press, 2005), 57–58; Bernice Pescosolido and Sharon Georgianna, "Durkheim, Religion and Suicide: Toward a Network Theory of Suicide," *American Sociological Review* 54 (1989): 33–48; see Miller McPherson, Lynn Smith-Lovin, and James Cook, "Birds of a Feather: Homophily in Social Networks," *Annual Review of Sociology* 27 (2001): 415–44.

14. Peter Berger, *The Sacred Canopy: Elements of a Sociological Theory of Religion* (New York: Anchor, 1990).

15. Christian Smith et al., *American Evangelicalism: Embattled and Thriving* (Chicago: University of Chicago Press, 1998).

16. Thanks to Mark Regnerus for suggesting this point to me.

## Chapter 4 Subsidiary Problems with Biblicism

1. To be clear, to suggest that the inerrancy debate is largely fruitless is not to say that inerrancy is either right or wrong. In either case, it seems to me that major differences exist *within* "the" (allegedly single) inerrancy "position"—between an unqualified, flat-footed version (popular among lay Bible readers and many pastors but not among most knowledgeable evangelical academic scholars) versus well-qualified, highly nuanced versions of "inerrancy" (to which many evangelical scholars subscribe, but which may be too tricky for many people at the popular level to work with). I hear both approaches in the 1978 Chicago Statement on Biblical Inerrancy, for example, which on close reading reflects less consensus than at first glance. The devil, so to speak, is often in the details and qualifications, however the more visible political positioning around terminology is negotiated. My sense is that affirmations of the simple version of inerrancy provide reassurance to many constituents that evangelicalism is not getting "soft" on scripture, that it is resisting liberalism; while the nuances and qualifications in the fine print provide sufficient political

"cover" and intellectual wiggle room for many evangelical scholars in academia who know better. It seems to me, however, that, at the very least, evangelicals categorically share a belief that it is wrong to attribute error to God. How exactly to express and sustain that belief, in view of the Bible as it is, is the challenge that often leads in divergent directions. For a more recent, fair-minded, nonliberal rethinking of inerrancy, see John Goldingay, *Models for Scripture* (Toronto: Clements, 1994), 261–83.

2. Some evangelical scholars do attempt to systematically sort through these issues (e.g., William Webb, *Slaves, Women, and Homosexuals: Exploring the Hermeneutics of Cultural Analysis* [Downers Grove, IL: InterVarsity, 2001]; I. Howard Marshall, *Beyond the Bible: Moving from Scripture to Theology* [Grand Rapids: Baker Academic, 2004]), but, however admirable and perhaps successful such attempts may be, evangelical biblicists generally cannot come to anything like agreement on them, so the differences continue and the larger problem remains unresolved—in part because other, more biblicist evangelical scholars (e.g., Wayne Grudem, "Should We Move Beyond the New Testament to a Better Ethic? An Analysis of William J. Webb, *Slaves, Women, and Homosexuals: Exploring the Hermeneutics of Cultural Analysis*," *Journal of the Evangelical Theological Society* 47, no. 2 [2004]: 299–346) remain unpersuaded. And so strategic attempts to overcome interpretive pluralism fail. Applied to roughly similar problems among mainline Protestant interpreters, see Charles Cosgrove, *Appealing to Scripture in Moral Debate: Five Hermeneutical Rules* (Grand Rapids: Eerdmans, 2002); Charles Cosgrove, *The Meanings We Choose: Hermeneutical Ethics, Indeterminacy, and the Conflict of Interpretations* (London: T&T Clark, 2004).

3. In the case of the Pauline Epistles, this is complicated by the "problem of particularity," namely, "that Paul wrote mainly to particular congregations [unlike many other New Testament books] for specific reasons weighs against the understanding that these letters were relevant to the church as a whole." Craig Allert, *A High View of Scripture? The Authority of the Bible and the Formation of the New Testament Canon* (Grand Rapids: Baker Academic, 2007), 128; referencing N. A. Dahl, "The Particularity of the Pauline Epistles in the Ancient Church," *Novum Testamentum* 7 (1962): 261–71. Biblicists take for granted as a default that a New Testament document that was written for someone else is also always written for them—except, as we've seen, in cases when an argument for cultural context or relativity is needed to distance the text from contemporary application.

4. The 1978 Chicago Declaration on Biblical Inerrancy attempted (unsuccessfully, in my view) to sustain universal applicability in the face of cultural relativity by distinguishing between "bound" and "conditioned": "Holy Scripture is nowhere culture-*bound* in the sense that its teachings lack *universal* validity, [but] it is sometimes culturally *conditioned* by the customs and conventional views of a particular period, so that the application of its principles today calls for a different sort of action" (italics added for emphasis). See chap. 1, note 29 for the URL.

5. This, by the way, being a classic illustration of the philosophers' "self-referential paradox" generally (coined specifically as the "Epimenides paradox," since it was Epimenides's statement), by virtue of its own asserted truth, has to be untrue because he himself was a Cretan.

6. Noted in John Goldingay, *Models for Scripture* (Toronto: Clements, 1994), 254.

7. William Webb, "A Redemptive Movement Model," in *Four Views of Moving Beyond the Bible to Theology*, ed. Stanley Gundry and Gary Meadors (Grand Rapids: Zondervan, 2009), 218–19.

8. Brian Malley, *How the Bible Works: An Anthropological Study of Evangelical Biblicism* (Walnut Creek, CA: Alta Mira, 2004). Ted Jelen ("Biblical Literalism and Inerrancy:

Does the Difference Make a Difference?" *Sociological Analysis* 49, no. 4 [1989]: 421–29) also shows that the difference between belief in biblical literalism and biblical inerrancy relevant in elite controversies over biblical authority appears to be fairly meaningless in effects on social attitudes among the United States mass public.

9. James Bielo, *Words upon the Word: An Ethnography of Evangelical Group Bible Study* (New York: New York University Press, 2009); also see James Bielo, "On the Failure of 'Meaning': Bible Reading in the Anthropology of Christianity," *Culture and Religion* 9, no. 1 (2008): 1–21.

10. John Bartkowski, "Beyond Biblical Literalism and Inerrancy: Evangelicals and the Hermeneutic Interpretation of Scripture," *Sociology of Religion* 57, no. 3 (1996): 259–72, quote at 266.

11. Ibid., 269. A large literature in the sociology of religion also shows that, while evangelicals are highly likely to profess to believe that the Bible teaches the "spiritual headship" of husbands, in actual practice they live out relatively egalitarian marriages—see, e.g., Sally K. Gallagher and Christian Smith, "Symbolic Traditionalism and Pragmatic Egalitarianism: Contemporary Evangelicals, Family, and Gender," *Gender and Society* 13, no. 2 (1999): 211–33.

12. Webb, "A Redemptive Movement Model," 228–41, quote at 234–35, italics added for emphasis.

13. James Bielo, ed., *The Social Life of Scriptures* (New Brunswick, NJ: Rutgers University Press, 2009). Also see Vincent Wimbush, ed., *Theorizing Scriptures: New Critical Orientations to a Cultural Phenomenon* (New Brunswick, NJ: Rutgers University Press, 2008). These are the first two titles in a book series on "Signifying (on) Scripture" developed by the Institute for Signifying Scriptures, http://www.signifyingscriptures.org/. Also see Matthew Engelke, *A Problem of Presence: Beyond Scripture in an African Church* (Berkeley: University of California Press, 2007); Susan Harding, *The Book of Jerry Falwell: Fundamentalist Language and Politics* (Princeton: Princeton University Press, 2000); Kathleen Boone, *The Bible Tells Them So: The Discourse of Protestant Fundamentalism* (Albany: State University of New York Press, 1989); Fenella Cannell, ed., *The Anthropology of Christianity* (Durham, NC: Duke University Press, 2006), esp. 273–94.

14. To borrow a word from Maurice Wiles, "Scriptural Authority and Theological Construction: The Limitations of Narrative Interpretation," in *Scriptural Authority and Narrative Interpretation*, ed. G. Green (Philadelphia: Augsburg Fortress, 1987), 43.

15. But, again, see Carlos Bovell, *By Good and Necessary Consequence: A Preliminary Genealogy of Biblicist Foundationalism* (Eugene, OR: Wipf and Stock, 2009).

16. See Paul Seely, *Inerrant Wisdom: Science and Inerrancy in Biblical Perspective* (Princeton: Evangelical Reform, 1989).

17. Nicholas Wolterstorff, *Divine Discourse: Philosophical Reflections on the Claim That God Speaks* (Cambridge: Cambridge University Press, 1995).

18. Goldingay explains: "There *is* force to the deductive argument from *dictation* to inerrancy. What God says is without error, so if God dictated scripture, then scripture is without error. But the claims that inspiration implies inerrancy rests on the prior identification of inspiration with dictation, which [most] inerrantists do not maintain. . . . They are inspired but not dictated, and therefore their inspiration is not an argument for being inerrant." Goldingay, *Models for Scripture*, 275–76. Also see Brian Rosner, "'Written for Us': Paul's View of Scripture," in *A Pathway into the Holy Scripture*, ed. Philip Satterthwaite and David Wright (Grand Rapids: Eerdmans, 1994), 81–105.

19. The Chicago Statement on Biblical Inerrancy also adds these qualifications: "We deny that it is proper to evaluate Scripture according to standards of truth and error that are alien to its usage and purpose. We further deny that inerrancy is negated by Biblical phenomena such as a lack of modern technical precision, irregularities of grammar or spelling, observational descriptions of nature, the reporting of falsehoods, the use of hyperbole and round numbers, the topical arrangement of material, variant selections of material in parallel accounts, or the use of free citations. . . . Differences between literary conventions in Bible times and in ours must also be observed: Since, for instance, nonchronological narration and imprecise citation were conventional and acceptable and violated no expectations in those days, we must not regard these things as faults when we find them in Bible writers." These provisos are needed, of course, to be realistic and honest, but they do begin to kill the strong meaning of "inerrancy" with the proverbial "death of a thousand qualifications"—inerrantists begin by taking a very strong stand but then inevitably have to back off into a much more compromising position. See chap. 1, note 29 for the Chicago Statement URL.

20. On this point, also see George Mavrodes, "The Bible Buyer," *The Reformed Journal* (July/August 1968): 12–14.

21. David Bentley Hart, *Atheist Delusions: The Christian Revolution and Its Fashionable Enemies* (New Haven: Yale University Press, 2009), 205.

22. David Yeago, "The New Testament and the Nicene Dogma: A Contribution to the Recovery of Theological Exegesis," in *The Theological Interpretation of Scripture*, ed. Stephen Fowl (Oxford: Blackwell, 1977), 88, quoted in Daniel J. Treier, *Introducing Theological Interpretation of Scripture: Recovering a Christian Practice* (Grand Rapids: Baker Academic, 2008), 60.

23. Gerhard May, *Creation Ex Nihilo: The Doctrine of "Creation Out of Nothing" in Early Christian Thought* (Edinburgh: T&T Clark, 1994). The only other possible evidence for ex nihilo is Heb. 11:3.

24. Nathan Hatch, "*Sola Scriptura* and Novus *Ordo Seclorum*," in Nathan Hatch and Mark Noll, *The Bible in America: Essays in Cultural History* (New York: Oxford University Press, 1982), 62.

25. Mark Noll, *America's God: From Jonathan Edwards to Abraham Lincoln* (New York: Oxford University Press, 2002), 373, italics added for emphasis; also see Conrad Wright, *The Beginnings of Unitarianism in America* (Boston: Beacon, 1955), 187, 194, 209. More generally, see Mark Noll, "Evangelicals, Creation, and Scripture: An Overview," BioLogos Foundation paper, presented at "In Search of a Theology of Celebration," Harvard Club, New York City, 2009, http://biologos.org/uploads/projects/Noll_scholarly_essay.pdf.

26. Noll, *America's God*, 140.

27. D. H. Williams, *Evangelicals and Tradition: The Formative Influence of the Early Church* (Grand Rapids: Baker Academic, 2005), 98.

28. Thomas Worcester, *Divine Testimony Received without Any Addition or Diminution* (Hanover, NH: Charles Spear, 1813).

29. Charles Beecher, *The Bible a Sufficient Creed* (Boston: Himes, 1850), 24, 26.

30. Roger Lundin, "Interpreting Orphans: Hermeneutics in the Cartesian Tradition," in *The Promise of Hermeneutics*, ed. Roger Lundin, Clarence Walhout, and Anthony Thiselton (Grand Rapids: Eerdmans, 1999), 34–35; also see John Franke, "Scripture, Tradition, and Authority: Reconstructing the Evangelical Conception of Sola Scriptura," in *Evangelicals and Scripture: Tradition, Authority, and Hermeneutics*, ed. Vincent Bacote, Laura Miguélez, and Dennis Okholm (Downers Grove, IL: InterVarsity, 2004), 192–210.

31. Reprinted in 2003 by Eerdmans.

32. Jim Wallis, *Agenda for Biblical People* (1976; repr., New York: Harpercollins, 1984); Stephen Mott, *Biblical Ethics and Social Change* (New York: Oxford University Press, 1982); James Skillen and Rockne McCarthy, eds., *Political Order and the Plural Structure of Society* (Grand Rapids: Eerdmans, 1991); also see James Skillen, *In Pursuit of Justice: Christian-Democratic Explorations* (Lanham, MD: Rowman and Littlefield, 2004); R. J. Rushdoony, *The Institutes of Biblical Law* (Nutley, NJ: Craig, 1973); Gary North and Gary DeMar, *Christian Reconstructionism* (Tyler, TX: Institute for Christian Economics, 1991); Gary DeMar, *The Debate over Christian Reconstruction* (Atlanta, GA: American Vision Press, 1988); Greg Bahnsen, *Theonomy in Christian Ethics* (1977; repr., Nacogdoches, TX: Covenant Media, 2002); Greg Bahnsen, *By This Standard: The Authority of God's Law Today* (Tyler, TX: Institute for Christian Economics, 1991). Also see David Gushee, *The Future of Faith in American Politics* (Waco: Baylor University Press, 2008).

33. See Carlos Bovell, *Inerrancy and the Spiritual Formation of Younger Evangelicals* (Eugene, OR: Wipf and Stock, 2007); Bovell, *By Good and Necessary Consequence*, 126–37. Also see Scot McKnight and Hauna Ondrey, *Finding Faith, Losing Faith: Stories of Conversion and Apostasy* (Waco: Baylor University Press, 2008).

34. Goldingay, *Models for Scripture*, 278.

35. Peter Enns, *Inspiration and Incarnation: Evangelicals and the Problem of the Old Testament* (Grand Rapids: Baker Academic, 2005), 172.

## Chapter 5 The Christocentric Hermeneutical Key

1. Joseph Lienhard, *The Bible, the Church, and Authority: The Canon and the Christian Bible in History and Theology* (Collegeville, MN: Michael Glazier, 1995), 80.

2. This term is Peter Enns's, which he prefers because he thinks it conveys a clear sense that scripture is always approached from the start with Christ as the end in mind. Enns, *Inspiration and Incarnation: Evangelicals and the Problem of the Old Testament* (Grand Rapids: Baker Academic, 2005), 154–55. For present purposes, I am treating these three terms as interchangeable, even though conceptually they are not identical.

3. Quoted in Donald Bloesch, *Holy Scripture: Revelation, Inspiration, and Interpretation* (Downers Grove, IL: InterVarsity, 1994), 171. Spurgeon also rightly pressed out this Christocentric belief in preaching, insisting, "That sermon which does not lead to Christ, or of which Jesus Christ is not the top and the bottom, is a sort of sermon that will make the devils in hell to laugh, but might make the angel of God to weep, if they were capable of such emotion. . . . This is the way to preach. From every little village in England—it does not matter where it is—there is sure to be a road to London. Though there may not be a road to certain other places, there is certain to be a road to London. Now, from every text in the Bible there is a road to Jesus Christ, and the way to preach is just to say, 'How can I get from this text to Jesus Christ?' and then go preaching all the way along it. . . . Suppose I find a text that has not got a road to Jesus Christ? . . . I will go over hedge and ditch but what I will get to him, for I will never finish without bringing in my Master. . . . You must not think of reading [Scripture] without feeling that he is there who is Lord and Master of everything that you are reading, and who shall make these things precious to you if you realize him in them. If you do not find Jesus in the Scriptures they will be of small service to you." Spurgeon, Sermon #1503, delivered at the Metropolitan Tabernacle, Newington (London), England, 1879.

4. Keith Ward, *What the Bible Really Teaches: A Challenge for Fundamentalists* (London: SPCK, 2004), 27.

5. Dietrich Bonhoeffer, *No Rusty Swords* (London: Fontana, 1970), 312.

6. John Webster, *Holy Scripture: A Dogmatic Sketch* (Cambridge: Cambridge University Press, 2003), 12.

7. Ibid., 12.

8. Which Merold Westphal correctly notes is a backfiring strategy in any case, since "The quest for certainty is the mother of skepticism." Merold Westphal, "Post-Kantian Reflections on the Importance of Hermeneutics," in *Disciplining Hermeneutics: Interpretation in Christian Perspective*, ed. Roger Lundin (Grand Rapids: Eerdmans, 1997), 61.

9. Webster, *Holy Scripture*, 13, 16.

10. Ibid., 16–17.

11. Enns, *Inspiration and Incarnation*, 110. Again, Enns writes about the Old Testament: "There is a coherence between the parts, but that coherence transcends the level of simple statements or propositions. It is to be found precisely in the unfolding drama of Israel and the world, where the nature of Israel's relationship to the Gentiles develops over time. . . . We must step back and view the big picture" (96–97).

12. This approach seems very closely related to that of the current movement for a "theological interpretation of scripture." See Daniel J. Treier, *Introducing Theological Interpretation of Scripture: Recovering a Christian Practice* (Grand Rapids: Baker Academic, 2008); also see John Goldingay, *Models for Scripture* (Toronto: Clements, 1994), 21–82.

13. John Stott, *Understanding the Bible* (Grand Rapids: Zondervan, 1999), 14. Elsewhere, Stott approvingly quotes the Anglican archbishop Christopher Chavasee in saying, "The Bible . . . is the portrait of our Lord Jesus Christ. The Gospels are the Figure itself in the portrait. The Old Testament is the background, leading up to the divine Figure, pointing toward it, and absolutely necessary for the composition as a whole. The Epistles serve as the dress and accoutrements of the Figure, explaining and describing it. . . . And, stepping from the canvas of the written word, the everlasting Christ of the Emmaus Story becomes Himself our Bible teacher to interpret to us in all the Scriptures the things concerning Himself." Stott, *Christ the Controversialist* (Downers Grove, IL: InterVarsity Press, 1972), 104.

14. Stott, *Understanding the Bible*, 16, 18–19, 20.

15. Ibid., 28.

16. G. C. Berkouwer, *Holy Scripture* (Grand Rapids: Eerdmans, 1975), 123, 125, 126. Another Reformed thinker, J. Gresham Machen, who many associate with biblicist Reformed fundamentalism, actually insisted on this Christocentric point: "Almost nineteen hundred years ago, outside the walls of Jerusalem, the eternal Son was offered as a sacrifice for the sins of men. To that one great event the whole Old Testament looks forward, and in that one event the whole of the New Testament finds its center and core. . . . Christianity depends, not upon a complex of ideas, but upon the narration of [that] event." Unfortunately, however, Machen then draws this misguided conclusion: "Christianity is founded upon the Bible" (J. Gresham Machen, *Christianity and Liberalism* [Grand Rapids: Eerdmans, 1923], 70, 79). In fact, Christianity is founded upon Christ, to whom the Bible is a witness.

17. Berkouwer, *Holy Scripture*, 165, 166, 178.

18. Ibid., 180.

19. Ibid., 179, 184, italics added for emphasis.

20. Ibid., 166, 179, italics added for emphasis.

21. Geoffrey Bromiley, *The Unity and Disunity of the Church* (Grand Rapids: Eerdmans, 1958), 69–71.

22. Donald Bloesch, *Holy Scripture: Revelation, Inspiration, and Interpretation* (Downers Grove, IL: InterVarsity, 1994), 37–38.

23. Ibid., 38, 39.

24. Ibid., 180, 181–82, 194.

25. Ibid., 193. Luther, quoted in Timothy George, *Theology of the Reformers* (Nashville: Broadman, 1988), 83, 193. Richard Muller also points out that Luther was firmly Christocentric about scripture, including in his view of what even belonged in scripture, citing Luther's remarks in his "Preface to the Epistles of St. James and St. Jude": "All the genuine sacred books agree in this, that all of them preach and inculcate Christ. And that is the true test by which to judge all books, when we see whether or not they inculcate Christ. For all the Scriptures show us Christ, Romans 3[:21]; and St. Paul will know nothing but Christ, 1 Cor. 2[:2]. Whatever does not teach Christ is not apostolic, even though St. Peter or St. Paul does the teaching. Again, whatever preaches Christ would be apostolic, even if Judas, Annas, Pilate and Herod were doing it." Richard Muller, *Post-Reformation Reformed Dogmatics*, Vol. 2, *Holy Scripture: The Cognitive Foundation* (Grand Rapids: Baker Academic, 1993), 213. Nevertheless, Muller cautions, "the Reformation era christocentrism that identified Christ as the *scopus Scripturae* never intended that Christ be understood as the interpretive principle of *all* points of doctrine, the heuristic key to the *entire* range or extent of doctrinal meaning. . . . [It] simply placed Christ at the doctrinal center of Scripture and, therefore, at the doctrinal and specifically soteriological center of Christian theology" (218, italics added for emphasis). If so, then the Christocentric approach advanced here carries the Reformation principle even further than some of the Reformers did.

26. Luther, quoted in R. Newton Flew and Rupert Davies, *The Catholicity of Protestantism* (London: Lutterworth, 1951), 118–19, 120.

27. Kevin Vanhoozer, *The Drama of Doctrine: A Canonical Linguistic Approach to Christian Theology* (Louisville: Westminster John Knox, 2005), 46.

28. Ibid., 195, 249. This christological hermeneutic Vanhoozer extends to all of life and history: "The focus of divine action is the history of Jesus Christ. The history of Jesus is thus the hermeneutical key not only of the history of Israel but to the history of the whole world, and hence to the meaning of life" (223).

29. The last quote comes from Kevin Vanhoozer, "A Response to William J. Webb," in *Four Views of Moving Beyond the Bible to Theology*, ed. Stanley Gundry and Gary Meadors (Grand Rapids: Zondervan, 2009), 267.

30. Vanhoozer, *Drama of Doctrine*, 297.

31. D. H. Williamson, *Evangelicals and Tradition: The Formative Influence of the Early Church* (Grand Rapids: Baker Academic, 2005), 155; Treier, *Introducing Theological Interpretation of Scripture*, 57–63.

32. John Barton, *People of the Book? The Authority of the Bible in Christianity* (Louisville: Westminster John Knox, 1988), 30–31, italics in original. Also see Joseph Lienhard, *The Bible, the Church, and Authority: The Canon and the Christian Bible in History and Theology* (Collegeville, MN: Michael Glazier, 1995), 95–100.

33. Paul Gavrilyuk, "Scripture and the *Regula Fidei*: Two Interlocking Components of the Canonical Heritage," in *Canonical Theism: A Proposal for Theology and the Church*, ed. William Abraham, Jason Vickers, and Natalie Van Kirk (Grand Rapids: Eerdmans, 2008), 27–42.

34. Craig Allert, *A High View of Scripture? The Authority of the Bible and the Formation of the New Testament Canon* (Grand Rapids: Baker Academic, 2007), 54–55, 79–80, 82–84, 121–26.

35. John Armstrong, "Introduction: Two Vital Truths," in *The Coming Evangelical Crisis: Current Challenges to the Authority of Scripture and the Gospel*, ed. John Armstrong (Chicago: Moody, 1996), 23. However, much of the rest of Armstrong's book does not stay consistently with this Christocentric focus but, as so often happens, shifts into what I have called a "handbook model" of the Bible.

36. J. I. Packer and Thomas Oden, *One Faith: The Evangelical Consensus* (Downers Grove, IL: InterVarsity, 2004), 17.

37. At the same time, many evangelical denominational statements of faith say nothing about Jesus Christ in their beliefs about the Bible. The Presbyterian Church in America's "What We Believe" statement on the Bible, for instance, states only this: "We believe the Bible is the written word of God, inspired by the Holy Spirit and without error in the original manuscripts. The Bible is the revelation of God's truth and is infallible and authoritative in all matters of faith and practice." The Evangelical Free Church's "Statement of Faith" says only the following: "We believe that God has spoken in the Scriptures, both Old and New Testaments, through the words of human authors. As the verbally inspired Word of God, the Bible is without error in the original writings, the complete revelation of His will for salvation, and the ultimate authority by which every realm of human knowledge and endeavor should be judged. Therefore, it is to be believed in all that it teaches, obeyed in all that it requires, and trusted in all that it promises." The Church of the Nazarene "Articles of Faith" state simply that, "We believe in the plenary inspiration of the Holy Scriptures, by which we understand the 66 books of the Old and New Testaments, given by divine inspiration, inerrantly revealing the will of God concerning us in all things necessary to our salvation, so that whatever is not contained therein is not to be enjoined as an article of faith." And the Assemblies of God document, "Our 16 Fundamental Truths," says of the Bible merely that "The Scriptures, both the Old and New Testaments, are verbally inspired of God and are the revelation of God to man, the infallible, authoritative rule of faith and conduct." Clearly, the priorities in these and many other similar evangelical statements on the Bible are divine inspiration, inerrancy, and Bible-only authority for belief and practice—Jesus Christ, unfortunately, is nowhere to be found in such doctrinal statements about the Bible.

38. Vern Poythress, *Symphonic Theology: The Validity of Multiple Perspectives in Theology* (1987; repr., Phillipsburg, NJ: P&R, 2001), all quotations in this paragraph are from page 18.

39. Ibid., italics added for emphasis.

40. Goldingay, *Models for Scripture*, 78.

41. Enns, *Inspiration and Incarnation*, 67. Elsewhere Enns writes, "The primary purpose of Scripture is for the church to eat and drink its contents in order to understand better who God is, and what he has done, and what it means to be his people, redeemed in the crucified and risen son" (170).

42. G. K. Beale, *The Erosion of Inerrancy in Evangelicalism: Responding to New Challenges to Biblical Authority* (Wheaton: Crossway, 2008), 220. The related objection in the inerrancy debate, furthermore, asserts that "If even only one error can be found in scripture, then the truthfulness and reliability of the entire Bible is destroyed," which I also think is untrue, or, rather, only true within a particular presupposed theory of inspiration, language, truth, error, and so on, which we should not presuppose—but inerrancy is not really the issue I am addressing here. See Goldingay, *Models for Scripture*, 280.

43. That no doubt also unintentionally helps to promote the Moralistic Therapeutic Deism that I describe in my books *Soul Searching: The Religious and Spiritual Lives of*

*American Teenagers* (New York: Oxford University Press, 2005), 118–71; and *Souls in Transition: The Religious and Spiritual Lives of American Young Adults* (New York: Oxford University Press, 2009), 154–56.

44. John Goldingay, *Models for the Interpretation of Scripture* (Grand Rapids: Eerdmans, 1995), 10.

45. Barton, *People of the Book?* 26.

46. Enns, *Inspiration and Incarnation*, 170.

47. C. S. Lewis, *Letters of C. S. Lewis* (Harvest Books, 2003), 247.

48. Ignatius, "Philadelphians 8," in *Early Christian Writings: The Apostolic Fathers*, trans. M. Stanifort (London: Penguin, 1987), 95.

49. Jeffrey McSwain, "Jesus Is the Gospel" (2007), unpublished paper.

50. Matthew 24:35 notwithstanding, since "my words" and the Bible are not identical.

51. James Barr, "Bibelkritik als Theologische Aufklärung," in *Glaube und Toleranz: Das Theologische Erbe der Aufklärung*, ed. T. Rendtorff (Gütersloh: Gütersloher Verlagshaus G. Mohn, 1982), 41, quoted in Barton, *People of the Book?* 33–34. Also see Donald Bloesch, *Holy Scripture*, 25–28, 127–29, 204; Donald Bloesch, *The Ground of Certainty* (Grand Rapids: Eerdmans, 1971), 74.

52. John Webster, *Holy Scripture: A Dogmatic Sketch* (Cambridge: Cambridge University Press, 2003), 36, italics added for emphasis.

53. Allert, *A High View of Scripture?* 145.

54. In N. T. Wright's words, the issue is not so much "the authority of Scripture" but rather "the authority of God exercised *through* Scripture." Wright, *The Last Word: Beyond the Bible Wars to a New Understanding of the Authority of Scripture* (San Francisco: HarperSanFrancisco, 2005), 23–25.

55. George Marsden, *Fundamentalism and American Culture* (New York: Oxford University Press, 2006); also note the kind of reactions to events at Fuller Seminary, documented in George Marsden, *Reforming Fundamentalism: Fuller Seminary and the New Evangelicalism* (Grand Rapids: Eerdmans, 1995). Also see Doug Frank, *Less than Conquerors: How Evangelicals Entered the Twentieth Century* (Grand Rapids: Eerdmans, 1986).

56. Mark Noll, *Between Faith and Criticism: Evangelicals, Scholarship, and the Bible in America* (Vancouver: Regent College Publishing, 2004), 92. See Gary Dorrien, *The Remaking of Evangelical Theology* (Louisville: Westminster John Knox, 1998), 107–10, 113, 126.

57. Cornelius Van Til, *The New Modernism: An Appraisal of the Theology of Barth and Brunner* (Phillipsburg, NJ: P&R, 1946). For a full history, see Phillip Thorne, *Evangelicalism and Karl Barth: His Reception and Influence in North American Evangelical Theology* (Allison Park, PA: Pickwick, 1995).

58. A comprehensive list that fits this description would be very long, but two examples are Vern Poythress, *Symphonic Theology: The Validity of Multiple Perspectives in Theology* (1987; repr., Phillipsburg, NJ: P&R, 2001), 72–74; and G. K. Beale, *The Erosion of Inerrancy in Evangelicalism: Responding to New Challenges to Biblical Authority* (Wheaton: Crossway, 2008), 281–83.

59. One among many examples is Richard Gaffin, "Biblical Theology and the Westminster Standards," *Westminster Theological Journal* 65 (2003): 168–69.

60. Wheaton College's professor of theology, Daniel J. Treier, names Barth as the key Protestant catalyst for the renewed current movement for a "theological interpretation of scripture" (*Introducing Theological Interpretation of Scripture: Recovering a Christian Practice* [Grand Rapids: Baker Academic, 2008], 14–20).

61. Bloesch rightly notes: "Plenary inspiration means that all of Scripture is inspired. It does not imply that all of Scripture has equal value. . . . I oppose a 'flat view of Scripture' that does not make a distinction between what is essential and what is marginal, what is in the foreground and what is background material." Donald Bloesch, *Holy Scripture: Revelation, Inspiration, and Interpretation* (Downers Grove, IL: InterVarsity, 1994), 121.

62. Thomas F. Torrance, *Reality and Evangelical Theology* (1981; repr., Eugene, OR: Wipf and Stock, 2003), 17, 18.

63. The best starting points for learning Barth, besides *Church Dogmatics*, is Eberhard Busch, *The Great Passion: An Introduction to Karl Barth's Theology* (Grand Rapids: Eerdmans, 2004); George Hunsinger, *How to Read Karl Barth* (New York: Oxford University Press, 1990); John Webster, *The Cambridge Companion to Karl Barth* (Cambridge: Cambridge University Press, 2000); Eberhard Busch, *Karl Barth: His Life from Letters and Autobiographical Texts* (Eugene, OR: Wipf and Stock, 2005); also see Bruce McCormack, "The Being of Holy Scripture Is in Becoming: Karl Barth in Conversation with American Evangelical Criticism," in *Evangelicals and Scripture: Tradition, Authority, and Hermeneutics*, ed. Vincent Bacote, Laura Miguélez, and Dennis Okholm (Downers Grove, IL: InterVarsity, 2004), 55–75. For a neo-Barthian view of scripture, see John Webster, *Holy Scripture: A Dogmatic Sketch* (Cambridge: Cambridge University Press, 2003), esp. 5–41.

## Chapter 6 Accepting Complexity and Ambiguity

1. Peter Enns, *Inspiration and Incarnation: Evangelicals and the Problem of the Old Testament* (Grand Rapids: Baker Academic, 2005), 108.

2. John Goldingay, *Models for Scripture* (Toronto: Clements, 1994), 274.

3. Enns, *Inspiration and Incarnation*, 15, 169.

4. Gordon Fee, "Hermeneutics and the Gender Debate," in *Discovering Biblical Equality: Complementarity without Hierarchy*, ed. Ronald Pierce, Rebecca Groothuis, and Gordon Fee (Downers Grove, IL: InterVarsity, 2005), 370.

5. The following draws heavily from Kenton Sparks's work on accommodation, in Sparks, *God's Word in Human Words: An Evangelical Appropriation of Critical Biblical Scholarship* (Grand Rapids: Baker Academic, 2008), 229–59; Sparks, "The Sun Also Rises: Accommodation in Inscripturation and Interpretation," in *Evangelicals and Scripture*, ed. Bacote, Miguélez, and Okholm, 112–32. Also see G. C. Berkouwer, *Holy Scripture* (Grand Rapids: Eerdmans, 1975), 174–78; Jon Balserak, *Divinity Compromised: A Study of Divine Accommodation in the Thought of John Calvin* (Dordrecht: Springer, 2006); Ford Lewis Battles, "God Was Accommodating Himself to Human Capacity," *Interpretation* 31 (1977): 19–38.

6. Michael Tinker, "John Calvin's Concept of Divine Accommodation," *Churchman* 118, no. 4 (2004): 332–33.

7. Sparks, *God's Word in Human Words*; Nick Wolterstorff, *Divine Discourse: Philosophical Reflections on the Claim That God Speaks* (Cambridge: Cambridge University Press, 1995); Enns, *Inspiration and Incarnation*, 56, 109, 132.

8. D. A. Carson, *The Gagging of God* (Grand Rapids: Zondervan, 1996), 130. I should note, however, that while I quote Carson here, I do not believe that he would endorse my larger argument in this book.

9. Augustine, *On Christian Teaching* (Oxford: Oxford University Press, 1999), 32–33 (originally published circa AD 395–97).

10. Brian Brock, *Singing the Ethos of God: On the Place of Christian Ethics in Scripture* (Grand Rapids: Eerdmans, 2007), 168–69.

11. John Barton, *People of the Book? The Authority of the Bible in Christianity* (Louisville: Westminster John Knox, 1988), 85.

12. Keith Ward, *What the Bible Really Teaches: A Challenge for Fundamentalists* (London: Society for the Promotion of Christian Knowledge, 2004), 25.

13. G. C. Berkouwer, *Holy Scripture* (Grand Rapids: Eerdmans, 1975), 275.

14. Craig Allert, *A High View of Scripture? The Authority of the Bible and the Formation of the New Testament Canon* (Grand Rapids: Baker Academic, 2007), 162.

15. Vern Poythress, *Symphonic Theology: The Validity of Multiple Perspectives in Theology* (1987; repr., Phillipsburg, NJ: P&R, 2001), 9–21, 43, italics added for emphasis.

16. In the second century, a Syrian Christian named Tatian actually proposed replacing the four Gospels of the New Testament with a single, harmonized gospel that he composed, named the Diatessaron—a proposal that was firmly rejected by the church, even though the Christian church in Syria read this book for more than two centuries. At issue in the West were both Tatian's orthodoxy and a right-minded shying away from harmonizations. Joseph Lienhard, *The Bible, the Church, and Authority: The Canon and the Christian Bible in History and Theology* (Collegeville, MN: Michael Glazier, 1995), 34–35.

17. Roger E. Olson, *Reformed and Always Reforming* (Grand Rapids: Baker Academic, 2007), 95–98; also see Michael Meiring, "Toward a Biblical Unity," in *Preserving Evangelical Unity*, ed. Michael Meiring (Eugene, OR: Wipf and Stock, 2009), 11–25; Rob Warner, "Disagreement and Evangelical Unity," in *Together We Stand*, ed. Clive Calver and Rob Warner (London: Hodder and Stoughton, 1996), 139–50.

18. Double predestination as a particular way of reading Augustine was explicitly condemned by the Council of Orange in 529.

19. See Brad Gregory, *Salvation at Stake: Christian Martyrdom in Early Modern Europe* (Cambridge, MA: Harvard University Press, 1999).

20. See, e.g., http://www.gospelway.com/salvation/baptism_action.php.

21. Peter Enns, *Inspiration and Incarnation: Evangelicals and the Problem of the Old Testament* (Grand Rapids: Baker Academic, 2005), 170.

22. Thanks to Douglas Campbell for first suggesting to me this "need to know" language as related to what is and is not in the Bible.

23. Christian Smith, Michael Emerson, and Patricia Snell, *Passing the Plate: Why American Christians Do Not Give Away More Money* (New York: Oxford University Press, 2008).

24. Mark Noll, *The Scandal of the Evangelical Mind* (Grand Rapids: Eerdmans, 1995).

25. Augustine, *Sermons* 52.16 (PL 38:360). Many translations of the New Testament Greek word *mysterion* (e.g., Rom. 11:25; 16:25; 1 Cor. 15:51–52; Eph. 1:9–10; 3:1–9; 5:25–33; 6:19; Col. 1:25–27; 2:2–3; 4:3; 1 Tim. 3:16; Rev. 1:20; 10:7; 17:5, 7) render the word in English as "mystery," when the better meaning for contemporary English speakers would be something like "revealed secret"—so those are different matters than what I speak of in this section. Thanks to Douglas Campbell for pointing out this distinction to me.

26. See Andrew Louth, *Discerning the Mystery: An Essay on the Nature of Theology* (Oxford: Clarendon, 1990); William Placher, *The Domestication of Transcendence* (Louisville: Westminster John Knox, 1996).

27. Richard Hooker, *Of the Laws of Ecclesiastical Polity*, Book II (1594; repr. London: J. M. Dent, 1964), 8.

## Chapter 7  Rethinking Human Knowledge, Authority, and Understanding

1. The literature on critical realism is vast, though still largely unknown in American church circles. For starters, see Christian Smith, *What Is a Person? Rethinking Humanity, Social Life, and the Moral Good from the Person Up* (Chicago: University of Chicago Press, 2010), and the many references therein.

2. "Alethic" comes from the Greek *aletheia*, meaning "truth." Regarding the particular alethic theory of truth to which I refer, see William Alston, *A Realist Conception of Truth* (Ithaca, NY: Cornell University Press), 1996; Smith, *What Is a Person?* 207–19.

3. "The modern dispute [over inspiration] is just that—modern. The Fathers of the Church made many incidental comments about inspiration, but never reflected on it as such, and certainly never wrote books about it. . . . Theological speculation on inspiration, among both Protestants and Catholics, began only after the first waves of the Reformation and Counter-Reformation." Joseph Lienhard, *The Bible, the Church, and Authority: The Canon and the Christian Bible in History and Theology* (Collegeville, MN: Michael Glazier, 1995), 79.

4. But see Paul Seely, *Inerrant Wisdom: Science and Inerrancy in Biblical Perspective* (Portland, OR: Evangelical Reform, 1989).

5. More thoughtful versions are then forced to qualify the argument by acknowledging having to take into account "ancient thought forms," etc., but the more serious those qualifications become, the more they undermine and compromise the original logic. Note that, according to Greene-McCreight's study of Augustine, Calvin, and Barth's reading of Genesis 1–3, "the pursuit of the text's 'plain sense' did not imply belief in 'single meaning' according to the modern sense of that concept: 'One cannot conclude that the plain sense of scripture is an objective, static "given" to be mined from the text like a diamond from the river bed.'" Kathryn Greene-McCreight, *Ad Litteram: How Augustine, Calvin, and Barth Read the "Plain Sense" of Genesis 1–3* (New York: Peter Lang, 1999), 243, quoted in Treier, *Introducing Theological Interpretation of Scripture*, 60.

6. Goldingay, *Models for Scripture*, 10.

7. Interpreters who want to use this passage to establish the supremacy of scriptural authority have to (but usually do not) grapple with the fact that it more broadly argues that the teachings of *other reliable people*, including Timothy's mother and grandmother (1:5) "from infancy" (3:15), and Paul (3:14), in whom Timothy rightly places confidence, do and should function as authority for Timothy.

8. See, e.g., H. Y. Gamble, *The New Testament Canon: Its Making and Meaning* (Philadelphia: Fortress, 1985); L. M. McDonald, *The Formation of the Christian Biblical Canon* (Peabody, MA: Hendrickson, 1995); Bruce Metzger, *The Canon of the New Testament: Its Origins, Development, and Significance* (Oxford: Clarendon, 1987); John Barton, *Holy Writings, Sacred Text: The Canon in Early Christianity* (Louisville: Westminster John Knox, 1997); Hans von Campenhausen, *The Formation of the Christian Bible* (Philadelphia: Fortress, 1972).

9. Craig Allert provides an excellent review of the relevant issues in *A High View of Scripture? The Authority of the Bible and the Formation of the New Testament Canon* (Grand Rapids: Baker Academic, 2007), 37–145.

10. See Peter Fritzsche, *Stranded in the Present: Modern Times and the Melancholy of History* (Cambridge, MA: Harvard University Press, 2004).

11. See, e.g., D. H. Williams, *Evangelicals and Tradition: The Formative Influence of the Early Church* (Grand Rapids: Baker Academic, 2005); Bryan Litfin, *Getting to Know the*

*Church Fathers* (Grand Rapids: Brazos, 2007); Robert Webber, *Ancient-Future Faith* (Grand Rapids: Baker Academic, 1999); D. H. Williams, *Retrieving the Tradition and Renewing Evangelicalism: A Primer for Suspicious Protestants* (Grand Rapids: Eerdmans, 1999); D. H. Williams, *Tradition, Scripture, and Interpretation: A Sourcebook of the Ancient Church* (Grand Rapids: Baker Academic, 2006); Ronald Heine, *Reading the Old Testament with the Ancient Church: Exploring the Formation of Early Christian Thought* (Grand Rapids: Baker Academic, 2007); Christopher Hall, *Reading Scripture with the Church Fathers* (Downers Grove, IL: InterVarsity, 1998); James Custinger, ed., *Reclaiming the Great Tradition: Evangelicals, Catholics, and Orthodox in Dialogue* (Downers Grove, IL: InterVarsity, 1997); William Abraham, Jason Vickers, and Natalie Van Kirk, eds., *Canonical Theism: A Proposal for Theology and the Church* (Grand Rapids: Eerdmans, 2008).

12. Enns, *Inspiration and Incarnation*, 169.

13. See George Marsden, *Reforming Fundamentalism: Fuller Seminary and the New Evangelicalism* (Grand Rapids: Eerdmans, 1987), 97–116. Vassady was a Hungarian evangelical theologian of international renown and unimpeachable credentials hired by Fuller Theological Seminary in 1949, only in great controversy to be dismissed soon thereafter as a result of intense pressures put on Fuller by a constituency of strict conservative evangelicals.

14. Here I draw on and slightly adjust J. L. Austin's landmark book on speech-act theory, *How to Do Things with Words* (Oxford: Clarendon, 1962). Nick Wolterstorff makes much of Austin's distinctions in his book, *Divine Discourse: Philosophical Reflections on the Claim that God Speaks* (Cambridge: Cambridge University Press, 1985), which I find helpful for thinking through present concerns, even though I do not necessarily accept all of Wolterstorff's conclusions. Concerning the latter, see, e.g., I. Howard Marshall, "'To Find Out What God Is Saying': Reflections on the Authority of Scripture," in *Disciplining Hermeneutics: Interpretation in Christian Perspective*, ed. Roger Lundin (Grand Rapids: Eerdmans, 1997), 49–55.

15. Donald Bloesch, *Holy Scripture: Revelation, Inspiration, and Interpretation* (Downers Grove, IL: InterVarsity, 1994), 127–28.

16. Some of the *clauses* that go into making up promises certainly may entail error, though. For instance, if I were to make you the promise, "If you read this entire book I will give you the million-dollar house that I own," that promise *as a promise* would only be empty, not in error; yet the clause "million-dollar house that I own" in the promise would be a factual aspect of it that *would* in fact be in error, since I do not own a house of such value.

17. To be clear, I am not here somehow recommending the jettisoning of propositionally formulated truth claims, which are indispensable in human knowledge systems. Evangelicals notably overemphasize theology as biblical propositions, but that itself does not make propositions from or about the Bible useless or illegitimate. As noted above, the *person* of Jesus Christ is of supreme importance, more so than propositions *about* him. But even persons, including Christ, cannot finally be really known or understood apart from some truthful propositional descriptions and representations of them. Whatever else changes in a postbiblicist world, in short, propositions stay and maintain their rightful, though limited, place.

18. See Barton, *People of the Book?* 74.

19. Max Weber, *The Theory of Social and Economic Organization* (New York: Free Press, 1964), 152.

20. Colin Campbell, "Distinguishing Power of Agency from Agentic Power: A Note on Weber and the 'Black Box' of Personal Agency," *Sociological Theory* 27, no. 4 (2009): 407–18, esp. 409; Anthony Giddens, *New Rules of Sociological Method* (London: Hutchinson,

1976), 110; Talcott Parson and Neil Smelser, *Economy and Society* (Glencoe, IL: Free Press, 1955), 181.

21. This approach may comport with Walter Brueggemann's "compost pile" metaphor for biblical authority (as providing material for new life) in his book *Texts under Negotiation* (Minneapolis: Augsburg Fortress, 1993); and perhaps with N. T. Wright's "five-act play" image in his article, "How Can the Bible Be Authoritative?" *Vox Evangelica* 21 (1991): 7–32.

22. Having said this, I do think it is possible to begin with a number of traditional statements about biblical authority without either falling into the biblicist trap or heading down avenues that generate pervasive interpretive pluralism. Many Christians, for example, find helpful the idea that scripture is the "norming norm." A norm is that by which something else is measured, evaluated, and perhaps corrected. Many authorities in life and the church, not only the Bible, can and do function as norms. But, in this view, the Bible—again, read Christocentrically—entails an authority over other norms, by which they are to be evaluated and perhaps revised when necessary. A postbiblicist evangelical can and ought to be able to affirm that idea.

23. We know that the apostle Paul wrote other letters that were lost, which we do not possess, yet that were likely treated in some early churches as "scriptural" before they were lost, and that perhaps were divinely inspired; if, hypothetically, one or more of them were to be discovered today, that would raise interesting questions about the possibility of adding them to the biblical canon.

24. I draw here particularly on the approach of William Webb, *Slaves, Women, and Homosexuals: Exploring the Hermeneutics of Cultural Analysis* (Downers Grove, IL: InterVarsity, 2001); also see a similar approach modeled in Gilbert Bilezikian, *Beyond Sex Roles*, 2nd ed. (Grand Rapids: Baker Academic, 2006); Enns, *Inspiration and Incarnation*, 85–97, 107–11.

25. For a similar argument, see Kenton Sparks, *God's Word in Human Words: An Evangelical Appropriation of Critical Biblical Scholarship* (Grand Rapids: Baker Academic, 2008), 289–93.

26. See David Bentley Hart, *Atheist Delusions: The Christian Revolution and Its Fashionable Enemies* (New Haven: Yale University Press, 2009); Christopher Dawson, *Religion and the Rise of Western Culture* (Garden City, NY: Image Books, 1991); also see, with some caution, Rodney Stark, *The Victory of Reason: How Christianity Led to Freedom, Capitalism, and Western Success* (New York: Random House, 2006); Rodney Stark, *The One True God: Historical Consequences of Monotheism* (Princeton: Princeton University Press, 2003).

27. Following this point, I am tempted to include among my proposals in this chapter the idea of progressive revelation within scripture. However, enough reservations present themselves about this idea that I opt not to actively suggest it here. Still, because the issues involved are significant enough and at least some evangelical biblical scholars are friendly to the idea, a review is perhaps warranted. Had I chosen to propose the idea of progressive revelation in scripture in the main body of this chapter, it would sound something like the following, stated in the form of a proposal argued with conviction: *Recognize that scripture itself reflects a progressive clarifying, sharpening, and intensifying of God's purposes in human history and must be read with that progressive or teleological frame in mind.* This insight about theological and moral development in scripture would require an entire book to explore and understand well. Here I will be able to suggest only the basic idea for present purposes. To do so, I will focus on two points of illustration. The first, which is obvious, is God's progressive unfolding in history of his plan of redemption. The

second concerns the morality of marriage relationships. These are not the only two ways in which the progressive clarifying, sharpening, and intensifying of God's purposes in history are evident in scripture, but they suffice for now to make the point. Once we see the basic principle at work, we can extend our understanding of it in ways that might help address biblicism's problems, particularly pervasive interpretive pluralism.

God did not lay out his plan for the salvation of the world on the final day of creation or on the same day of the first sin. For innumerable years, millennia in fact, God slowly unfolded his redemptive intentions. In his original curse on sin, God (rather cryptically) promised to crush the serpent's head (Gen. 3:15). With Noah and Abraham, God established covenants of love, fidelity, and care—yet God also explained relatively little and only asked them to live in faith in his promises. Centuries upon centuries passed—with the lives of Isaac, Jacob, Joseph, Moses, Joshua, Saul, Boaz, David, Solomon, Josiah, Daniel, Isaiah, and many, many more, up until Mary and Joseph—as God gradually worked in history toward the decisive redemptive event of the incarnate coming of Jesus Christ. Along the way, God gave many promises, visions, and prophesies. Divine event by divine event, the picture of what was coming by way of salvation grew gradually less murky. Yet during most of the old covenant period, God's people had only a dim awareness of what was to come in Christ. Even during Jesus's own lifetime on earth, the disciples were often clueless about the larger significance of the person they were following. Not until Christ's resurrection and the coming of the Spirit at Pentecost did more of the fullness of God's redemptive plan become evident. Even so, there was and is much about salvation and its completion that the church in history—which sees only "a poor reflection as in a mirror" (1 Cor. 13:12)—still does not know or understand. Across much of the narrative of scripture, in short, the mystery of God's salvation in Jesus Christ had been hidden "for ages and generations" (Col. 1:26) and "for long ages past" (Rom. 16:25). It was only with the coming of Jesus that believers could "make plain to everyone the administration of this mystery, which for ages past was kept hidden in God," namely, "the unsearchable riches of Christ." With the coming of Christ, God's "intent was that now, through the church, the manifold wisdom of God should be made known" (Eph. 3:8–10). Consequently, what anyone today has to learn about salvation from the Bible must be conditioned by an understanding of any given scripture passage's particular place in this unfolding historical story. Not every biblical text is "equal" to every other in this regard. So, once again, the Bible cannot be read as a "flat" text. The discerning reader must perceive internal theological development within scripture. For this reason, Sparks argues, "It seems to me that if God does reveal himself to us in written, historically contingent textual installments, then the result will be progressive. That is, to say that revelation is progressive is merely to notice how revelation necessarily works" (Sparks, *God's Word in Human Words*, 246; also see Webb, *Slaves, Women, and Homosexuals*, 30–66; I. Howard Marshall, *Beyond the Bible: Moving from Scripture to Theology* [Grand Rapids: Baker Academic, 2004], 33–54; Walter Kaiser, "A Principlizing Model," in *Four Views of Moving Beyond the Bible to Theology*, ed. Stanley Gundry and Gary Meadors [Grand Rapids: Zondervan, 2009], 45–50). And, read evangelically, that progressive development always anticipates, references, and culminates in Jesus Christ.

The big picture of salvation history is not the only thing in the Bible reflecting an unfolding of revelation and understanding. Within that, God also works a more specific, progressively clarifying, sharpening, and intensifying process of (at least some) religious and moral teachings and expectations. Take marriage, for instance. Genesis 2:20–25 and Jesus's teachings on it (Matt. 19:4–6) seem to make clear that God originally intended marriage to be a lifelong monogamous relationship between a man and a woman. Sin introduced a distorting and damaging power into marriage, as with all relationships, unfortunately, producing shame, domination, unfaithfulness, polygamy, and divorce. In God's larger economy of salvation, however, God accommodated some of the destructive effects of sin, for a time, which were present in the cultures of his people. God, for instance, clearly allowed and tolerated men of his people having multiple wives and concubines (e.g., Gen. 32:22; Deut. 21:15; 2 Sam. 5:13; 2 Chron. 11:20–21). And Jesus acknowledged that "Moses permitted you to divorce your wives because your hearts were hard" (Matt. 19:8). Even so, God sometimes advised against multiple wives (e.g., Deut. 17:17) and condemned divorce (Mal. 2:16). In the course of time, however, in part through the natural workings of cultural evolution and partly through explicit teaching, God led his people back to the creation standard of marriage as faithful, lifelong monogamy between men and women. About this Jesus was clear (Matt. 5:31–32; 19:9), as were apostolic teachings (1 Cor. 7:10–13; Eph. 5:33; 1 Tim. 3:2, 12; Titus 1:6). In brief, what was morally acceptable for God's people regarding marriage varied and developed at different stages of salvation history. Any reading of scripture seeking to understand a Christian view of marriage must therefore take seriously those changes across time. Again, that means that the Bible cannot be read for moral instruction as a "flat" document containing a set of instructively equal pieces on various topics that readers simply need to fit together into a single, noncontradictory picture. God's leading his people along in moral development complicates the picture. Not, however, that I think it leads to a clear and rigid dispensationalism. It demands a more theologically sophisticated reading of the Bible that understands all of God's doings in history as leading to and pivoting on salvation in Jesus Christ. And that realization itself creates problems for the kind of simple biblicism described in chapter 1.

I, of course, am not the only Bible reader who has recognized this theological and moral development in scripture. It would be hard for any serious reader to ignore it. So, e.g., the evangelical biblical scholar Peter Enns has noted the developmentally dynamic nature of the law, morality, and theological understanding in the Old Testament: "God seems to be perfectly willing to allow his law to be adjusted over time. . . . Within the Old Testament there is a dynamic quality." And again, speaking of the early Israelites, Enns observes that "they were taking their first baby steps toward knowledge of God that later generations came to understand and we perhaps take for granted. [That was a specific] point in the process of redemption" (Enns, *Inspiration and Incarnation*, 87, 94, 102). Somewhat similarly, Keith Ward points to instances of "sublation" in scripture (the etymology of which is Latin, *sublatus*, the past participle of *tollere*, to take away, lift up; from *sub*- up + *latus*, past participle of *ferre*, to carry), in which something taught prior is later negated and fulfilled at the same time. Jesus, e.g., says, "Do not think that I have come to abolish the Law or the Prophets; I have come not to abolish them but to fulfill them" (Matt. 5:17). Thus, "eye for eye and tooth for tooth" is in time fulfilled and displaced by "do not resist an evil person" (Matt. 5:38–39). Likewise, the hatred of those who hate God in Ps. 139:21–22 is in time sublated by Jesus's command to love our enemies (Matt. 5:43). Ward observes, "The Law has been negated in its obvious sense, but only because its inner meaning has been fulfilled by a 'higher law.' That is what sublation is, cancelling an obvious or literal meaning by discovering a deeper spiritual meaning that can be seen to be the fulfillment to which the literal meaning points." And so what then are the implications of this recognition? According to Ward, for starters, "we must be very cautious when we claim, 'The Bible says . . .'" (Ward, *What the Bible Really Teaches*, 23).

Beyond that, one might suggest that evangelicals should appreciate the relevance of this kind of progressive clarifying, sharpening, and intensifying of God's purposes in human history when it is evident in scripture. Such an appreciation complicates the simple practices of biblicism. It might also contribute to a frame of biblical understanding and interpretation that holds some promise for reducing pervasive interpretive pluralism by suggesting a coherent approach for making sense of apparently conflicting passages in different parts of scripture that have at times generated disagreement and conflict. This will itself hardly be a panacea for all interpretive problems. But, again, some believe that it promises to make one contribution to a larger, more constructive rethinking of biblicism and its alternatives.

The problems with this kind of argument—which is why I am not including it in this chapter's constructive proposals—are at least threefold. One is that it is in fact not consistently true about moral development in scripture. It may arguably be true about marriage. But it is also arguably not true when it comes to issues like distributive justice and private property, e.g., where the Old Testament laws about the Year of Jubilee (Lev. 25 and 27) might be considered more progressively moral than some of the assumptions and teachings about property in the latter Old Testament and in the New Testament. Progressive revelation might also arguably not be true when it comes to gender relations, where the "moral progress" evident in Gal. 3:28 (see also 1 Cor. 11:5 and 14:1–33 regarding women praying and prophesying) seems to be lost by, say, the injunctions of 1 Tim. 2:11–15—which, to the best of our knowledge, was written later—for women to be silent in church. Second, this kind of progressive-revelation thinking is highly vulnerable to self-congratulating, quasi-Hegelian, liberal assumptions about progress in history (see Goldingay, *Models for Scripture*, 241–42; Charles Cosgrove, *Appealing to Scripture in Moral Debate: Five Hermeneutical Rules* [Grand Rapids: Eerdmans, 2002], 104–9; Edgar McKnight, *Postmodern Use of the Bible* [Nashville: Abingdon, 1988], 67–69; Kevin Vanhoozer, "Into the Great 'Beyond': A Theologian's Response to the Marshall Plan," in I. Howard Marshall, *Beyond the Bible: Moving from Scripture to Theology* [Grand Rapids: Zondervan, 2004], 81–95). I am not convinced that this is a necessary and fatal problem. But very strong is the modern temptation to believe the self-affirming story that the closer history and the world get to *us*, the better, smarter, and more moral both get. In some ways that may be true, but in other ways it is not. At the very least we should be extremely cautious about applying such a progress-driven hermeneutical notion to scripture for fear of projecting onto scripture misguided modern notions. Third, the Christocentric approach advanced at the start of this chapter trumps the need to argue for progressive revelation in scripture. Sparks points out: "The height of divine revelation was and is in Jesus Christ himself, who came to humanity in an historical context that lay chronologically *between* the two Testaments" (Sparks, *God's Word in Human Words*, 246). When we understand Christ as the center and purpose of the Bible, there is less need for the interpretive lens of progressive unfolding to address scripture's multivocality. Given these concerns, then, I suggest foregrounding the christological reading of the Bible and being very cautious about progressive-revelation perspectives.

## Conclusion

1. Mark Twain, when once asked if he believed in infant baptism, is reported to have replied, "Believe in it? Hell, I've *seen* it!" My case in this book is something like the reverse of that answer. Do I believe in the practice of evangelical biblicism? "How could I? It doesn't exist!"

2. This, again, is a clearly Barthian move, about which Jeff McSwain never ceases to remind his friends.

3. Again, merely for starters, see Scot McKnight, *The Blue Parakeet: Rethinking How You Read the Bible* (Grand Rapids: Zondervan, 2008); William Webb, *Slaves, Women, and Homosexuals: Exploring the Hermeneutics of Cultural Analysis* (Downers Grove, IL: IVP Academic, 2001); Willard Swartley, *Slavery, Sabbath, Women, and War: Case Issues in Biblical Interpretation* (Scottdale, PA: Herald, 1983); also see Ellen Davis and Richard Hayes, eds., *The Art of Reading Scripture* (Grand Rapids: Eerdmans, 2003); and Timothy Geddert, *All Right Now: Finding Consensus on Ethical Questions* (Scottdale, PA: Herald, 2008); Charles Cosgrove, *Appealing to Scripture in Moral Debate: Five Hermeneutical Rules* (Grand Rapids: Eerdmans, 2002). There is also the answer of (evangelical) Catholicism, see Christian Smith, *How to Go from Being a Good Evangelical to a Committed Catholic in 95 Difficult Steps* (Eugene, OR: Cascade Books, 2011).

# Index

Paul (apostle), 31, 72, 73, 79, 80, 104, 110,
   131, 139, 169, 188, 195, 200, 207
   new perspective on, 34
penal satisfaction doctrine of atonement,
   24, 25, 33, 135
Pentecost, 166, 168
pentecostal Christians, viii, 33, 38, 135
perlocutionary acts, 156–63
perspectivalism, 133
perspicuity of scripture, viii, 4, 17, 26, 39,
   53, 80, 133, 176
pervasive interpretive pluralism, x, xi, xiii,
   16, 17, 27, 28, 33, 37–38, 42, 43, 52, 60,
   62, 65, 67, 87, 89, 95, 97, 113, 116, 120,
   121, 130, 137, 139, 147, 153, 162, 170,
   171, 173, 207
Peter (apostle), 28, 47, 133
Philip (apostle), 131
Philippi, 169
picture theory of language, 56, 58, 59
Pierce, Ronald, 189
Pilate, Pontius, 200
Piper, John, 189
plausibility structures, 61, 88
poison, drinking, 71, 135
polysemy, 21, 47, 48, 50, 52, 53, 58, 78, 95,
   124, 173, 175, 177
polyvalence. *See* multivalence
Poole, Allan, xiv
popular religion, 6, 7, 12, 16, 162, 181
populist evangelicalism, 36
pork, 70
positivism, 30, 152
postconservative, 96
postmillennialism, 24, 26, 87
postmodernism, 65, 95, 96, 149, 151, 152
post-traumatic stress disorder, 122
poverty, 32, 51
Poythress, Vern, 22, 109, 110, 133
pragmatism, 30, 96, 145
predestination, 23, 26, 29, 38, 138, 144,
   204
premarital sex, 68
premillennialism, 24, 26, 144
Presbyterian, 20, 34, 125
Presbyterian Church of America (PCA),
   25, 201
presuppositionalism, 79

primitivism, 84
Princeton Theological Seminary, xi, 55,
   57, 88, 153
Promise Keepers, 15
prooftexting, 99, 169
prophetic-apocalyptic literature, 159
Prophets, 79, 99, 110, 143, 188
Protestant Reformers, 59
providence, 24
Psalms, 99, 132
psychological, 23, 55, 64, 65, 122, 156
puzzle, reading scripture as, 5, 45–48, 82,
   102, 113

quasi-papal Magisterium, 14
Queen's Road Church, 190
"quiet times," 11

racism, 110
Rapture, 23
rationalism, 145, 150, 151
Reality Ministries Center, xiv
Reformation, 20, 21, 29, 121, 153, 155,
   180, 189, 205
Reformed evangelical denominations and
   seminaries, 14
Reformed Theological Seminary (Orlando),
   4, 185
Reformed tradition, 24, 34, 189
regulative principle of worship, 34, 35
Reid, Thomas, 56
relativism, 65, 150, 152
Renaissance, 59
Republican Party, 32, 87
*res scripturae*, 132
restorationism, 35
revivalism, 188
Ricoeur, Paul, 50
Rio Grande river, 68
Roman empire, 140
rule of faith, 107, 108, 154
rules, 141, 164, 176
Rushdoony, R. J., 87

sabbatarians, 29
sabbath, 29, 30, 141
Samaria, 143
Samaritan woman at the well, 48–50